Praise for *If You Tell*

"There's only one writer who can tell such an intensely horrifying, psychotic tale of unspeakable abuse, grotesque torture, and horrendous serial murder with grace, sensitivity, and class . . . a riveting, taut, real-life psychological suspense thrill ride . . . all at once compelling and original, Gregg Olsen's *If You Tell* is an instant true crime classic."
—*New York Times* bestselling author M. William Phelps

"We all start life with immense promise, but in our first minute, we cannot know who'll ultimately have the greatest impact on our lives, for better or worse. Here, Gregg Olsen—the heir apparent to legendary crime writers Jack Olsen and Ann Rule—explores the dark side of that question in his usual chilling, heart-breaking prose. Superb and creepy storytelling from a true-crime master."
—Ron Franscell, author of *Alice & Gerald: A Homicidal Love Story*

"Bristling with tension, gripping from the first pages, Gregg Olsen's masterful portrait of children caught in the web of a coldly calculating killer fascinates. A read so compelling it kept me up late into the night, *If You Tell* exposes incredible evil that lived quietly in small-town America. That the book is fact not fiction terrifies."
—Kathryn Casey, bestselling author of *In Plain Sight*

"A suspenseful, horrific, and yet fascinating character study of an incredibly dysfunctional and dangerous family by Gregg Olsen, one of today's true crime masters."
—*New York Times* bestselling author Caitlin Rother

"A master of true crime returns with a vengeance. After a decade detour into novels, Gregg Olsen is back with a dark tale of nonfiction from the Pacific Northwest that will keep you awake long after the lights have gone out. The monster at the heart of *If You Tell* is not your typical boogeyman, not some wandering drifter or man in a van. No. In fact, they called her . . . mother. And yet this story is about hope and renewal in the face of evil and how three sisters can find the goodness in the world after surviving the worst it has to offer. Classic true crime in the tradition of *In Cold Blood* and *The Stranger Beside Me*."

—James Renner

"This nightmare walked on two legs and some of her victims called her mom. In *If You Tell*, Gregg Olsen documents the horrific mental and physical torture Shelly Knotek inflicted on everyone in her household. A powerful story of cruelty that will haunt you for a long time."

—Diane Fanning

"A true-crime tour de force."

—Steve Jackson, *New York Times* bestselling author of
No Stone Unturned

"Even the most devoted true-crime reader will be shocked by the maddening and mind-boggling acts of horror that Gregg Olsen chronicles in this book. Olsen has done it again, giving readers a glimpse into a murderous duo that's so chilling, it will have your head spinning. I could not put this book down!"

—*New York Times* bestselling author Aphrodite Jones

IF
YOU
TELL

ALSO BY GREGG OLSEN

Fiction

Lying Next to Me

The Weight of Silence

The Last Thing She Ever Did

The Sound of Rain

Just Try to Stop Me

Now That She's Gone

The Girl in the Woods

The Girl on the Run

Shocking True Story

Fear Collector

Betrayal

The Bone Box

Envy

Closer Than Blood

Victim Six

Heart of Ice

A Wicked Snow

A Cold Dark Place

Nonfiction

A Killing in Amish Country: Sex, Betrayal, and a Cold-Blooded Murder

A Twisted Faith: A Minister's Obsession and the Murder That Destroyed a Church

The Deep Dark: Disaster and Redemption in America's Richest Silver Mine

Starvation Heights: A True Story of Murder and Malice in the Woods of the Pacific Northwest

Cruel Deception: The True Story of Multiple Murder and Two Devastated Families

If Loving You Is Wrong: The Teacher and Student Sex Case that Shocked the World

Abandoned Prayers: The Incredible True Story of Murder, Obsession, and Amish Secrets

Bitter Almonds: The True Story of Mothers, Daughters, and the Seattle Cyanide Murders

Bitch on Wheels: The True Story of Black Widow Killer Sharon Nelson

If I Can't Have You: Susan Powell, Her Mysterious Disappearance, and the Murder of Her Children

IF
YOU
TELL

A TRUE STORY OF MURDER,
FAMILY SECRETS, AND THE UNBREAKABLE
BOND OF SISTERHOOD

GREGG OLSEN

THOMAS & MERCER

Published by Thomas & Mercer, Seattle

www.apub.com

Amazon, the Amazon logo, and Thomas & Mercer are trademarks of Amazon.com,
Inc., or its affiliates.

ISBN-13: 9781542005227 (hardcover)
ISBN-10: 1542005221 (hardcover)
ISBN-13: 9781542005234 (paperback)
ISBN-10: 154200523X (paperback)

Cover design by Rex Bonomelli

Printed in the United States of America

First Edition

For Nikki, Sami, and Tori

AUTHOR'S NOTE

Shared memories are like jagged puzzle pieces. Sometimes they don't exactly align with complete precision. I've done my best to put all of the pieces of this complex story in the most accurate sequence as possible. In instances where the narrative includes dialogue, I used investigative documents and recollections from interviews conducted over a two-year period. Finally, for reasons related to privacy, I elected to use a pseudonym for Lara Watson's first name.

PROLOGUE

Three sisters.

Now grown women.

All live in the Pacific Northwest.

The eldest, Nikki, lives in the moneyed suburbs of Seattle, in a million-dollar home of gleaming wood and high-end furnishings. She's in her early forties, married, with a houseful of beautiful children. A quick tour through a gallery of family photos in the living room touches on the good life she and her husband have made for themselves, with a successful business and a moral compass that has always kept them pointed in the right direction.

It takes only the mention of a single word to take her back to the unthinkable.

"Mom."

Every now and then, she literally shudders when she hears it, a visceral reaction to a word that scrapes at her like the talons of an eagle, cutting and slicing her skin until blood runs out.

To look at her, no one would know what she's lived through and survived. And outside her immediate family, no one really does. It isn't a mask that she wears to cover the past but an invisible badge of courage.

What happened to Nikki made her stronger. It made her the incredible woman that she is today.

The middle daughter, Sami, eventually returned to live in her hometown, the same small coastal Washington town where everything happened. She's just turned forty and teaches at a local elementary school. She has corkscrew hair and an infectious sense of humor. Humor is her armor. It always has been. Like her older sister, Sami's own children are what any mother dreams for their little ones. Smart. Adventurous. Loved.

When Sami runs the shower in the morning before getting the kids ready for school and heading off to the classroom, she doesn't pause a single beat for the water to warm. She jumps right in, letting the icy water stab at her body. Like Nikki, Sami is tied to things in the past. Things she can't shake.

Things she can't forget.

The youngest, like her older sisters, is a beauty. Tori is barely in her thirties: blonde, irreverent, and brilliant. Her home is farther away, in Central Oregon, but she's very connected to her sisters. Adversity and courage have forged a strong, impenetrable bond between them. This young woman has made an amazing life for herself developing social media for a major player in the hospitality industry. Her posts for work and for her personal life never fail to bring a smile or even a laugh out loud.

She did it on her own, of course, but says she couldn't have managed it without her sisters.

Whenever she's in the cleaning supply aisle of the local grocery store and her eyes land on the row of bleach, she turns away. Nearly a wince. She can't look at it. She certainly can't smell it. Like her sisters, it's the little things—duct tape, pain relievers, the sound of a weed eater—that propel her back to a time and place where their mother did things they swore they'd hold secret forever.

Enduring their mother was what bound them together. And while they might have had three different dads, they were always 100 percent sisters. Never half sisters. Their sisterhood was the one thing the Knotek girls could depend upon, and really, the only thing their mother couldn't take away.

It was what propelled them to survive.

PART ONE

MOTHER

SHELLY

CHAPTER ONE

Some small towns are built on bloody earth and betrayal. Battle Ground, Washington, twelve miles northeast of Vancouver, near the Oregon state line, is one such place. The town is named for an incident involving a standoff between the Klickitat nation and the US Army. The native people freed themselves from imprisonment in the barracks, but while a surrender was being negotiated, a single shot rang out, killing the Klickitat's Chief Umtuch.

It's fitting for Michelle "Shelly" Lynn Watson Rivardo Long Knotek's hometown to be known for a major conflict and a false promise.

As it turned out, it was pretty much the way Shelly lived her life.

For those who lived there in the 1950s, Battle Ground was quintessential small-town America with good schools, neighbors who looked out for each other, and a bowling league that kept the pins falling every Friday and Saturday night. Dads worked hard to afford the new car and nice house. Most moms stayed home taking care of the children, maybe later returning to the workforce or taking classes at Clark College to continue dreams thwarted by conventions of the day and marriage.

If Battle Ground had a Mr. Big Shot of sorts, it was Shelly's father.

At six feet, two inches tall, with broad shoulders, Les Watson, former Battle Ground High School track and football star, was a big deal around town. Everyone knew him. He was quick-witted and could pour on the charm, a smooth talker and a master of BS. Handsome too. All the girls in town thought he was a catch. Not only did he and his mother own and operate a pair of nursing homes, Les also owned the Tiger Bowl, a ten-lane bowling alley complete with a twelve-seat snack counter.

That was where Lara Stallings worked in 1958. She'd just graduated from Fort Vancouver High School and was selling hamburgers to save money for college. Lara's curly hair was blonde, with a ponytail that swung back and forth as she took orders. With sparkling blue eyes, she was undeniably beautiful. She was also smart. Later, she'd lament that her brain wasn't in full gear when she agreed to date, and then eventually marry, Les Watson.

Les was also ten years older, though he'd lied and told his teenage bride that he was only four years her senior.

"I got caught up in all he had going for him," Lara said years later, bemoaning the choice she made. "I fell hook, line, and sinker. He just wasn't a great guy."

Lara's jolt into reality came the day after she put her hair up in a French twist—like Tippi Hedren in the Hitchcock classic, *The Birds*—and married Les in a civil ceremony in 1960 in Vancouver, her hometown. Only Lara's family was present, though her parents had been against the marriage. Les had had good reason not to invite his.

They knew what was coming.

When the phone rang early the next morning, Lara answered. It was Les's first wife on the line, calling from California.

"When are you coming to get these damn kids?" Sharon Todd Watson spat into the phone.

Lara didn't know what she was talking about. "What?"

Les had never mentioned to Lara that he'd promised to raise his children by Sharon: Shelly, Chuck, and Paul Watson. The omission of that little detail was typical of Les, though Lara knew that she'd never be able to fix that—and that her parents' concerns had been justified.

After the early-morning call, Les told Lara that his ex-wife, Sharon, couldn't raise the kids; she was a depressive and an alcoholic. Lara took a deep breath and agreed. And really, what could she do about it anyway? They were her husband's children, and she knew she would need to buck up.

It turned out to be a very big request. Shelly was six and Chuck was just three when they moved in. Lara took on the role of stepmother—Sharon had kept the youngest son, Paul, still then an infant, with her. Shelly was a beautiful little girl, with wide eyes and thick, curly auburn hair. Lara noticed a strange dynamic, however, between Shelly and her brother. Chuck didn't speak a word. It was Shelly who did all the talking. She seemed to control the boy.

And as Shelly grew more comfortable with her new environment, she often voiced complaints or unkind words.

"She told me every single day that she hated me," Lara recalled. "I'm not joking. It was honestly every day."

))(

Sharon Watson returned home to Alameda, California, after dropping off her two oldest children with Lara and Les in the fall of 1960. Once Sharon was gone, it was like she'd never existed. She never called or sent birthday cards to either Shelly or Chuck. No Christmas wishes either. There were few excuses for this "out of sight, out of mind" approach to child-rearing, though Lara later wondered if the course had been set long before Shelly's mother had married and divorced Les Watson.

"Sharon came from a very dysfunctional family," Lara recounted, having heard about Les's first wife. "Her mother was married five, six, seven times and she was an only child. I understood she had a twin that died at birth. I don't know if that's really true or not, but that's one of the stories I'd been told."

Regardless of what had led her to that point, it was understood that while Sharon had serious problems with alcohol, there was more pulling her down. She'd gotten caught up in a dangerous lifestyle. Family members speculated she might even be a prostitute.

Finally, in the spring of 1967, a call from the Los Angeles County Sheriff's Department came to the Watsons' home in Battle Ground. A homicide detective said that Sharon had been murdered in a seedy motel room and the coroner needed someone to identify her body—and to pick up her little boy, Paul.

Les didn't want to go get his son, whom he knew had exhibited myriad behavioral problems, but Lara insisted. It was the right thing to do. Reluctantly, they made the trip to California to get him and to identify Sharon's body.

Les reported to Lara what he'd learned from the police and the coroner.

"She was living with a Native American, but they were homeless," he told her. "Drunks. Living on Skid Row. She was beaten to death."

Later, when Sharon's cremains were sent to Washington, her mother refused to take them. Nor did anyone hold a memorial service for her. It was tragic but it fit her story. In images culled from a tattered old family album, there are only a handful of pictures of Sharon, almost never with a smile. Her perpetual despondency preserved forever in black and white.

When Shelly was told what had happened to her mother, the thirteen-year-old didn't seem the least bit interested. She barely reacted. Lara thought it was strange. It was as if there had been no true connection between Shelly and Sharon.

"She never once asked about her mother," Lara recalled.

CHAPTER TWO

The newest member of the Watson family brought a host of problems to Battle Ground. Paul possessed zero impulse control and positively no social skills. He didn't even know how to sit at the table at dinnertime. His first or second day in the house, Lara caught the boy on the kitchen countertop stomping around looking for food, opening cupboards and tossing out whatever didn't meet with his approval.

"Paul was wild," she acknowledged. "He was like an animal. He even carried a switchblade. Really. Not kidding. He did."

Lara did what she could, but she knew almost right away that she was in way over her head. Les was busy with his businesses, and Lara didn't fault him too much for not having much time for his children, but she was doing all she could as a stepmother to three hand-fuls—willful Shelly, wild Paul, and silent Chuck. Chuck, who still didn't speak unless Shelly put words in his mouth, was a loner. People who knew their birth mother suspected that his difficulties might have come from some kind of child abuse, though in the 1960s little of that was actually put into words.

"A neighbor told me one time that they'd seen Chuck in his room with the window open and he was just standing there crying," Lara said. "It was something that he did all the time."

As difficult as Paul and Chuck could be, the child who created the most difficulty for Lara was Shelly.

The Watsons put extra emphasis on getting the most out of their family time on the weekends, shutting out all other distractions and focusing on the kids, which by now also included a daughter and a son Lara and Les had had together. They made regular trips to the Oregon or Washington coasts for boating in the summer months, and in the winter, they skied the slopes of Mount Hood. It would have been a fine and happy life, if not for Shelly.

She pitched fits, started fights, and would flat out refuse to go. If something wasn't Shelly's idea, it was a nonstarter. Whenever she didn't get her way, Shelly was crafty enough to find a suitable solution. Usually it involved a lie. Her excuses were vague and often ridiculous. She didn't like doing her homework, for example. So she'd complain that her youngest siblings had destroyed all of her hard work. When that ruse didn't work anymore, she'd simply refuse to go to school.

"I'd try to find ways to make [things] easier for her in the morning," Lara recalled. "I would set her clothes out at night, so she wouldn't have to worry at the last minute to decide. I would set cereal and fruit out on the dining table—all ready to go. Anything to make the mornings go a little more smoothly. But that didn't matter. Shelly didn't want to do what she didn't want to do."

Each morning, a sullen and frequently angry Shelly would head off to school and the morning battle would be over.

At least that's what Lara believed at the time.

"I got a phone call one time from the Standard Oil service station down the street from the school. They said, 'This is the craziest thing! We've been seeing this little girl come in and going in [to] use the bathroom, and she brings in a sack of clothes [and then] she goes out,' and they say, 'She's got a pile of clothes here. But she leaves with another set of clothes, jeans.'"

Lara got in her car and drove to the Standard station. She was astounded by what she found.

Shelly had indeed left behind a stash of clothes. "Probably had four or five dresses and skirts of hers squirreled away there. Beautiful brand-new things that Shelly didn't want to wear to school."

The impasse on clothing was only a fraction of the discord between Shelly and Lara, though Lara kept trying to find a way to get her stepdaughter on the right path. When Shelly was a little older, Lara took her to dance lessons, but half the time the girl refused to go inside the studio. She'd skip the recitals too.

"Everything was a big drama with her. Every little thing. Shelly always looked distraught and upset, whatever we did, wherever we went. No matter what it was. Even doing something nice for her like getting her a gift brought anger. 'What are you being mad about?' I'd ask. No answer, but I knew from the way she acted that nothing was good enough. Nothing whatsoever. Nothing satisfied her."

In time, Shelly's behavior began to change from being merely disruptive and ungrateful to dark and vengeful. She especially resented her siblings. Every bit of attention to another person meant a deficit in what she felt was owed to her. Whenever the deficit wasn't paid, Shelly sought revenge. Her tactics were brutal and, frequently, sadistic. There would be lies about family members, stolen money, and even suspicion of arson in the Watson house.

Years later, Lara took a deep breath, recalling, "She used to chop up bits of glass and put them in the bottom of [the kids'] boots and shoes," she said. "What kind of person does something like that?"

Lara didn't have to look far for an example.

Grandma Anna, Shelly's paternal grandmother, was just that kind of person too.

CHAPTER THREE

For Lara, seeing her mother-in-law, Anna Watson, meant a tightening of the muscles along her spine, hoping that Les's mother wouldn't cast her sharklike eyes in her direction. If Anna passed by, it brought Lara a shudder of relief. Only then could Lara take a breath. A very deep one. At least that's how Shelly's stepmother felt whenever she faced the singular terror that was Anna Watson.

Born in Fargo, North Dakota, and transplanted to Clark County when she was a teen, Shelly Watson's paternal grandmother was tall and large, with muscled, shot-put shoulders and the sinewy trace of tendons that ran from her neck into the collar of her plain blue blouse. Anna tipped the scales at more than 250 pounds, and her left foot dragged when she walked, emitting a scraping noise that let people know when she was coming or going. Like her physical size, Anna's self-certainty was formidable. She was absolutely right about everything, so much so that no one ever dared challenge her. Not Les, and certainly not his young wife, Lara. Anna ran one of the Watsons' nursing homes, and there was no mistaking that everything had to be done her way. "Iron fisted" often came to the lips of those recalling Anna Watson's style.

Anna's husband, George Watson, was the opposite of his wife. He was kind. Sweet. Endearing, even. He was smaller than Anna, standing four inches shorter, and did whatever his wife told him to do. For more than twenty years, Lara recalled, George slept in a small eight-by-eight-foot shed just outside the back door to the kitchen. He never slept in the house, because Anna insisted he stay in the shed.

Not long before Les and Lara married, two women from Western State Hospital, near Tacoma, came to work for Anna at one of the nursing homes the family owned in Battle Ground. While their names were Mary and Pearlie, Lara only ever heard Anna refer to them as her "retards." She lorded over them as a cruel queen might order around less-favored house servants. There was no task too low for the women to attend to in a nursing facility where there were more than enough such tasks.

From Lara's perspective, the women were nearly slaves to Anna. At home, Anna made them clean her house, do the dishes, wash the floors. She'd order them to stop whatever task they were engaged in to wash her feet, do her hair. If the women moved too slowly, Anna would punch them, kick them, or pull their hair.

One time when Lara went over to Anna's to pick up Shelly, she noticed that Mary was upset about something. Pearlie's hair was wet and wrapped in a towel. Lara asked Mary what was wrong, and she confided that Anna had stormed out of the house with Shelly. She had been so angry about something that she had held Pearlie's head in the toilet bowl and repeatedly flushed.

Lara was stunned. She'd never heard of such a thing.

"Why would she do something like that?" she asked Mary.

"She does it all the time when she gets mad," she said.

"They were always afraid of Anna," Lara said later.

Everyone was.

Everyone, it seemed, but little Shelly.

Lara started working in the nursing home office shortly after Les's children came to live in Battle Ground. She had wanted to go to college, but those plans had been waylaid by instant motherhood. Since Shelly's school was next to the nursing home, Shelly would often go to Grandma Anna's after school instead of taking the bus home. Lara would call to see if she was there, and Anna would seethe that her granddaughter was being neglected and needed to stay with her to have a "proper" meal or be bathed correctly.

"You don't need to wash her hair, Anna."

"You don't do it right. It's filthy."

Anna knew what was best for Shelly.

Indeed, she knew what was best for everyone.

Lara held her tongue, a practice she'd come to master over time.

Another time, Lara came to pick Shelly up and found her beautiful red hair all cut off. Grandma Anna stood next to her granddaughter with a pair of scissors and a mean smile.

Lara was shocked. "What happened?"

Grandma Anna snapped at her. "You can't keep her hair brushed properly, so I cut it!"

It was a cruel, frenzied hack job. It looked awful. Shelly looked demoralized.

"She has very thick hair," Lara said, fully aware that Shelly was going to blame her for what her grandmother had done. "I brush it every day," she insisted, glancing at Shelly, who would scream every time a brush came near her.

Grandma Anna made a dismissive face and turned away, sliding her bum leg over the polished wooden floor.

She'd done exactly what she'd wanted to do.

Making people unhappy was her way of having fun.

Lara could see it even then. Shelly and Grandma Anna were inseparable, constant companions. While occasionally her victim, Shelly mainly served the role of protégé in her grandmother's life. Grandma Anna's favorite, her shadow, her mimic, was paying close attention to everything she did.

In time, Shelly would reveal just how good a student she'd been.

CHAPTER FOUR

Shelly's first real strike came when she was almost fifteen. It was a stealth attack, the kind of tactic a practitioner of discord learns is the most effective means to wreak the most damage.

She was a no-show after school in March 1969. While she'd been tardy before, this time felt a little different. She was later than normal. Lara stared at the clock in her spotless kitchen. She drummed her fingertips on the surface of the table.

Where are you, Shelly?

What are you up to?

Who are you with?

Growing anxious, Shelly's stepmother finally phoned the principal's office, and what she learned took the air from her lungs. Shelly hadn't come home because she'd been taken to the juvenile hall detention center in Vancouver. Shelly, a month shy of her fifteenth birthday, had told a counselor that something was going on at home and she couldn't handle it anymore.

"What are you talking about?" Lara pressed the school employee for additional details. "You need to tell me what's going on here."

"I really can't say anything more," the woman on the other end of the line said. Her tone was cool. That alarmed Lara even more.

She hung up and immediately phoned her husband, Les, at the nursing home and told him to get home. She was sharp and direct. "Right now," she said. "Something's happening with Shelly."

After another frantic call to juvenile hall, the Watsons were on their way to find out just what had happened at school that afternoon.

"No one was telling us anything," Lara said later, looking down at photos of Shelly as a child, then a teenager. There was no denying Shelly's beauty. Red hair framed a face with a freckled nose, and her blue eyes had thick lashes like the undulating fringe of a sea anemone. But to Lara, the kind of beauty Shelly possessed was like that of nightshade berries. They appear to be delicious but are actually dangerous.

Innocent. Sweet. A mask.

Lara was frantic.

"I even called the principal at home, but he wouldn't say anything either. I'm thinking Shelly just stole something because she used to steal my things and take money out of my purse. I thought that maybe Shelly stole some kid's purse or something like that. I had no idea what she'd done this time."

It was frustrating. Painful. It had to be something very, very bad.

When the Watsons arrived at the juvenile detention center in Vancouver, they asked to see their daughter right away but were denied the request by the superintendent of the facility.

"Under investigation now," he said.

"What investigation?" Les asked.

"Shelly has accused you of raping her," said the grim-faced man.

Les's eyes nearly popped from their sockets, and his face went completely red with anger. He immediately pushed back.

"Oh Jesus!" he exclaimed. "What in the world is Shelly saying that for?"

Lara stood there feeling sick. The accusation was the most disgusting thing she'd ever heard in her entire life. Shelly was a known liar, but this was too, too much. Even for her. As Shelly's stepmother saw it, there were a lot of things people could call her husband, but "rapist" wasn't on the list.

"She doesn't probably know what it means," Lara finally said, reaching over to calm her husband.

"We need to see her now," Les insisted.

"Absolutely not," the superintendent snapped. "You can't. We're investigating a crime here."

Les threw his hands upward. "Fine. We're calling our doctor. We're going to demand he examine her. Now."

Family doctor Paul Turner ordered Shelly to St. Joseph's Hospital in Vancouver, and the Watsons returned to Battle Ground.

That night, Lara went into her stepdaughter's bedroom. She really didn't know what she was looking for. An answer, maybe? The truth. *Something.* As usual, Shelly's room was a mess, with clothes and dirty dishes everywhere. Papers too. Scribblings in notebooks. Shelly fancied herself a poet and was always writing something, but nothing Lara saw as she picked through the mess provided a clue. After a while, she found herself poking around the bed to see what she could unearth there. Bending down, she reached between the mattress and the box springs. Her fingertips grazed the edges of a magazine and she pulled it out.

The air leaked from her lungs.

It was a dog-eared copy of a *True Confessions* magazine.

The cover screamed in bold type: "I WAS RAPED AT 15 BY MY DAD!"

Lara felt her blood pressure rise. It was unfathomable that Shelly could've made such an accusation, one that mirrored exactly the cover of a magazine.

"Look here," she said, showing Les her discovery.

Les shook his head in disgust and disbelief. He'd been crushed by the accusation, but he was more troubled by his daughter's behavior.

"What's wrong with her?" he asked.

Lara didn't know. She'd never heard of anyone making up such a destructive story. It didn't make sense.

The next morning, when Dr. Turner arrived at the hospital to conduct the exam, Lara brandished the magazine.

"She's made it up," Lara said.

In the Watsons' view, the magazine was proof nothing had actually happened, that the lurid story had merely been Shelly's inspiration. But this was more than just another beat in a drama that Shelly created with her destructive and outrageous behavior. Les and Lara had had it with her. They had their other kids to consider. Les's career too. He was the president of the chamber of commerce. If even a whisper of Shelly's lie got out, the scandal would ruin him.

"This is really bad, Lara," Les said as they waited outside Shelly's hospital room.

Lara let out a sigh. "It's Shelly," she said. "It's what she does."

A little while later, Dr. Turner emerged with the results of his exam.

"This girl's completely intact," he said. "No bruising. Nothing. She's never even been touched."

Shelly was released on one condition later that night.

"Your daughter needs serious counseling," Lara said the juvenile hall superintendent told them. "She needs a psychologist."

※

Unfortunately, rounds of family therapy and private sessions with a psychologist proved less than successful. Shelly wouldn't entertain the idea that she might have problems that needed fixing. Even though she'd been confronted with the truth, Shelly remained adamant that nothing was her fault. Nothing had *ever* been. Lara and Les came to know something that few understood in the late sixties and seventies: no one can help a troubled person who doesn't think they need it. Indeed, Shelly never even admitted to fabricating the story of her rape. She didn't even seem to grasp the magnitude of what she'd done to her father.

Instead, she seemed happy to have tossed a grenade into the circle of her family, and to have received the attention she craved because of it.

Shelly wanted to return to Battle Ground High School, but administrators declined to take her back.

"You burned that bridge," the principal said. Shelly sat blank eyed in his office while Les and Lara looked on. "We don't want you in class here. We just don't want any more trouble."

Hearing that, the Watsons were beside themselves. Shelly was only fifteen. She *had* to go to school. Lara immediately tried to get her enrolled in Annie Wright, a prestigious and expensive boarding school in Tacoma, but that was a no-go too.

"They researched her," Lara recalled later. "They turned her down flat."

While the Watsons made a good income, the truth was they'd have paid just about anything to get Shelly out of Battle Ground and into a classroom somewhere. Anywhere. Eventually, they found a spot for Shelly in Hoodsport, Washington, living with Lara's parents, who quickly learned to walk on eggshells around the teenager. No one wanted to set Shelly off. There simply was no telling what she would do next. She was volatile, unpredictable. She had a mean streak that was sometimes hidden by a pretense of caring about someone or something. For instance, she'd volunteer to help Lara's mother with the dishes, but would end up throwing the unwashed utensils, plates, and even pots and pans into the garbage. When she was in a more productive mood, she would wipe the plates "clean" with a cloth instead of washing them.

Shelly said she loved kids and wanted to babysit for the neighbors. Even better, she loved babysitting so much, she said, she even volunteered to watch them for free. She seemed to enjoy being seen as a benevolent, caring girl. It was an affectation that didn't last long. When the parents came home from a night out, they found their children in bed with clothes still on and tales of how Shelly had barricaded them in their rooms with heavy furniture.

Shelly also turned on her grandparents after only a few weeks under their roof.

"With all their grandchildren, my mom and dad never had a problem," Lara said, looking back many years after Shelly returned to Battle Ground. "I found out later that my parents were so glad when school finally finished and they could send Shelly home." Shelly had apparently also accused Lara's father of abuse. "I learned that Shelly actually told the neighbors that her grandpa was messing with her. And they contacted my mother immediately." It was baffling to Lara. "I don't understand Shelly's constant need to try to ruin people's lives."

CHAPTER FIVE

Lara Watson would sometimes brace herself at the sound of the phone's grating ring, dreading another call about something Shelly had done, something new to test Lara's resolve to make things work. Lara was capable. She was good with people. She had a bright spirit. But even without Shelly at home, the Watsons' marriage was under unbearable strain. Certainly family businesses required constant attention, and Les was up for the challenge. It was probably what he was best at doing. Lara, for her part, was mired in the quicksand of raising five children, two of her own with Les and the three from his ex-wife, Sharon. The older children continued to wreak havoc on the household, though none to the degree that Shelly did. Chuck was mostly quiet—timid, even. Lara would have him sit on her lap while she read to him and listened to him pretend to read to her. Whenever he tried to speak, Shelly was right there answering for him. School was difficult for him too. For his part, Paul was a habitual liar, like his older sister. While Shelly controlled Paul, Paul, in turn, mimicked his sister and tried to control Chuck. It was as if all of the kids had coalesced into a mob, with Shelly as their ultimate leader.

The queen bee.

The one who always knew what was best.

Just like Grandma Anna.

Shelly was always a master of disruption and chaos. It was a foregone conclusion that adding her back in the mix after her exile from Battle Ground was not going to work out for anyone. Lara spent half of that summer on the phone trying to find a school that would enroll Shelly that fall. Every place she called turned her down. Lara was nearly at her wit's end when she finally got a yes from St. Mary of the Valley in Beaverton, Oregon, about forty minutes south of Battle Ground. It might not have been as far away as Lara hoped, but it was the best of a very short list of options.

She would later admit that she did hold back some about the challenges that would follow Shelly to boarding school, because she was so desperate. She also figured that a bunch of no-nonsense nuns would see right through Shelly's most obvious manipulations and put a stop to them.

After a few weeks, the sisters started calling to ask the Watsons if they could come and get Shelly for the weekend.

"Friday nights we'd pick her up and take her with us and we go up to our mountain cabin and go skiing. I always tried to do it on weekends, though honestly it was hard. Every weekend I would just grit my teeth. It was so peaceful without her. Even the boys, who had big problems, were doing better."

It seemed like the more anyone did for Shelly, the more she'd take. If she didn't get what she wanted, she'd pitch a fit.

"The sisters didn't want her back the next year," Lara said. "They told me she had behavior problems."

The problems were familiar.

According to the sisters, Shelly would often wake up in the middle of the night screaming. She stole another girl's homework and destroyed it. She was caught stealing things from other girls. Shelly even resurrected an old favorite guerilla tactic: she put broken glass in a classmate's shoe.

Near the end of the school year, the sister administrator at St. Mary of the Valley told Les and Lara that they would not accept Shelly as a returning student.

"We were willing to pay anything to keep her there," Lara said. "No dice. The sisters stayed firm."

That summer, Shelly took a scorched earth approach to her life in Battle Ground. She spent her days telling Lara how much she hated her and how she wished Lara would curl up and die. Lara, weary of holding back, let Shelly know more than a few times that she was no prize either.

"What's the matter with you?" she asked. "You are never happy or appreciative about anything."

That was true. Lara didn't need to look any further than her husband to see why. He gave Shelly everything she ever wanted. Despite all she'd done to him, literally smearing his name, Les treated Shelly like a little princess.

Princess Shelly couldn't stay in Battle Ground.

✕

Les Watson's sister, Katie, was the next unwitting but well-meaning person to hurl a lifeline in the direction of the Watsons. Shelly had a way about her that could get people to take pity on her and side with her against the rest of the world. *Her mother was murdered. Her dad was abusive. Her stepmom was mean to her.* Katie offered to have Shelly stay with her for the summer after Shelly complained to her about how rotten her folks—especially Lara—were to her.

Lara overheard some of the conversations. Shelly was never one to hide her feelings. She spoke loudly and in a manner that made certain everyone heard.

"She was on the phone telling Katie how bad and how mean and how abusive I was," Lara recalled. "How I wouldn't let her have anything and that I didn't buy her anything. [That] I called her bad names."

Shelly's pity party was a complete success.

The Watsons had a pickup and a camper, and they made plans to go to Disneyland that summer. The entire family packed up, put Shelly on a plane, and had a wonderful time without her.

A few weeks later, Katie phoned and said Shelly had told her everything. She and her husband, Frank, had decided to have "the poor girl" stay with them for the school year in their home on the East Coast where Frank was a mining engineer and the president of a coal company.

Lara couldn't believe her good fortune. She knew Shelly had lied through her teeth about how things were in Battle Ground. That was fine with her.

Oh Lord! she thought at the time. *God is so good at answering my prayers!*

As it turned out, the East Coast was Shelly's last stop on the high school education tour that had had her moving from school to school, family member to family member.

"It was awful," Lara said of the two years Shelly strained her relatives. In Lara's opinion, "The problems that [Shelly] caused between Katie and Frank were so bad they ended up getting a divorce."

Shelly didn't seem to mind any of that drama at all. She was moving on. She was not yet eighteen and she'd already met her future husband.

CHAPTER SIX

Every guy knows the moment when he meets the girl. *The One.* The one who spins him around like a top that turns so quickly it digs deep. Randy Rivardo first laid eyes on Shelly Watson in the summer of 1971, when she was seventeen. There was no denying she was a knockout, this new girl. Shelly caught the attention of a lot of local boys when she was staying with her aunt and uncle in Murrysville, Pennsylvania, and attending high school at Franklin Regional High. She and Randy started dating, and they went steady Shelly's senior year. The two made a striking couple: Shelly with her red hair and flawless skin, and Randy with the dark eyes and hair of his Italian heritage. But it was a teenage romance, destined to be only a passing fancy and a happy memory. They went their separate ways after graduation in 1972, with Randy staying in Pennsylvania to earn money for college tuition, and Shelly eventually returning to Washington, where she took a job as a nurse's aide at her father's nursing home.

Later that summer, however, Randy's old flame called. Shelly not only missed him, but she also knew of an opportunity. Her father had a job offer for Randy.

"Do you want to come out to Battle Ground?" she asked. "My dad will hire you as a maintenance man."

Randy wasn't sure. It was a good offer, but it was completely out of the blue.

Shelly sweetened the deal.

"My dad will put you up in a rent-free apartment," she said. "You can save up for school faster."

The idea intrigued him. The job only paid five dollars an hour, but after researching the cost of tuition at Clark College in Vancouver, Randy made up his mind. He drove out to Battle Ground and right into Shelly's open arms.

Open like a Venus flytrap, that is.

Not long after he arrived, it grew clear that the Watson family had more in mind for Randy than being just a maintenance man. They wanted a husband for Shelly. Truth be told, by the time he'd pulled his car into Battle Ground, wedding plans were likely already in the works. It didn't take long for the hook to be reeled in. Shelly told everyone how much she loved Randy. Les treated Randy like a long-lost son. Anything he needed, Les was right there to offer it, going above and beyond.

However, Randy had an inkling that something else was afoot. Shelly's father appeared too eager to pass his daughter off to another man.

"They rushed this thing so much that Les picked out my best man because I didn't have any friends or family in the area," Randy recounted. "It was that quick." Randy wasn't a passive guy, but he kept his mouth shut. "I sat back and let it all happen."

None of Randy's relatives or friends made it to the wedding.

Later, a family member discovered the reason: Shelly never mailed them the invitations.

)X(

Shelly and Randy, both nineteen, were married in February 1973 at the Methodist church in Vancouver. Shelly wore a long white dress with a high collar, deliberately echoing what actress Olivia Hussey wore in the 1968 film *Romeo and Juliet*. The groom wore a pink tuxedo that Shelly had selected for the occasion. A reception followed at the historic Summit Grove Lodge in nearby Ridgefield. Everyone agreed it was a lovely ceremony, a lifelong dream for Shelly. The couple was young but very much in love. At least Randy thought so.

The couple honeymooned at the Watson cabin at Government Camp, Oregon—a place Shelly had loathed as a teenager—and afterward, they lived rent free in a forty-foot trailer owned by the Watsons. Shelly complained about its shabbiness, but Lara pointed out that it was only a starting point for her life with Randy. They really didn't have the income for a house anyway.

"But I don't want to live in this trailer!" Shelly repeated over and over.

Shortly after the wedding, Shelly started to complain of severe menstrual cramping and began to miss work at the nursing home. Her "troubles," as she called them, came in a tsunami that lasted from the beginning to the end of the month. She'd go to work, leave, and then do it all over again. Finally, in what must have been a difficult decision for Les Watson, he fired his daughter.

"Hard work and dependability were never two of her strong points," Randy said later of his young bride.

After that, Shelly went to work at another relative's nursing home. But the pattern of serial absenteeism repeated there too, and she was terminated.

"She would then revert back to her dad's nursing home," Randy said. "Like a ping-pong ball."

Eventually fired for good, a stay-at-home Shelly brought no benefits to the new household whatsoever. She didn't cook. She didn't clean. All she seemed to like to do was lie around and tell everyone in earshot what they should be doing, though she was never shy about telling others what *she* deserved, and how they should help her get whatever she wanted.

She was a lot like Grandma Anna that way.

)(

Shelly had designs on a new car, so she did what she always did—she made a beeline for her daddy. It didn't matter that she'd nearly cost him his reputation, or worse, by claiming to authorities that he had raped her. That appeared to be water long under the bridge. In reality, the Watsons were afraid of Shelly and what she might do. It was easier to give her everything she wanted, just to keep her happy and at bay. If Shelly wanted to go to the movies, or to a concert, or to an event somewhere out of town, they'd immediately fork over the cash.

Of course, even the Watsons had their limits. As successful as Les's businesses had been, he wasn't made of money.

With the demand for a new car, Shelly showed her dad and step-mom once more how far she'd go to get what she wanted.

Shelly insisted on a VW Beetle.

"Daddy, that's the car I want! The car I have to have!"

Les agreed and went to Vancouver to see what he could find. However, he didn't come home with a VW. Instead, he returned to Battle Ground with what he thought was even better—a nearly brand-new pale-pink Buick convertible.

Shelly's eyes narrowed, and her face went ten shades darker than the new car. She stomped her feet. She pitched a fit so loud that the windows of the house rattled. She screamed at her father that he'd bought her a "horrible old maid's car."

Les took a step back. Though he should have known better, he just didn't expect that.

Randy thought the car was nice, but he was unable to calm his wife down. Shelly couldn't be consoled.

What happened next sent everyone into a tailspin.

That night, Shelly collapsed in a stupor, apparently having overdosed on sleeping pills and booze. When Randy couldn't revive her, he called the Watsons in a panic and they immediately rushed her to Vancouver Memorial Hospital. Everyone was worried that she might not make it. The ER doctor on duty pumped her stomach and reported his findings to the family.

"We found out she'd taken aspirin of all things," Lara recalled many years later. "And only a small amount. There had been no sleeping pills."

X

One day after Randy returned from classes at Clark College, he found their trailer in complete shambles and his wife with a bloody face.

He ran to her. "What happened?"

"A man came in," Shelly sobbed. "He came in [and] attacked me. Raped me." She indicated some scratches on her face. "He took your rifle and ran outside."

Randy called the Clark County sheriff as well as his father-in-law. Both arrived within minutes of each other. Randy and Les stayed outside while the sheriff questioned Shelly in the trailer.

A bit later, the sheriff emerged and with a grim expression said that Shelly's wounds had been self-inflicted. There had been no intruder. He gave Les and Randy a look before telling them he wouldn't file charges against Shelly.

When the sheriff left, Shelly changed her story again.

"She reverted back to claiming she was raped," Randy said later. "She said she only gave up the story because the sheriff forced her to. She said she watched as the attacker buried the rifle not far from the house."

To prove her story, Shelly led her husband and father to the rifle.

"Right here," she told them. "That's where he hid it."

Randy knew better than to believe this story. He suspected his father-in-law did too. Shelly's stepmother did for sure.

Shelly simply didn't want to live in that trailer anymore. It wasn't good enough. She was Les Watson's daughter, for God's sake. She deserved better.

"She said it was too dangerous for her to live there," Lara said, rolling her eyes years later. "Instead, she wanted to live in a cute little house in town."

⋈

Whatever Shelly wanted, she got. Shelly acted like she owned Battle Ground. She left unpaid bills at the gas station and the grocer. She bounced check after check. She grew such a tab over time that some business owners thought it necessary to strong-arm Randy into paying. He'd tell them never to let Shelly charge a penny again, and they'd agree. And then they'd always give in.

Now Randy knew why Les had been so quick to welcome him into the family. It was more than handing off a daughter to be married; he'd been passing along a very big problem.

When Shelly announced she was pregnant in the summer of 1974, everyone took a gulp of air.

Maybe this would help?

⋈

Randy's parents announced they wanted to make the trip from Pennsylvania to Washington, bringing along baby gifts and the excitement that comes with the anticipation of a new addition to the family.

Shelly, however, told Randy that she didn't want his family to come. He brushed her off. They were coming and that was that. When the Rivardos finally arrived, she sequestered herself in her bedroom. She never once came out during the time they were there. It was embarrassing, but Randy put on a brave face and he and his family had a great time without her.

That, in turn, made her even angrier.

The fallout came later. Books brought as gifts from Randy's little brother to the new baby went missing. Randy couldn't find them anywhere. Shelly said she didn't have a clue what happened to them either. After looking all over the place, they gave up.

After the family left, Randy sampled homemade candy his grandfather had sent as a gift. His grandfather had made it a hundred times. Randy took a bite and had to spit it out. It tasted of nothing but salt. He called his grandfather to tell him of the mistake with the latest batch. The old man couldn't understand what had gone wrong—none of the other family members tasted anything but marshmallow.

The only bad batch was the box delivered to Battle Ground.

When it was discovered that Randy's sister left some new clothing behind, Shelly offered to mail the articles back.

The package arrived in perfect condition. Its contents, not so much. Someone had taken a pair of scissors and shredded the garments.

Shelly told Randy she had no idea how that could have happened.

"Someone at the post office must have done it," she said.

PART TWO

SISTERS

NIKKI AND SAMI

CHAPTER SEVEN

"Love Will Keep Us Together" by the Captain & Tennille and the Bee Gees's "Jive Talkin'" played on repeat on Shelly Rivardo's cassette player when her daughter Nikki came into the world in February 1975. It wasn't a moment too soon either. Shelly had complained for weeks about her pregnancy, and how she was sure it was going to ruin her figure.

With both her mother's coloring and features, Nikki could not have been a more beautiful baby. Everybody said so, even Shelly, who saw her daughter as the perfect extension of herself. She told everyone how excited she was to be a mother. How she had big dreams for her little girl. Those who knew Shelly were skeptical, but hopeful that having a baby would refocus her attention away from herself.

Instead of taking her newborn back to Battle Ground, Shelly decided that it would be best if Nikki was cared for at her parents' rambling Tudor home in Vancouver. Lara couldn't tell if Shelly was indifferent or worried about caring for a baby. With the exception of the disastrous stretch of babysitting for her grandparents' neighbors in Hoodsport, Shelly had zero experience caring for a child.

"I don't think she'd ever held a baby in her life," Lara said later.

Lara was the opposite. She was born to be a mom, delighted to be a grandmother. When she'd first felt Nikki's kick inside of Shelly, Lara had dubbed the baby Thumper after the rabbit from *Bambi*, and she had loved that baby from that little kick.

What Lara thought was going to be a few days' stay, however, turned into three months before Randy finally put his foot down and the three of them returned to Battle Ground.

Lara drove up to see the baby every day.

"I just didn't trust her," Lara admitted of Shelly.

Randy didn't either. Trouble in the Rivardo marriage escalated. His wife locked him out of the house at night. Whatever money he brought in, Shelly would spend without any regard for what the family needed.

He told Lara something that stuck with her for decades.

"Shelly is only nice to me when there are other people around."

Randy started sleeping in his car, something that became a nightly occurrence. Shelly wanted only his paycheck, which she insisted he hand over on Fridays. The checks weren't a magnificent sum. Far from it. Even with a decent job and no rent payments, things were tight. Shelly was used to getting more of everything. She complained to her father, so Les Watson interfered and made it so Randy's check got delivered straight into Shelly's hands.

"So I was sure to go home," Randy said later.

It didn't take too much longer for Randy to decide that he couldn't take it anymore—no matter how much he loved Nikki, he couldn't ignore that his marriage, which had started on tenuous grounds, was now falling apart.

Lara didn't blame Randy for leaving his family, for leaving Shelly. No one did. Except Shelly.

He got airfare from his parents and left Washington—and Shelly—as fast as he could. "I needed a fresh start," he said. Yet when Shelly called him at his parents' house two weeks later and professed a genuine desire to repair their marriage, Randy agreed to let her and Nikki come stay with him and his family, albeit reluctantly. He missed his daughter, and cared more for her than whatever he felt for Shelly.

The reunion was short-lived, lasting just two weeks.

"Even my grandparents were disgusted by her behavior. She created such a furor there that I had no recourse but to file for divorce."

Shelly retaliated immediately by buying everything in sight and sticking Randy with a growing bill. This put her ex further and further into debt. Shelly didn't care. Randy sent her an income tax refund check that needed to be countersigned. Randy told Shelly that the money would get him caught up with the collectors who had been hounding him.

No such luck. Shelly double-crossed Randy and had another man forge his signature.

She cashed the government check and kept the money for herself.

And then suddenly Shelly simply dropped out of sight. Lara tried every number she had—friends, relatives. Anyone. She was worried about the baby.

"I kept calling Shelly," Lara said. "She wouldn't answer. And I was frantically trying to get ahold of her. Trying to see her and she wasn't home or wouldn't answer the phone. She just stopped being a mother. Shelly got a job as a waitress in a bar on Main Street in Vancouver and that seemed to be enough for her."

This went on for some time. At one point, a relative in Battle Ground told Lara that she'd better come and get Nikki, for whom the relative was caring.

"Shelly's gone."

"Where?" Lara asked.

"I don't know."

"When is she coming back?"

"Don't know that either."

Shelly stayed gone. What she was doing and who she was with was a bit of a mystery, though frankly, Shelly being gone was a very good thing. Less drama. Less worrying. Less of everything that tied the stomachs of those around her into knots.

It would be almost a year before Shelly would return to collect her daughter from Lara. Shelly's absence wasn't even explained. She just popped back in and took Nikki. Lara's love for Nikki was deep. She'd wanted to keep her—to have her declared abandoned by Shelly, to adopt her and raise her as her own.

Lara vowed she'd do whatever she could to stay close to her granddaughter.

In 1978, when Nikki was just three, her mother lovingly wrote about her feelings for her firstborn.

Shelly dotted her i's and underscored exclamation points with hearts to emphasize her unbridled devotion. She wrote in verse how seeing Nikki's face brightened up the drudgery of a long day.

"A face as darling as can be, her laughter . . . a bubbling brook . . . while her smile dimples her sweet little chin . . . All framed by her hair of gold . . . and those eyes—big and brown . . . sparkling with laughter."

She tempered her love letter with a splash of cheerful reality too.

". . . she's in my jewelry box! My purse! My lipstick! Or pulling off some mischievous trick!"

Shelly concluded with a telling rhyme:

"Oh Nikki, though our tempers increase our love for her will not ever cease!"

For a time, Shelly perpetuated a kind of "you and me against the world" story line. She told Nikki that her daddy had abandoned them, that her paternal grandparents didn't love her. She said all of that to her daughter with sad eyes and her arms wrapped around her, but added that it was fine because she loved Nikki so, so much.

Unsurprisingly, this turned out to be carefully curated fiction. Many years later, Nikki found a cache of letters from her dad and his side of the family, and discovered that her father's family had sent birthday and Christmas gifts as she was growing up. Her mother had cut off the tags and put her own name on them.

⋊⋉

Lara and Les were concerned that Shelly was leaving Nikki alone while she went out, so they went over to her apartment in Vancouver to check up on her. There they met Danny Long, who was living across the hall from Shelly. Lara knew Danny's mother because she'd bowled at Tiger Lanes. Danny was thin, with longish dark hair and a pleasant smile. He said he had keys to his neighbor's apartment.

"You must know my daughter pretty well if you have her keys," Les said.

Danny mumbled something and let them in.

Shelly and Nikki weren't there, but the Watsons did find a box full of things stolen from the cabin on Mount Hood, plus a full set of keys to their home, their cars, and, of course, the cabin. The keys had been missing from Lara's purse for several weeks.

Not long after, Shelly and Danny moved into the house in Battle Ground that Grandma Anna had always promised would be her favorite grandchild's. Soon Shelly had a second baby on the way. The couple married in a small wedding chapel near the courthouse in Vancouver on June 2, 1978. Shelly was on her second marriage by twenty-four. A couple of months later, in August 1978, Samantha was born. She was a beautiful baby—blonde, with big, expressive eyes.

Danny was good to the girls but pushed back on Shelly more than she'd been used to experiencing. The two of them fought constantly, hard and physically. Dishes shattering. Yelling. Running out the door. All that kind of drama. One time when Lara visited—on a rare occasion when she was allowed to—she noticed holes punched into the drywall. The smart money might've been on Danny, though in truth Lara couldn't be sure which of the adults had slammed a fist into the wall.

Indeed, Shelly's marriage to Danny was very tempestuous, as had been the case with her marriage to Randy, and ended just the same. When a spat ended and Danny left to cool off or get away, Shelly would pack the girls in the car and start looking for him.

Shelly, her family would later say, always liked to hunt.

Whenever there was a new boyfriend, Shelly had a singular instruction for Nikki.

"You need to call him Dad," she said.

So Nikki did. When she went to school, her mom would simply enroll her under her new man's surname. No legal formalities at all, just Shelly's insistence and good word that she'd created a new family.

Just like that.

Five years into her marriage to Danny, Shelly phoned her father and said she needed money for a divorce. She complained that Danny had betrayed her.

As usual, Les didn't question any of it.

Anything for Shelly.

It was 1983 and, at twenty-nine, Shelly had a new guy on the string.

"I thought of Danny as my dad," Nikki recalled, many years later. But once Danny was out of the picture, Shelly set her sights on mild-mannered Dave Knotek. "I remember Mom bringing Dave around at our place in Battle Ground and telling me that he was our new dad. I hated him because I loved Danny. And not too much later, we were packed up for Raymond."

X

Even now, Nikki holds on to a memory that comes to her occasionally, visiting her like a ghost.

It was just before the move to Raymond. She was asleep in her bed in the house behind the nursing home in Battle Ground. All of a sudden, she woke up, unable to breathe through a pillow pressed over her face. Nikki started screaming for her mother, and suddenly—as in that very instant—Shelly appeared.

"What is it?" she asked. "Baby, what's wrong?"

Nikki, crying, said someone had put a pillow over her face.

"It was a bad dream," Shelly said.

Even then, Nikki knew better.

"It wasn't a dream, Mommy."

Shelly fixed her eyes on her little girl and insisted she was wrong. She wouldn't back down. She didn't have to. She was, as always, right about everything.

The encounter stayed with Nikki. The speed with which her mother responded. The peculiar look on her face—more interested than concerned.

Later, she would wonder if that was the first time her mother had messed with her mentally, and if she'd done the same thing to others in her life.

CHAPTER EIGHT

Timber. Oysters. And decades later, marijuana.

Soggy and exceedingly gray, Pacific County, Washington, has always relied heavily on nature. It's been on a boom-or-bust trajectory since the first white settlers came to the rainy, windy spot in the state's southwest corner in the 1850s. It seems almost dismissive to call the people who live there a hardy lot, but there's really no denying it. The place where the Pacific Ocean meets the Willapa River and various tributaries is the kind of place in which abundance wasn't given, it was earned. Its triad of towns—county seat South Bend, Raymond, and Old Willapa—are the county's backbone. Huge Craftsman homes run along the hills above the bay that empties into the ocean. They speak of a time before the economy ebbed, as it always does in places that depend on natural resources. Only the courthouse, with its Beaux Arts design and magnificent art glass rotunda, still does a booming business. Its annex is where the welfare office is located.

Soggy as it is, the region along the Willapa River to the bay has made its mark in popular culture. Maybe more of a smudge than a mark. Nirvana, originally from Aberdeen, one county away, played its very first gig in Raymond, a town of less than three thousand. Lyricist Robert Wells, who wrote "The Christmas Song" with Mel Tormé and the theme from TV's *Patty Duke Show*, grew up there. Author Tom

Robbins wrote his first novel, *Another Roadside Attraction*, in South Bend.

And yet most of those who live there—especially those who have grown up with sawdust and oyster shells—are not famous. Not by a long shot. They fit mostly in that tight space between salt of the earth and hardscrabble.

Dave Knotek was a local Pacific County boy through and through, having lived his first four years in nearby Lebam, before his parents, Al and Shirley, moved along Elk Creek into a little wood-frame house in Raymond. Al was a timber faller, but work in the woods could be spotty. That the Knoteks never had a lot of money was an understatement. Dave and his brother and sister made their own toys—bows and arrows out of sticks and chicken feathers. Country kids like the Knoteks could often be spotted in a Raymond classroom. Their clothing was older, not always in the best shape.

"A few times I started the school year with the same clothes I wore the year before," he recalled. "No disrespect to my parents. They worked very hard. We just didn't have the money."

The daughter of a sawmill worker, Shirley picked up the slack by working in an oyster cannery for quite some time, and then later at J. C. Penney.

Of the three kids, Dave was the hellion of Al and Shirley's brood—messing around, stealing his dad's smokes, even a half-hearted attempt at running away with a buddy in the fourth grade. And because of that, he was disciplined in the way his father had been. Al had a razor strap and wasn't averse to using it on the kids if needed. Dave felt its sting more than a time or two, but never thought he didn't deserve it. It was the way it was.

At the time, Raymond was bustling. The mills were running three shifts, and the endless supply of timber kept logging trucks on the roads all day long. The river was nearly clogged with log rafts.

In 1971, Dave graduated from Raymond High School—home of the Seagulls—with the idea that he wanted to follow in his father's footsteps and be a logger, though his dad did his best to convince him otherwise.

"Dad didn't want me to do any of that. Too hard. But that's what I ended up doing." He worked in logging for a year before enlisting in the navy.

"I wasn't going to be a timber faller like my dad, but I enlisted in the navy like my dad had and learned to run heavy equipment. And that's what I did for twenty-two years—running a dozer in the woods."

The military gave Dave a much-needed boost of self-confidence. When he came home to Raymond after serving in Hawaii and Alaska, Dave Knotek was suddenly viewed as a very eligible bachelor. He was a nice-looking, athletic guy, having learned to surf in Hawaii. He had a kind, gentle personality, though he could also party. Best of all, he had a good job at timber giant Weyerhaeuser. Upon his return, he became a member of fraternal orders like the Elks and the Eagles, and his popularity surged. He got serious with a couple of local girls, but those relationships didn't pan out.

"The girls chased me a little," he said later with a smile.

At the time, he didn't know that the wrong one would end up catching him.

)(

There was no particular reason why Dave Knotek drove down to Long Beach, Washington, on a Saturday near the end of April 1982. It wasn't beach weather—that doesn't hit the Washington coast until the end of August. Dave, recently dumped by a girl, was in search of a beer and a little distraction. In fact, when he left his place in Raymond and drove his orange VW surf buggy toward the highway, he didn't know if he should turn right to Westport or left to Long Beach. Long Beach won.

When he arrived at a tavern called The Sore Thumb, it was packed with young men not doing much of anything.

Shooting the breeze.

Shooting pool.

Talking about shooting.

Yet amid all the guys was the most beautiful girl Dave had ever laid eyes on.

Though there were hiccups in Shelly's life when it came to choosing men, there was no denying she was very good-looking, with light eyes, red hair that she wore big and long, and the kind of figure that little girls hope for when they are growing up. Curves in all the right places. Shelly understood that men liked a girl who flaunted what she had, and in her early years, she was more than happy to work it.

By Dave Knotek's estimation, Shelly Watson Rivardo Long was way out of his league. He just knew it. He watched her from the sidelines. She was all auburn hair and had a killer body. Dave had been a late bloomer. No girlfriend to speak of in high school. He was shy back then. Even after the navy, he was still shy. He sipped his beer, and tried to get up the nerve to ask the pretty redhead to dance.

"She really looked like a movie star in some of them old films. A wow. Other guys were hitting on her right and left and I just looked at her. Pretty soon, she came over to my table just as I was ready to ask her to dance."

Shelly told Dave she had two little girls and was living down south in Clark County, in a nice little house that her Grandma Anna had left her when she passed.

"Can I get your phone number?" he asked Shelly after they'd danced for a few songs.

"Okay," she said, playing it cool.

They parted ways later that evening. Dave never expected to see her again, but he couldn't stop thinking about her. He certainly wouldn't see her there at the bar. The Sore Thumb burned to the ground the night after they met.

He finally sucked up the courage and dialed Shelly's number and asked if he could come down to see her in Vancouver. She said yes. In time, he made it a weekly trip. Dave fell hard for Shelly *and* her little girls.

"They were nice kids. Really good kids. They needed a dad. I could see that. Anyone could."

About that time, Shelly needed a savior—someone she could use. Danny was long gone. So was Randy. She was in trouble with the house that Grandma Anna had left her. It had gone into receivership when she couldn't come up with the money for the taxes or the loan. She quitclaimed it over to Dave Knotek.

"Dave wants to try to save it for me," she wrote the judge, *"but it needs much needed repairs. I can barely afford to care for my children. I think I'll have to let Dave have claim to it."*

Shelly lamented the legacy of the house adjacent to the nursing home. It had been in her family for three generations.

"My grandmother lived there. My natural mother before her death. And I was raised there for the first twelve years of my life. It has been common knowledge between my family and my relatives that the house would go to me at the right time. That came in 1981. It wasn't before that because I had a very bad marriage and my parents didn't want me to lose it in a divorce settlement. In 1979 I separated from my husband and moved in. I know this for sure because my daughter started kindergarten in the fall . . . Save my home for my children. I would like to work with U.S. Creditcorp to see what I can do. I haven't hurt anyone. I just want to make a future for myself."

Later, Dave made a promise that he'd give the house back to Shelly, but in time, the house was lost to foreclosure.

As the new couple grew a little closer, Shelly tearfully confided after a doctor's appointment that she had a bigger problem than merely trying to make ends meet for herself and her girls.

"I have cancer," she said. "I probably won't live to thirty."

Dave was stunned. Shelly looked completely fine. Besides, by then he was in love with her. And now, he was held completely captive by her disclosure.

"I thought to myself," he said many years later, "that she was going to probably die. And if she died, who was going to take care of Nikki and Sami? They really didn't have anyone. The whole time we were together she played the cancer card. I should have known better, but I didn't."

After about a month in Dave's studio apartment, the four of them moved into a red house on Fowler Street in Raymond's Riverview neighborhood.

"I didn't marry Shell because her kids needed me," Dave said, "but I have to admit that was a pretty big reason behind my wanting to marry her."

Indeed, they finally made it official in Raymond on December 28, 1987. One of the witnesses to the wedding was a young woman named Kathy Loreno, Shelly's hairdresser and best friend. No one knew at the time that Kathy would eventually play a far bigger role in the Knotek marriage than anyone could have imagined.

✕

Les Watson was only too glad to have his daughter get married for a third time. Indeed, he couldn't have been more relieved. It meant that she'd probably not come around anymore for money. He'd never truly forgiven her for the rape story, though he'd learned to play nice. While her accusations hadn't ruined him, they'd left a scar.

Shelly continued to bad-mouth her dad behind his back, though to his face she tried to worm her way back in with indirect apologies and promises to be a better person. She claimed she had cancer and she thought he'd want to know directly from her, not Lara, with whom she'd started a war over seeing the girls more frequently. When Les didn't take her calls, Shelly wrote to him:

"I'll always be so proud to have you as a Dad. The older I get the more I've realized how much I appreciate you. Dad, I'm so full of pain I just want out. You've known so little of my life for such a long time. Maybe the next time around . . . I won't make the same mistakes. I'm not strong enough to go through the months ahead. But I love you, Dad, and I've missed you. Love, Shell."

CHAPTER NINE

From Nikki's perspective, it was like her mother and stepfather had started their life together with a poisoned kiss and a declaration of war. It was apparent to many, including Nikki, that Dave Knotek had been made less of a man by marrying Shelly. It was clear that her stepfather could barely function in his marriage to her mom.

Nikki recalled an incident she'd watched with the gaping eyes of a child—unblinking but petrified at the same time. Dave, thin with longish hair and tattoos that portrayed his love of the sea from his stint in the navy, was on the front porch of the Fowler house with a shotgun in suicide position. He was shaking and crying. It was after another row with her mother, another heavy spate of hatred and disgust directed at him because he didn't make enough money or care enough about the kids.

Her mom hurled nasty invectives at him, one after another.

"You are a worthless excuse for a husband!" Shelly yelled before slamming the door with one last parting shot. "You don't even love me or the girls! If you did, you'd work harder!"

Dave sat still and composed himself. He got in his truck and drove off like he always did after a big fight.

He was like that. Compliant. Passive. Submissive.

"I never once saw him strike her," Nikki remembered later. "I mean rarely would he even use a cuss word toward her."

The same couldn't be said of Shelly.

"She'd get violent. Really violent. She'd slapped me around a few times and I didn't hit her back because that's not what a man does," Dave recalled. "She'd push. Shove. Scream. Really violent. I wasn't used to that."

"We need to talk things out," Shelly said more than one time, trying to keep him where she wanted him.

"I can't be around you like this," he said.

Shelly snuggled up to him. "This is normal. This is the way people work things out."

"Not normal to me," he told her.

The first time things got really bad was when Dave had a few too many drinks at a Christmas party at the Weyerhaeuser sorting yard. His coworkers brought him home to find Shelly at the door, angry as all getout. Bugged eyes and red-faced. She pushed him and screamed so much that he ended up going to his folks and spending the night there. That, in turn, made Shelly even angrier. Shelly wanted her husband home to face the music for which she was the conductor. He had no place of refuge. After that, she did everything she could to separate Dave—and later the girls—from his family. She insisted on total control all the time, everywhere they went. If an argument ensued while they were in the car, Shelly would make Dave get out.

"Right now! Out!"

In time, Dave couldn't function normally. It crept up on him. He didn't know what was happening or why. He couldn't sleep. He was always wondering when the other shoe would drop and Shelly would go into attack mode.

I need a break. Some rest. I need time away from her.

Sometimes he'd get in his truck and head up to the hills above Raymond to camp. On other occasions he'd stay with friends. He knew that life with Shelly was not like anyone else's marriage. He didn't miss work or climb into the depths of a whiskey bottle. He dealt with her by being away.

To survive Shelly meant avoiding her whenever possible. Even early in their marriage, Dave would retreat from her constant barrage of angry demands. Yes, she could be sweet. Yes, she could be fun. But as time went on, those attributes took a back seat to her uncontrolled anger, a temper that scared him. He knew that something wasn't right with her. She was off. The screaming. The violent temper. The slamming of the doors until the hinges broke from the wooden frame. All of that. Dave would sit in his truck with a sleeping bag and pillow and ask God what to do.

"Lord, this isn't right," he'd say. "This isn't normal. This isn't how a family operates. I know it. Help me."

"When somebody pushes, pushes, and pushes you into a corner, pretty soon you're not going to want to be in that corner anymore. People would ask me later why I just didn't leave. Take the kids and go. You just didn't do that with Shelly. You can't. She wouldn't allow it. She'd hunt you down."

Often when he'd return home after considerable introspection, Shelly would flip the switch and be sweet, soft voiced, and affectionate. That might last a few weeks, days, or merely a few hours.

And then the cycle would spin out of control again.

CHAPTER TEN

Years later, the house on Fowler Street in Raymond burned to the ground, leaving a big, gaping scar in the landscape—in its own way, a metaphor for the beginning of the Knotek marriage. When they passed by the spot, Nikki would frequently recall her mother's tirades against her stepdad and herself. She'd fight to hold on to the good memories, scant as they were. Her mom loved her. That had to be true. Her mom loved Sami. That was obvious.

Painfully so.

Sometimes hitting the pause button on a life beginning to spiral out of control by moving to a new house can actually reset the situation and make things better.

Nikki hoped that would be the case.

It had to be.

Dave and Shelly Knotek moved their family into a big Craftsman rental home in Old Willapa, which they always referred to as the Louderback House, so named for its original owners, a family associated with the region's historic maritime industry. The residence was at the end of a long private drive that snaked past farmland. The road turned sharply up a hill, where the house was tucked into the fringe of the forest. Painted dark evergreen with contrasting trim, it boasted a wide porch that swept around the corner, connecting the entry into the living room to a side door accessing the kitchen. Inside, the ceilings were at least twelve feet high; the floors, battered but beautiful hardwood; a large masonry fireplace filled a front room paneled with wide planks. Across from the living room, adjacent to the staircase, was a large bathroom with a big tub. Off to the right of the front door was the master bedroom with a window facing the front yard.

Nikki's and Sami's bedrooms were up a flight of improbably steep wooden stairs. Each girl had her own room, separated by an open space that they would use for a playroom. Nikki's overlooked the grassy and wooded hillside above the kitchen. Sami's windows took in a view of the side yard with its mature rhododendrons and the garden spigot. Two flights down, the basement was large and musty, with a furnace that burned diesel oil and smelled every bit of it—no matter the season. Shelly loved the house. She thought it was perfect and she wanted to buy, instead of rent, but that kind of expense wasn't in the cards. Dave was working in the woods then, pulling extra hours and doing everything he could. Shelly said she might look for a job, though she never seemed to get around to it.

It was a great house, charming and comfortable.

It was also the place where everything bad started.

X

Anything could be a weapon. The kids knew it. Dave too. A spatula from a kitchen drawer, a fishing pole, an electric cord. Shelly Knotek would employ all of those—and anything else within her grasp—to beat her girls if she perceived they'd done something wrong. No matter how big. Or how small. When she found a punishment that worked, she looked for ways to make it even more effective, more brutal. The act of beating her children seemed to fuel her and excite her. She seemed to savor the rush of adrenaline that came with being on the attack.

"Discipline" came mostly at night, the girls later recounted.

Nikki and Sami would be asleep upstairs, unaware that their mother had been seething on the couch, making sure that their punishment would be both severe and a surprise. Shelly was a stealth attacker. Her daughters learned to wear extra clothes to bed in the event that their mom would drag them out into the yard in the middle of winter.

"Sometimes there were reasons, I guess," Nikki said later. "Maybe we used her makeup or lost a hairbrush. Things like that. A lot of times we really didn't know for sure what we'd done."

Beatings like that nearly always ended in blood. On one occasion, Shelly pushed Nikki into a walk-in closet. *Hard.* Shelly was screaming at the top of her lungs.

"You fucking little bitch!"

Shelly jumped on Nikki and started punching and hitting while the girl cried out and begged her to stop.

"I'm sorry, Mom! I won't do it again!"

The truth was, Nikki had no idea what had set her mother off.

Something she said? Something missing? Something else?

Nikki got up and tried to make a run for the door, but her mom grabbed her, swung her around, and shoved her up against the wall, where she hit a protruding nail.

It was only then, with Nikki's head literally nailed to the wall, that Shelly backed off.

When she played volleyball at Raymond Elementary, Nikki wore opaque ballet tights under her shorts to conceal the bruises and bloody cuts on her legs from a phone cord—another of her mother's favorite implements of rage.

Later, she'd accept some of the blame for her abuse because her mom "had gotten carried away during the beatings because I was trying to get away."

While she had many opportunities to tell someone what was happening to her, Nikki didn't. She stayed private and guarded. She didn't want anyone to know that anything bad was happening to her or that her family was engaged in any kind of violence.

"I never even thought to tell," she said later. "I didn't want the attention. I didn't want people to think I was weird. And no one ever asked. Not even once."

Not all of the abuse was physical. Shelly employed a series of mind games on her daughters as well.

During the week before one Christmas, Shelly locked Nikki in her room. She'd told her that she was worthless and would never amount to anything.

"You fucking loser! You make me sick!"

And when Christmas Day came, Shelly acted like everything was perfect. She showered the girls with presents, served wonderful holiday treats, and for that one day, they were the happiest family in the world.

Then it was over.

Some things their mother did were routine. All of the presents were taken back from the kids within days. Shelly would tell them they were bad, or ungrateful, and that they didn't deserve anything she'd given them.

One year Nikki got a Cabbage Patch doll. She could not have been more excited. But Shelly took it away right after she'd given it to her, and put it in a closet. The girls knew that their mother set traps for them to see if they'd gotten into anything when she was away. She'd arrange things just so or would put tiny pieces of tape on the edge of the door to see if the trigger was tripped. Nikki learned to be as careful as she could. Especially with that Cabbage Patch doll.

"I'd wait for my mom to leave and then, very carefully, I'd get the doll out of Mom's closet, so I could hold it for a while," she said later. "Sometimes she'd catch me. Sometimes not."

Another Christmas, Shelly gave Nikki and Sami teddy-bear pins in their stockings. As the mountain of wrapping paper started to grow as present after present was opened, the little pins somehow went missing. Shelly became unhinged and beat both girls with an electric cord.

"You girls are the most selfish, ungrateful kids!"

With Dave's backing, Shelly kept them up all night looking for the pins. When they finally found them—tucked inside another Christmas gift—they instantly knew who had hidden them there.

A holiday drama culminating in a beating, it seemed, had been just what Shelly had wanted for Christmas.

ⅺ

As the kids got older, Shelly spent considerable effort concocting new techniques to make them suffer.

"The well's about to run dry," she announced out of the blue, referring to the water source at the new house. "No showers. Also, check with me before you try to use the bathroom."

It was a lie she'd use over and over—even when on city water at the house on Fowler.

Whenever Shelly left her daughters alone, they'd hurry into the bathroom and shower as quickly as they could. Sami would dry the floor, the shower walls, and the faucet. She'd hide the damp towels. There could be no hint left behind that they'd done what their mother had forbidden. After cleaning up, Sami would try to make herself look as if she hadn't had a shower at all.

"It was embarrassing going to school without a shower," she recalled. "You want to look clean and smell good. My mom wanted to control everything. She wanted to decide when we could bathe, even when we could use the bathroom. We had to have permission. Everything as simple as a shower was considered a privilege that only she could give us."

ⅺ

Sometimes after the beatings, Sami snuck into her sister's bedroom and crawled into bed with her. She and Nikki would lie there for hours talking about how much their butts hurt and thinking of what they could do to their mother to stop her from hurting them.

"I wish we could shrink her," Sami suggested. "Make her supersmall and put her in a cage."

Nikki liked the idea but saw a pitfall.

"She'd get out and bite our ankles!"

They laughed about it.

"Can you imagine our mother stabbing us with little sticks and stuff?" Nikki asked.

They could.

No, shrinking Mom wouldn't help. Not even a little.

CHAPTER ELEVEN

Though no one came over to visit, appearances were important in the Knotek household. Dave saw it. Nikki did. Even Sami would later say she understood the significance of making things look "nice" no matter how far the world was tilting toward crazy. It was makeup on a bruise. A fake rose in a garden of straw and twigs. It was as if making things appear pretty just inside the front door meant that whatever was going on in the bathroom, the back bedroom, the basement, the backyard couldn't be so bad.

Could it?

Indeed, wherever she lived, Shelly decorated with a homey country motif, decidedly more Holly Hobbie than Martha Stewart. Her favorite color was blue, so the dark oak furnishings in their new home were either upholstered in a faded denim blue or draped with blankets appliquéd with hearts and flowers. Some pink. Some blue. Baskets and doilies were everywhere. She had a penchant for knickknacks; Precious Moments, with their wide-eyed figurines, were a favorite. She could scarcely resist a teapot with flowers or butterflies. It seemed that if there was a space available for something cheerful—and country—Shelly would find something at the mall or through a mail-order company to occupy the space. She'd take great joy in setting it out, admiring it for a beat, before moving on to whatever she had her eye on next. Shelly also decorated nearly every room with an astonishing array of family photos. There was no surface left without pictures of her girls or, later, their cousin Shane, peering from the walls. Dozens of portraits hung around the redbrick fireplace.

"Yeah," Sami recounted many years later, "Mom had a thing for putting up pictures of us. It was weird to see Nikki's smiling face on the wall. It broke my heart. Seeing those pictures and knowing how she'd been punished, how she'd been abused. It hurts and makes me sick to even think about it."

Hundreds, if not thousands, of photos of the sisters exist. Each with a smile that was not only hopeful but often genuine. Years later, it would be hard for others to look at the images and wonder how a beautiful young girl like Nikki could manage a smile in front of the camera.

The girls watched their mother put up heart-themed wallpaper borders and dusty-rose wainscoting in the dining room. They gave their two cents as she tried out a lighthouse figurine on the mantel or a collection of scented candles on a side table. Those times were fun, and while later it would be easy to roll their eyes at their mother's design aesthetic, the girls knew that there was something within their mother that craved the kind of warmth and charm this style evoked. Yet it was, they also knew, completely at odds with the way she lived her life—and raised her daughters.

The truth was never far, of course. It was always easier to do what their mother asked than to fight it. Each day, each time, there was always the hope that the craziness would be over. That Shelly Knotek would just, inexplicably and without any fanfare, be the mom they dreamed she'd be.

That was a childhood fantasy that was beat into submission by a new punishment.

Shelly called it "wallowing."

It was her way of proving she was the supreme being over the entire family. Like all her best inventions, wallowing was a mix of humiliation and physical pain. It was also the kind of punishment that she could direct from the sidelines.

Wallowing was a nighttime activity, and an all-seasons endeavor.

Nikki was almost always the primary focus.

It started with Shelly flipping on the bedroom lights.

"Get up! Clothes off! Get the fuck downstairs. You are a worthless piece of shit!"

Tears came instantly as Nikki complied. There was something about her mother's voice, the force of it. It was loud, guttural. It scared her. Behind her words was the kind of rage that made Nikki think that anything could happen and that, whatever form that took, she'd be on the losing end of things.

"I'm sorry!"

"Shut the fuck up!"

Nikki would squat naked in the mud as her father sprayed her with the hose. Dave was mostly mute as he went about what he'd been told to do. Nikki cried and begged for a second chance.

Her mother watched from a few yards away, telling her husband what to do.

"Make her wallow! She's a pig, Dave! Teach her a lesson!"

More water tumbled over her shivering body.

"Wallow, Nikki!" Dave said.

"I'm sorry, Dad."

"Wallow!"

On one occasion, as she tried to lift herself, Nikki's fingertips felt frozen shards of ice. It was the depth of winter. The mud puddle of the wallowing hole was frozen at its edges. She was all but sure she'd get pneumonia and die.

Dying, she thought, *is the only way out of what is happening to me.*

From her window on the second floor, Sami watched the scene below. She wished she were there too—not to rescue her sister, exactly, but to be punished in the same way. Sami was keenly aware that, for some reason, Nikki's punishments were so much worse than the ones Shelly meted out to her. It wasn't fair that Nikki had to endure that kind of trauma for the same kinds of transgressions that would merit Sami the ripping sting of a belt or a hard slap from the back of a hand.

"I remember thinking that it was unfair that I didn't get the same kind of treatment," Sami said years later. "I knew that whatever she'd done didn't deserve the wallowing but that's what happened to her. That's what my parents did to her."

After what seemed like a very long time, Shelly dragged Nikki up to the bathroom, berating her the entire time. She switched on the hot-water faucet and filled the tub. No cold water. Just hot. Nikki was tough, but she cried the whole time.

"You are a pig," her mother said. "Clean up. Go to bed."

It was hard for Nikki to recall how long it went on. Or how many times she was made to wallow. *Dozens? More?* Some stretches were longer than others. It could have been twenty minutes. It could have been two hours. She'd crawl around in the mud in the dark, feeling the roots of the bushes, the spray of the hose, and the sting of her mother's cruel remarks.

Her sister watched it all, tears streaming down her face.

※

Without quite knowing why, Nikki could see that her position in the family had plunged downward. In her mother's eyes, she'd been diminished to almost nothing. A zero. Her little sister had somehow, she supposed, managed to find a way to work their mother to her advantage. It was true that Sami was abused too, yet she seemed to compartmentalize what happened better. She took the abuse and then found ways to sweet-talk her attacker with words of love. That singular ability worked in Sami's favor.

"She was good at buttering up Mom," Nikki recalled. "Sami always got her way by being her own advocate. It saved her. My mom didn't focus on Sami so much because Sami had friends and maybe it crossed through her head that Sami would tell on her one day. I didn't have what Sami had—the ability to butter her up or a social network. I also didn't think there was anyone that gave a shit."

Sami learned to be accommodating and not push too hard to wriggle out of a punishment that was going to happen no matter what she said. Nikki didn't quite get that. Or she refused to. Nikki continued to fight. She continued to resist.

Sami recalled one time when Nikki was lashed with a whip. The beating escalated because she didn't just take the punishment. She *fought* it.

"Nikki ran and Mom caught her," Sami recalled. "She just beat her and beat her until she couldn't walk. Her butt was all bloody."

Sami, though four years younger, figured out that if she aligned herself with her mother, she'd be able to bypass some of the violence. She didn't do it often, because she loved her big sister, but she did tell on her from time to time. Nikki, for her part, didn't trust Sami completely, yet she never wished for her to receive the same kind of treatment she had.

Indeed, Shelly loved to play favorites. Most of the time, that was Sami.

Shelly changed Sami's name to Sami Jo after the Heather Locklear character in *Dynasty*. Later, Sami would wonder if her mother had actually done it to hide her from Danny Long, her biological father, who she learned had been looking for his daughter at that time, but she couldn't be sure.

"You were born Sami Jo," Shelly insisted out of the blue one afternoon. "We just didn't call you that until now. Now we're going by your name as it was always supposed to be."

While Nikki seldom received her mother's affection, Sami—and her stuffed raccoon, Racoony—frequently did. Shelly used to create lavish parties—cakes, presents, decorations—for the plush animal that Dave had bought Sami when he was new in their lives. For years, Shelly even drove to Baskin-Robbins in Aberdeen for an ice-cream cake and went as far as setting up little scenes by restuffing the plush toy with her husband's athletic socks and old pantyhose and leaving out a half-eaten cake to show Sami what the little creature had done during the night.

"My mom could be sweet when she wanted to be," Sami said.

CHAPTER TWELVE

Nikki couldn't quite be sure how long her mother kept her locked in her upstairs bedroom in the Louderback House. Nor could she recall why her mother had dished out that particular punishment. There were no locks on the doorknobs, so Shelly employed a butcher knife lodged into the doorframe to keep her daughter inside. It was a technique she'd use whenever she wanted any of the kids to stay put.

Shelly told Nikki she was ugly and worthless, and she needed time to think about why she was such a rotten girl. She was told that she'd be there awhile.

"As long as it takes," Shelly said.

Nikki later recalled it might have been for the entire summer.

"I stopped counting the days," she said.

In reality, Nikki almost didn't mind the banishment, first to the bedroom, then the closet. The closet space was small, airless, and windowless. After a while, though, she even welcomed the imprisonment. It meant that she was away from her parents.

She'd hear the knife move. The door would be flung open. She'd snap to attention, never cowering. Just facing her mom with resolve.

"Use this," Shelly barked, handing Nikki a plastic bucket from the Aberdeen Home Depot.

She didn't have to ask what for.

Over the next few weeks, Shelly only let Nikki out to empty the bucket. She was not permitted to have any contact with Sami.

Shelly told Sami the reason behind the exile and the importance of her no-contact order.

"Your sister is bad," she said. "Do you understand?"

"Yes, Mom," she lied.

Sami was worried about Nikki. She'd been locked in her room too, but only for a day or two.

A few times, Sami was allowed to go into the room to retrieve Nikki's toilet bucket. She'd empty it in the bathroom downstairs and then hurry back up while her mom stood guard at the door. She also tried to stay in touch by tossing small pine cones up at her sister's window when their mother was sleeping during the day.

Nikki knew she was in prison. But prison, she decided, had its perks. She was away from her mother's nasty tirades. She didn't have to walk on eggshells only to find out she'd nevertheless done something wrong. In a way, she was free. The best part was the massive collection of books her mother stored in the walk-in closet in Nikki's bedroom.

"That summer I found out how much I loved to read. I read all of the Nancy Drew books that I had, then moved on to my mom's John Saul and Dean Koontz. She loved horror. She had boxes of paperbacks and I read every one of them."

When the family dog Freckles had her puppies, Sami alerted Nikki with a pine cone tossed against the bedroom window.

"There's eight of them!" she whisper-yelled.

"I want to see them," Nikki said, then touched her finger to her lips to remind her sister to be quiet.

Sami nodded.

Freckles and her puppies were the source of a happy time.

Nikki sent the bucket down on two bathrobe ties she'd fashioned together in a move that she'd seen on a prison-escape film. Sami gave the bucket a good scrubbing, and when she was sure their mother wouldn't see, she sent two puppies up, terrified they'd be caught.

Nikki cuddled the puppies for as long as she dared, then lowered them back to her sister.

✕

Nikki was eventually let out, though it wasn't long before their mother started up again. Shelly was like that. Dormant. Then suddenly alive and in a flash in search of a target. The target was almost always Nikki.

From the covered porch, Sami watched as her mother chased Nikki through the house and then into the kitchen. Shelly was screaming and telling Nikki to stop so she could punish her.

"I'm going to beat the shit out of you!"

Shelly shoved Nikki through the plate glass of the kitchen door. Shards flew everywhere, and Nikki let out a yelp that sounded like a wounded animal's. Shelly dropped the belt she was carrying and hurried to help her daughter, who was bleeding from dozens of cuts. Spikes of glass clung to her bloody shirt and shorts. Nikki started to cry, yet she didn't say anything. She'd immediately gone into shock. Sami, also crying, went to help.

Sami's eyes met her mother's. At that moment, she allowed herself to believe that her mother hadn't meant for any of that to happen. But Shelly's first response was always a denial couched in blame.

"Look what you made me do," Shelly said.

A beat later, as the blood dripped from her daughter's body, Shelly suddenly changed her tone.

Strange words came out of her mouth, like some foreign language.

"I'm sorry."

In its own way, the apology was as shocking as the blood that dripped from the kitchen floor to the bathroom.

Sami and their mother led Nikki into the bathroom where Shelly ran a hot bath. Not a scalding one. Just a nice warm bath. She gently removed Nikki's blood-soaked clothing and helped her step into the tub.

The water went red.

"Sorry," she said again.

The girls hoped that their mother *was* sorry. Maybe she could see that she'd gone too far, after all? There was reason for the hope. Shelly was actually kind to Nikki right after that incident. She took her out to dinner and even to a stylist to have her hair done.

"Just me and her," Nikki later recalled. "My mom never did that."

Even as a child who'd seen it all happen, Sami knew that her mother should have taken her sister to the hospital with the kinds of cuts her sister had all over her body.

"But she couldn't," Sami theorized. "Mom couldn't explain the cuts and all the belt welts and bruises on my sister's body. All of us had them. Nikki's were always worse. There probably wasn't a time for a lot of years that we didn't have visible marks of the abuse my mom inflicted on us."

Still, Shelly wasn't completely averse to taking her girls to the doctor whenever they needed medical attention.

Sometimes, however, she'd take matters into her own hands.

She had been around nurses all her life and had even taken a few courses at Clark College in Vancouver. She'd often talk about her desire to go back to school to get a nursing degree, but she said raising her daughters took precedence over her dreams and ambitions. She kept a stack of medical and first-aid books around the house, and when she wasn't reading a Stephen King or Dean Koontz novel, Shelly had her nose in one of the medical books.

Dave Knotek remembered a time his wife performed surgery to remove a large cyst from his back.

Shelly poured him several shots of whiskey to anesthetize him before taking a small knife to his skin and cutting out the cyst. He could feel the pain, but he was sure that Shelly knew what she was doing.

"Ain't no big deal. Her dad used to cut warts off her fingers and stuff like that," he recalled. "She pretty much lanced it off and it kind of popped out and [she] just cut it off. It was fine."

⚹

Despite the dire magnitude and appalling frequency of the abuse in the Knotek household, Lara Watson never heard her granddaughters say a bad word about their mother. Never once did they let on what was happening.

"Mom is weird," was the extent of any disclosure from Nikki or Sami.

Lara once came for a visit to celebrate Nikki's birthday. It was a hot summer evening, and she was to sleep in Nikki's bedroom on the second floor where all the heat was collecting. But when she tried to open the windows, she discovered they had been nailed shut. The girls indicated that their mom had done it, for some reason neither could recall.

The next morning, Lara noticed that each of the bedroom doors had a hasp on the outside.

She asked the girls about that too, but they shrugged it off as something their mom did.

Shelly *was* weird.

CHAPTER THIRTEEN

To a boy living on the streets in Tacoma half the time, the pull to Raymond was more of a hug than a tug. Shane Watson was Shelly's nephew by her brother Paul. Paul had been in and out of jail and prison, and Shelly focused on Shane, ostensibly to help him out of an intolerable position. For several years, Shelly and Dave talked about taking in the boy, possibly adopting him, but Dave resisted the idea. He was already struggling to keep up with Shelly's spendthrift ways.

Shelly patently ignored her husband. That was pretty much how she handled everything—and everyone —who got in her way. She was the one who was right and to disagree meant that you were stupid, a coward, a selfish prick.

Though Shane was hours away, Shelly directed a barrage of loving communication at him.

In October 1985, when Shane was ten, Shelly signed everyone's name after she wrote: *"You haven't been gone long, but we sure miss you. See you before you know it. Weekend before next for sure. We love you so much! Uncle Dave says 'Hi Big Guy! I miss you!'"*

In reality, Shane had nowhere else to go when he arrived in Raymond in the middle of 1988. His father, Paul Watson, had run away from Battle Ground at fifteen, when he thought he'd gotten a girl pregnant. That was a false alarm; however, Paul stayed away, vanishing into a life of crime and biker gangs, only turning up again briefly at eighteen with a pregnant girlfriend of Native Alaskan heritage. Shane was born in June 1975. He lived a hard, itinerant life surrounded by quick violence and clannishness, with a dad on the move and a mother with devastating problems of her own, including severe substance abuse, but Shane somehow managed to cope on his own.

It might have been an act or it might have been genuine, but Shane brought hope and an optimistic attitude with him to the Knotek home. He hadn't been beaten down by life. Certainly, he was more streetwise than the Knotek girls—Nikki was fourteen and Sami ten to Shane's thirteen—but he was also sweet too.

Shane was like a lot of kids in Raymond. He loved heavy metal and Bon Jovi. He had dark eyes and dark hair that alluded to his Native ancestry. Girls thought he was cute, not only because he was the new boy, but because he had a kind of fun, goofy personality that made everyone want to be his friend. The Knotek sisters took to him right away. He was more than a cousin to them, closer to a brother. Always smiling. Always telling someone a joke. Shelly applied for Department of Social and Health Services benefits to take care of him. She bought him new school clothes and fixed up a cozy bedroom in the basement, complete with new bedding, and helped him put up a few things that he'd brought along to make him feel at home.

Almost immediately, he started calling Shelly and Dave "Mom and Dad."

Shane was a friendly kid, but he was also a city boy from a rough neighborhood. He didn't talk too much about what his life was like before Raymond. One time when the family went on a trip, he and the girls slept in sleeping bags in the back of the truck. It was the one time when their cousin really opened up and told them about growing up with a biker dad and a drug-addicted mother. He was angry at what had happened to him back in Tacoma and how he'd been shuttled around until moving in with the Knoteks. After Raymond, he barely heard from anyone from his family other than his grandparents on his mother's side and, of course, Lara.

"Shane was nothing like his family. He was never going to be in trouble with police, addicted to drugs. None of that," Nikki said. "I never ever worried that he'd fall into the same trap as his parents. Shane was good."

Soon after her nephew arrived, Shelly put him to work on a mile-long list that never seemed to shrink.

"Mom worked Shane to the bone," Nikki said years later. "He did everything. Not willingly at first, but he eventually did whatever she told him to do."

Shane spent most of his time doing chores. Occasionally he found time to take his dirt bike up into the woods. Sometimes he took Sami for a ride, but mostly his confidant was Nikki, who was only a few months older. She understood what it was like to be an outsider—at school and at home. And like Shane, she knew what role her mother played in all of that.

Shane was scared of Shelly. Same as the girls, he would do anything not to make her mad. Shelly started to fixate on him and heap additional demands to do more around the house or in the yard. If things weren't done the way she wanted, Shane paid the price. Items from his basement room started to disappear. His pillow. His blanket, then his bed. He was told to sleep on the floor. He complained about it, but he quickly learned objections only made punishments worse.

Next, Shelly took away his every-other-week shower privileges and gave him only one set of clothes to wear to school. Shane went from cool new boy to smelly, greasy, and weird boy.

)(

Soon after Shane came to live with the Knoteks, Lara Watson made a trip up north. Such visits were always somewhat of a risk. Occasionally she'd arrive with gifts and have to leave everything on the doorstep as no one was home—despite making arrangements for the get-together. Other times, she'd park her car and wait for what seemed like hours for the girls and their mother to return home with a feeble apology that Shelly had mixed up the dates or had an unexpected errand in Aberdeen or Olympia. This time, however, Shelly, the girls, and Shane were at home when she arrived. While Shelly watched TV, Lara spent time with the girls in their rooms on the second floor. Everything upstairs looked wonderful. Nikki's and Sami's rooms were clean, organized, and uncluttered—the opposite of the way Shelly had kept her room when growing up in Battle Ground.

Lara was eager to see her grandson's bedroom too. With Shelly suddenly right behind her, she ventured down the steep wooden steps to the basement. Halfway down, Lara could barely breathe. The smell of the diesel oil used to heat the old house was so strong, acrid. It filled her lungs, making her eyes water.

"I just got the diesel tank filled," Shelly said. "The guy's coming back to fix the problem."

Lara went past the little door to the furnace room toward the front of the basement where Shane slept on a mattress on the concrete floor.

She spun around. She was confused. This wasn't acceptable at all.

"Where's his bed?" she asked.

Shelly didn't answer.

Lara, upset, looked at Shelly in complete dismay. "He needs a bed, Shelly. What's going on here? If you don't have the money . . . Let me give it to you."

Shelly just stood there.

Lara gave the room another quick scan.

"He needs a closet too."

Shelly made some vague excuse about being too busy to get Shane completely settled, but she took the money.

A short time later, Lara learned that Shelly had finally purchased Shane a bed. She wondered if she hadn't made a big stink about it if Shelly would have even thought to do it.

Or if she even cared.

CHAPTER FOURTEEN

Nikki saw how moms acted on TV. How they listened and comforted their children with words and a tender touch. She also observed other moms around town, and how they interacted with their children or husbands. There wasn't all the yelling and hitting. They didn't make their kids do weird things that were not only physically painful but humiliating, so much so that they couldn't even talk about it. Nikki *knew* her mother was *not* normal. When Shane arrived, he and Nikki spent hours talking about how messed up Shelly was.

He wasn't anywhere near as forgiving as Nikki.

"She's full of shit," he said.

"I know," Nikki said. "But there are times . . ."

Shane cut her off. "What times?"

"When I think she really loves us. She makes me feel loved and that all the craziness is just gone."

"For a minute, Nik," he reminded her. "Then it's back."

Nikki agreed. It might have been hard for Shane to really understand where she was coming from. She actually had been loved by her mother. It was fleeting and gone now, but she hoped down to her bones that it would come back.

In spite of all the things Shelly did.

Years later, she'd search for the words to make others understand how she could have loved an abuser like her mom.

"I think as a kid I depended on her, her being my mom, I don't think I ever thought I had any other options but to live with her. As an adult I kick myself for not doing something to help myself back then. My mother could show affection and say kind words when she wanted to . . . she would abuse me, then the very next day hug me or tell me how I was her baby and she loved me blah, blah. I think it worked like any abusive relationship . . . a person feels trapped, nowhere to go . . . they are abused and then the abuser reins them back in with kindness and the person being abused settles, not quite thinking about the next time they are beat etc. just relieved the abuse is over (for now). My mother was a ticking time bomb . . . I never knew when she would go off. Everything could be great for a few days then boom. I loved my mother because I didn't know I had a choice. I had to love her."

※

Some things Shelly made the kids do were embarrassing, others painful. Some were flat-out ridiculous. It was as if she was conducting tests, seeing how far she could go. Shane had been beaten and made to wallow. He'd been called every ugly name in the book. Like soldiers in a prison camp, he and Nikki joined forces, and the two of them became inseparable conspirators.

Shelly had a distressingly acute ability for finding new ways to humiliate the pair. She instructed them to take off their clothes in the living room for transgressions no one could remember. Sami watched as her sister and cousin were instructed to slow dance nude.

"Until I say you're done," Shelly said.

Sami watched, cringing at the sight. Glad it wasn't her. She was so modest herself that she could barely handle being in a bathing suit. This was beyond humiliating.

Which, of course, was the reason their mother had the two older kids do it.

Sometimes Dave would be there for the dancing.

"My dad would just sit there," Sami said. "My sister and Shane would be crying the whole time. You know, you just do it. You don't refuse my mom."

Years later, Lara Watson would struggle to come to terms with or make some sense of her stepdaughter's singular fascination with nudity. It came out of left field. Lara was unable to come up with a causal link between Shelly's childhood and that kind of behavior.

"None of my kids ever saw me in panties and a bra," Lara said. "I always had a robe on. Their father didn't walk around the house naked or even swim in the nude. Les showered with the boys when they went camping but never Shelly."

She had no idea where it came from.

Maybe something weird had gone on when Shelly was over at her grandmother Anna's. That was possible, though not likely.

"I think Shelly would have told me back then. I really do. I don't know where any of that came from."

Shelly's life with her birth mother—before Sharon Watson dropped off her kids and returned to California—was a bit of a mystery.

"Maybe something was going on with her? I don't know. Sharon was an alcoholic. Something could have happened with her. I don't think we'll ever know," Lara mused.

Growing up, Lara said, Shelly was very modest. She dressed in her room with the door shut. She never paraded around Battle Ground in a skimpy outfit. She didn't do anything like that at all.

The way the kids saw it, the nudity was more about power than sexuality. Sami came to see the nudity as her mother's way of humiliating her victims, and also to keep them from running away. Forced nudity was one component of Shelly's bizarre and demeaning methodology of stripping away a person's identity.

And their ability to leave.

CHAPTER FIFTEEN

It was winter, and the sun had already dropped behind the firs that shrouded the Louderback House on all sides. Icicles hung from eaves overloaded with leaves and fir needles. Snow crunched underfoot. The air had been heavy around the house since Nikki and Shane had gotten home from school. It was almost always an ambush with Shelly, who had been sitting around eating Oh Henry! bars, watching TV, and ruminating on a new plan to make the kids pay for one thing or another.

That something was going to happen was palpable, like some kind of strange energy in the atmosphere that grabbed the kids by their necks.

"Take your clothes off! Now!" Shelly screamed.

Not that.

Not again.

Why?

Sometimes Nikki and Shane fought her castigations. A lot of good that did. It just made Shelly angrier, and angering Shelly, with her red face and bulging eyes, was like daring a monster to annihilate its victim. In most cases, they simply acquiesced. Just as Nikki could almost never recall exactly what she'd done to make her mother so angry, she could never figure out why she and her cousin didn't fully resist.

"There had to be a reason for it," she said, struggling later to pin down a specific reason why she and Shane were singled out that day. "I honestly just don't remember what it was."

They peeled off their clothes, thinking they'd be forced to wallow together, but Dave wasn't home at the moment. He was almost always the commander of the wallowing, standing in the dark, running the hose and reinforcing his wife's very specific orders. This would be a new punishment, and neither knew exactly what it could entail. Shelly told Nikki and Shane to go to a spot on the hill behind the house and sit there with their backs to each other.

"You'll stay here until I say you are done."

Then she went back inside the house to watch TV with Sami.

Shane shuddered, freezing his ass off. "I'm tired of this shit, Nikki," he said.

Nikki, naked and half-frozen, agreed. "I am too."

Puffs of warm breath drifted from Shane's mouth. "I want out of here."

"I do too," Nikki said.

They kept their eyes fixed on the house, wondering if Shelly would emerge with the hose and douse them with water for good measure.

It would be like her to do that.

Or maybe even have Sami do it. Sami was the chosen one, the prison-camp favorite who walked between both worlds, telling on the others to curry favor.

And to survive.

There were times when Nikki and Shane could laugh about what Shelly did to them, but that frozen day on the hill behind the house wasn't one of them.

"This is completely fucked up," Shane said. "I really hate your mom."

"I do too."

It wasn't that Nikki was blindly agreeing with Shane. She really did hate her mother. Part of her believed, however, that despite how Shelly treated them, she was better than having no mother at all. Shane didn't have any other family. Didn't he see that this was better than nothing?

Shelly leaned over the porch railing a few times to observe while the teens shivered back to back. Neither spoke. Talking didn't distract Shelly; it only made her tighten the screws on whatever discipline she was meting out.

"She's crazy," Shane said when Shelly went back into the house.

Nikki couldn't argue against that. "Yeah," she said, "I know."

As they sat there, they played a favorite game: killing Mom. It wasn't a real game, of course. It was merely a kind of revenge fantasy they allowed themselves to indulge in.

Like bath time. Her robe always half-open, Shelly would enlist Shane and Nikki to prepare a hot bath.

"Draw me a bath," Shelly would demand whenever the mood struck her.

The kids would go into the bathroom and start to fill the tub. While Shane looked on, Nikki would add some bubble bath. Her mother didn't have a favorite, just whatever was on sale. Lavender. Rose. Jasmine. She'd sit on the edge of the tub as a billowy mountain of suds formed, testing the water. The temperature had to be just right.

Hot, but not too hot.

Shane would watch the suds grow and smile.

"We should bring a radio in here," he'd say.

Nikki always knew instantly what he was getting at. She'd look over and smile at him.

Shane would nod. "And throw it into the water when she gets in."

"Good idea," she'd say.

It was a joke, but not really. It was the kind of musing that tightened the bond between Nikki and Shane.

They'd stop talking when Shelly returned. She'd let her robe fall to the floor and climb into the tub. The fleeting fantasy of ending their torment with electrocution was gone. Despite all that she had done to them, they couldn't hurt her.

It was completely dark when Shelly finally told Nikki and Shane to come inside from the hill and get warmed up.

"I hope you learned your lesson," she said.

They said they did, though they didn't have a clue what she'd been so angry about.

PART THREE

BEST FRIEND

KATHY

CHAPTER SIXTEEN

Sami's favorite childhood home would always be the Louderback House in Old Willapa. Its seclusion at the end of the road made it seem like a special destination tucked away in the forest, a stand of massive old-growth Douglas firs that would eventually succumb to the sound and fury of a logger's chain saw.

At six, Sami had done two years of half-day kindergarten, because her mother had wanted to keep her home so she'd have company while watching the entire ABC TV lineup of soap operas. The bond between mother and daughter was forged on the couch while they watched soaps and ate pickle-and-tuna-fish sandwiches.

Nikki, on the other hand, did not have such fond memories of her days at the Louderback House.

She was nine when they moved in, and while she'd been disciplined by her mother at their previous houses, it was still within the margin of what some might consider acceptable. What Shelly dished out after moving to the Louderback House was far beyond routine. The dynamic also changed as new people came to live there.

First Shane came to live with them, then Kathy arrived.

Kathy Loreno first showed up on the scene as a friend, then a babysitter. She was Shelly's hairdresser and friend, the woman who'd served as a witness at Shelly and Dave's wedding. Kathy cut an imposing figure at almost six feet tall. Her hair was brown and she often wore it long in a tumble of curls, though like a lot of stylists, she changed her look nearly every season. Longer, shorter. Curly. Straight. She'd laugh about it and offer up her curling iron to the girls so they, too, could get a new style.

Sami, always the most ready to go along to get along, immediately took to Kathy. "Kathy was bossy. That's what [Shane and Nikki] thought. And she was. But I loved her. She was like a mom to me in a good way. Before she lived with us, she used to come over and give me spiral perms, my friends too. She brought her beautician stuff over and did our hair. She was great."

The older kids were annoyed that yet another person was running their lives. Nikki and Shane initially couldn't stand Kathy, though it wasn't really her fault. She was put in the role of acting like she was their mother. They didn't need another mom or a babysitter.

For Christmas 1988, Shelly, then thirty-four, was pregnant with her third baby, which added even more to the holiday spirit. Nikki, Sami, and Shane all shared in the excitement of a new member of the family. What none of them knew was Shelly's plan to add yet another head of the household.

"Kathy's moving in," Shelly announced.

The statement seemed to come out of the blue, and not just for the kids. Dave knew Shelly was good friends with her hairdresser, but live with them? This was a complete surprise to him.

"Why's she moving in here?" he asked.

"Her family doesn't want her," Shelly said. "She needs a place to live. Plus, she's going to help me with the baby. Like a midwife."

Dave didn't argue, though he wanted to. He'd tried to push back on Shane moving in, but Shane's dad was back in prison and the boy needed a stable environment if there was any hope to end the cycle of crime. He could see that Shelly had made up her mind and didn't care what he had to say anyway.

Shelly and Dave moved Kathy's twin bed and dresser to the open space between Sami's and Nikki's rooms on the second floor. They decorated the walls with some of Kathy's things and set out her yarn basket and other items that she'd brought along. She was thirty years old and out of work, having been let go at the salon, and grateful to be with such good friends.

To the kids, Shelly appeared to be rescuing Kathy from an old life that she didn't want anymore, and Kathy seemed fine with that. Appreciative, even. Early on, Shelly told her she didn't need to work and they would take care of her.

"You need to stay with us, Kathy," she said. "It will be so fun. Plus, I really need you."

The last part was the hook.

Shelly needed Kathy all right. She told her that it was for the medical appointments at first, then the new baby. Then it was her four unruly kids who needed Kathy's good judgment and support. Kathy seemed up for the challenge.

Nikki watched the interloper with skeptical and anxious eyes, scrutinizing her mother's bossy hairdresser/best friend. She could see the dynamic that was developing between Kathy and her mom. Kathy worshipped Shelly. She hung on Shelly's every word. Shelly stood upon a pedestal above all others, godlike. Kathy seemed to embrace that.

"No one works harder than your mom," Kathy insisted. "I don't know why you girls and Shane can't do more to help her."

If Kathy overheard anything that she thought was impertinent to Shelly, she'd pull the offender aside.

"Do you listen to yourself?" she hissed. "Don't be so disrespectful."

Likely because she was in a favored position with her mother, Sami adored Kathy right away. On the other hand, Nikki and Shane thought she was an overbearing busybody whose sole purpose was to make their lives more difficult by telling them what to do. It was like having two mothers. Shelly undoubtedly had briefed Kathy about what was up with the two oldest: Nikki was defiant and Shane was incorrigible.

"She wasn't mean to us kids," Nikki recounted. "She came into the house where my mom was yelling at us constantly. She thought we were just horrible kids. We were always in trouble for something. Shane had cigarettes occasionally and got caught with marijuana one time. She thought Shane was a bad kid."

And if Kathy didn't know much about the Knotek kids, they knew even less about her.

CHAPTER SEVENTEEN

Kathy Loreno's mother, Kaye Thomas, was a striking woman with a knack for short-lived marriages. Kaye's parents had raised her in North Hollywood, California, where her dad worked for NBC. Her mom took a job at Lockheed to support the family during wartime. When Kaye was older, she took a job at a high-end cosmetics counter in Hollywood. It was a life of hard work with a touch of glamor.

Kaye's youngest daughter, Kelly, remembers her mother as an unhappy woman who seldom smiled but worked hard and loved to read. By 1952, she had the first of her children, a son. Later, three more children would follow. Two were girls, Kathy and Kelly.

When Kathy was born in the summer of 1958, she came into the world with the most beautiful blue eyes, like big blue marbles. Blonde hair too. She looked like her mother, who had once posed as the Langendorf Bread model in the 1930s.

Husbands came and went while the family moved from place to place—Lompoc, Moorpark, Simi Valley. Kelly came four years after Kathy; another brother after that. While money was often tight, Kathy and her siblings grew up mostly in middle-class neighborhoods, places where parents worked as plumbers and printers and moms stayed home. Kids would go out to play in the summer and not come home until dinner. Kathy and Kelly always shared a bedroom, twin beds separated by a vanity. Barbies and the clothes their mother sewed were strewn everywhere. They read bedtime stories from their mother's childhood books nearly every night. Certainly, there was drama. Drama always found Kaye. But the kids were happy.

After Kathy's stepfather died, her mother bought a camper and took the kids camping around California. It became the source of indelible memories. Kathy made purses out of old jeans, and the two sisters would stuff their bags with snacks, climb into the top of the camper, and spend hours watching the road and talking about life. Kathy liked the boy across the street, but it was only a friendship. She lived for the monthly release of Harlequin and Silhouette books. She bought them all and devoured them long before the next month arrived. She also adored country music, with Dolly Parton and the Gatlin Brothers as her favorites.

When Kathy was about eighteen, Kaye told the kids they were headed up north to South Bend, Washington, for a family vacation. After days on the road and nights in Motel 6's—the kids dreaming of at least one Howard Johnson's with a pool—they arrived in Pacific County, Washington.

"It was summer and gray and dark," Kelly recalled. "Typical Washington Coast."

Shortly after the vacation trip up north, Kaye quit her job as a cook at a Thousand Oaks Steakhouse and made a big announcement to the three children still at home.

"We're moving up to Washington!"

The declaration landed with a thud. No one liked the idea. They lived in a big rental on a corner lot in Simi Valley. It had four bedrooms and six walnut trees—a much-needed source of family income at Christmas time. It was home in every sense, especially for a family that had seen dads come and go.

They had no idea what they were getting into, but all of them knew what they were leaving behind.

Little sister Kelly couldn't see any sense in the family moving up to Washington. Kaye had little money. No job. Still, she brought her kids and mother to South Bend in the summer of 1977. Kathy, nineteen, was in the middle of cosmetology training and transferred her credits from Simi Valley to a beauty school in Aberdeen. They settled in a tiny turn-of-the-century wood-frame house for which Kaye paid just over $25,000.

She didn't work and they had very little money left after she bought the house.

"I couldn't understand what my mom was thinking," Kelly said pointedly. "How are we going to get by?"

Kathy continued her studies at the beauty school and landed a job at a local salon. It was tough going, however, to build a client base in a place like Pacific County. Most stylists' clients were their friends. And most friends were the result of longtime relationships.

The county was small by population, but its walls were huge for a young newcomer to scale. For Kathy, a girl with a kind yet sometimes bashful personality, they were impassable.

✕

Of Kaye Thomas's daughters, Kelly was the stronger of the two. By far. She had a better understanding of what she wanted and didn't want out of life than her big sister. First of all, she needed to get out of South Bend. She wanted to go to college. She wanted to have a fulfilled and happy marriage.

Kathy was stuck, though. She had her dreams, but she didn't know how to get them going.

"My mom took advantage of Kathy, who was very much a pleaser," recalled Kelly. "When Kathy started working at the salon, she and my mom shared a single checking account. Mom worked, but Kathy's paycheck paid the bills."

When Kelly, who didn't drive until twenty-one, needed a ride, it was Kathy who drove her. She was glad for the ride, of course; she just didn't think why her sister was always so available. And always so kind.

When she was younger, Kathy often babysat for free when she knew a family was poor. She once lamented to a neighbor that her family didn't have enough money for the holidays, so a bunch of kind people showed up with gifts. It embarrassed Kaye, though, in truth, they *were* in need. Kathy scrimped and saved and bought their mother a "mother's ring" for Christmas. For their mother's forty-fifth birthday, it was Kathy who dreamed up and planned a surprise birthday party.

She was a complete giver.

Many years later, when Kathy went to visit Kelly in Seattle to see Neil Diamond in concert, they walked past a panhandler by the arena and Kathy immediately reached in her purse to offer him some money.

"I thought to myself that my sister could never make it here," Kelly said later of life in the big city. "She is too nice."

When her father was killed in a workplace accident on a TV production set, Kathy and her brother were awarded the proceeds of a wrongful death lawsuit. Kathy wanted more than anything to buy a new car, maybe a Camaro or a Trans Am, but at a family member's urging, Kathy ditched her car dreams and instead put money on a house not far from her mother's.

She was independent and working at the salon in Aberdeen.

Making a life.

It didn't last long.

As hard as Kathy tried, she couldn't get her sales volume to where the salon's corporate owners said it needed to be. She lost her job and became depressed. Nothing was going right. She started to drown financially, so much so that she lost the house and was forced to move back in with her mother. It was a stunning and sad reversal of fortune. Not long after she moved in with her mom, Kathy was told she needed to start paying rent. She'd done so much for her mother, but this time the tables had turned. She didn't have any money. She did, however, have a very good friend. She'd even been a member of her wedding party.

Her name was Shelly Knotek.

CHAPTER EIGHTEEN

Having a child of his own, and all the anticipation that comes with such an occasion, marked the one time in his marriage to Shelly when Dave Knotek was truly happy. Even so, with Kathy and Shane already in the household, a new baby would mean yet another mouth to feed. Dave felt the pressure of his role as the sole provider and worked harder than ever. Shane was family, and although he needed correction now and then when it came to doing chores around the house, Dave considered him mostly a good kid. For her part, Kathy was there to help with the pregnancy and prenatal appointments, as well as keep up with Shelly's cancer treatments. Though he never said it to anyone at the time, it passed through Dave's mind that it was extraordinary that his wife had even become pregnant, what with all the chemo she was taking to beat her cancer. This new baby? An undisputed miracle, that's what.

When Shelly said it was time to get to the hospital in Olympia, she told Dave that Kathy would be driving her.

It was the first he'd heard of that plan.

"I don't get to drive you?" he asked.

"No," she said. "You follow us."

Dave was stupefied. "Really?"

Shelly shut him down.

"You heard me, Dave."

When Tori Knotek was born the first week of June 1989, it was Dave, though, not Kathy, who got to hold her first. She was all wrapped up, a little gray in her skin tone but the most beautiful little thing he'd ever seen in his life. Her eyes were blue and her hair a fuzzy blonde.

"I will never forget that," he said. "She opened her eyes and I was the first thing she ever saw."

Tori, Shelly said, was a preemie with underdeveloped lungs. Dave thought at the time that Kathy being there to help was a godsend. He doubted Shelly could have found a better helper than Kathy.

Shortly after they returned home, Shelly announced in dramatic fashion that Tori had stopped breathing but she was able to revive her. The next day, she and Kathy took Tori back to the hospital where she stayed under the watchful eyes of the neonatal staff for about a week.

"I don't know if Shell saved her or not," Dave said later. "She said she did."

For a while, despite the drama, things seemed better. Shelly, then in her midthirties, appeared to revel in the worry that something might go wrong with the baby. While Tori was not really a preemie, Shelly told Nikki and Sami that the week-early birth had left their baby sister with some heart problem that needed to be watched. She was sent home with a special bed and the riggings of a heart monitor.

Every night after the girls had gone to bed, they'd be awakened by the sounds of alarms going off and a panic ensuing downstairs. They'd hurry down to find their mother cradling the baby with a terrified look in her eyes.

"Is she okay?" Sami worried about her little sister.

"She's fine now. She's fine," Shelly said, rocking Tori back and forth. Shelly was the calm in a terrifying storm, soaking in the concern and worry from her older girls and doing her best to put them at ease.

One time Nikki came downstairs to find their mother holding a pillow over Tori's face.

"She's okay now," Shelly said, looking up from the baby, a startled expression on her face.

The alarms hadn't gone off yet.

Nikki had arrived too early.

Later, she'd think of the time her mother had come into the room when she was little, the time she'd thought her mom had put a pillow over her face.

Had she done that to all of them?

After that, Nikki and Sami kept an eye out for their baby sister. No one talked about what they suspected had been going on. No one needed to push Shelly. She seemed interested in her new baby, but only in a peripheral way. As the weeks went on, Kathy and the older girls took on a greater role.

Shelly went back to watching TV and staying up at all hours of the night.

Dave, however, saw Shelly as the best mother he'd ever known.

"She was excellent with babies," he said later. "Really the best baby mom ever."

Shelly liked bathing and dressing her girls when they were infants, loved showing them off. She seemed to bask in the attention that came from new motherhood. However, as the girls grew older, Shelly seemed less interested in any of that. She moved from one daughter to the next youngest until her focus was on Tori all day, every day.

Many years later, Sami's father, Danny, came to see her, and he told her something that gave her a different perception of how her mother cared for babies than what she'd heard from Dave Knotek.

"I always thought that she was better with babies than kids, especially as we got older," Sami said of her mother, but eventually questioned even that. "My biological father told me he watched my mother pop up from the couch and run to the crib to get me. She wanted to appear as though she'd been holding me the whole time. But she hadn't."

He could tell that I'd been in my crib all day. Dirty diapers. Bottles lying in there. Diaper rash that was something terrible."

For someone who always had so much to hide, Shelly had become an expert at keeping things out of view. It was a skill that would help her keep the darkest secrets from her family.

And the authorities.

CHAPTER NINETEEN

The kids were gathered around Sami, the birthday girl, with flickering white candles on a pink birthday cake. Shelly liked to make a show of holidays and special occasions. Birthdays were an especially big deal. It didn't matter if money was tight or even nonexistent; Shelly found a way to pile up the presents and fill the refrigerator with treats. Sami dove through the mountain of presents stacked before her on the picnic table on their porch. Shelly gave her daughter a Popple, a stuffed toy that all the girls had wanted that year. Kathy gave Sami a gold necklace with a small heart pendant. Sami was thrilled and put it on right away. It was real jewelry, and it was special mostly because Kathy was special.

Everyone was having a great time, when the mood darkened with a question from her mother.

"What's your favorite present?"

Sami grinned from ear to ear and touched the necklace. "Kathy's present. I love this necklace so much! Isn't it pretty?"

"Yes, it is," Shelly said.

Later, after everyone had gone, Shelly got out a belt and beat the birthday girl.

"You ungrateful little brat! I put this party together. I got your friends here! I'm the one who made all of this happen. I got you beautiful things. Kathy's necklace wasn't even new! It was something she had around the house!"

In tears, and sore where her mom had beat her, Sami learned a valuable lesson— her favorite present must always be the one her mother had given.

⋇

Lara Watson had done all right for herself, working in the medical field, specializing in senior care facilities—a legacy from her time in Battle Ground as Les Watson's wife. Divorced for more than two years by then, she was living in a small house on NW Cherry Street in Vancouver when she took a call from a very distraught and, now, very specific Shelly Knotek.

"It's confirmed," Shelly said. "Non-Hodgkin's lymphoma."

The news sent a jolt through Lara's body. She started crying. Hard. For all of their differences, Shelly was family. She was also a mother and had little girls depending on her. It was heartbreaking news.

Shelly told Lara that she was getting treatment, but that it was very, very serious.

A few days later, Shelly called a second time. This time she said the doctors had been wrong. It wasn't lymphoma but cancer of the pituitary gland.

Lara had never heard of such a thing. She wondered how the doctors could make such a colossal mistake and change the diagnosis in the middle of a treatment plan.

"It didn't really make sense to me," she said later. "And I was in the medical field."

She asked Shelly about treatment.

"It's pretty bad," she said. "I'm not sure how much time I have left. I'm going to see a specialist."

It passed through Lara's mind that if Shelly didn't make it, she'd be called upon to raise her granddaughters. That was fine with her. She loved them all.

Lara offered to come to Raymond to help, but Shelly told her that she had a helper already.

"My friend Kathy is here."

"Who's Kathy?" Lara asked.

"My hairdresser," Shelly said. "My best friend. She's wonderful with the girls. She can watch them while I get my treatments."

Lara was a little uncertain, but she didn't push. Cancer be damned— no one pushed Shelly.

Over the next few weeks, Kathy would make the calls to Lara to let her know that Shelly's treatments were progressing, and the girls were doing great too.

"Kathy was perfectly wonderful," Lara recalled. "This was at the very beginning. Oh gosh she was just wonderful. Bless her heart she's going to do this and that. And whenever I called, she'd answer the phone."

"Shelly's really tired," Kathy told Lara one time. "I'm cooking dinner now and keeping the house up. Kids are doing their homework. Doing the best I can."

There were early signs of cracks in the relationship, however. Another time when Lara was talking to Nikki, she heard screaming in the background.

"What's going on there, Nikki?"

"Oh," she said, "Mom's just mad at Kathy again."

※

Shelly's cancer treatments lasted for a very long time. Too long. Lara Watson became increasingly suspicious. She'd tell oncologists she worked with about her daughter's symptoms and the vague treatment she was getting from God knows who, and they couldn't make sense of it either.

One day, Shelly phoned and Lara pressed the point. She used a tone she'd never used before.

"Shelly, you know what?" Lara said. "I'm tired of this cancer crap."

Shelly started to scream.

"I've talked to some doctors and we think you're lying again."

Shelly slammed down the phone.

A few minutes later, Kathy called Lara back.

"You've really upset Shell," she said.

"Kathy, this is a bunch of BS. Cancer isn't like this."

"I don't know what you're talking about."

"You're being suckered," she said.

Next, Dave got on the line.

"What kind of mother are you, Lara? Shell's going through the fight of her life. You couldn't care less about her."

Lara knew that Dave took everything his wife said at face value. He needed proof.

"Dave, have you been taking her to the doctor?"

"Yes," he said.

Lara persisted. "Have you actually gone inside? You know that doctors insist on that. Family is a very important part of treatment."

"No," he said. "Shell's too proud. She has me wait."

"You've never been there while she's getting her IV?"

"No, but that's no reason to say she's lying, Lara."

Lara wouldn't let up. "Where are you waiting? In the car?"

Dave tried to stay firm. "In the waiting room. All day."

"All day," she repeated.

"Yeah," Dave said. "Eight hours."

"It doesn't take eight hours," Lara said. "Have you ever gotten a bill from the insurance company?"

Dave said that Shelly got the mail and he hadn't seen one. But that didn't mean anything. The truth was there was no convincing Dave. He hung up on Lara.

"He's there sitting in the waiting room," Lara said later. "I don't doubt that. Dave's not a liar. She probably went out the back door to go to the movies or out to lunch. I don't know that for sure. But it's a good guess."

CHAPTER TWENTY

With Kathy there, the dynamic in the Louderback House continued to shift. It was slow. Frog-in-boiling-hot-water slow. Kathy didn't appear to grasp what Shelly's game really was all about. She was lonely, estranged for the most part from her family, and had no money of her own. Kathy was big. Brassy. Fun. She played softball on a local league. She attended church regularly. She was the kind of woman who would gather all the girls together and make them laugh with stories of her hairdressing days at the salon in Aberdeen. After moving in with the Knoteks, Kathy started to fade away. Her personality began to dissolve right in front of everyone's eyes. She just started to fade away.

By then, whatever Shelly wanted was always of the highest order.

Yes!

Right away!

I'll clean it again.

Kathy's upbeat spirit ebbed. No matter how hard Kathy worked, Shelly didn't seem satisfied. It was never enough to take care of the baby, clean the house, and fix dinner. Whenever Kathy displeased Shelly, Shelly would grab whatever was handy—a kitchen utensil, an appliance cord, a book from the coffee table—and strike her. *Hard.* Kathy would cry, sometimes even threaten to leave. In the end, Shelly would tell her that it was her fault.

"You forced me into doing that," Shelly told her. "Don't make me do that again. I need to count on you. Don't argue. Do what I need done."

Kathy would indicate she was sorry and promise never to do it again.

Shelly would give her a hug, then a bunch of pills.

And the kids watched it all, wondering what was happening.

Shane and Nikki talked about it.

"Your mom is a freak and Kathy is stupid to put up with her," Shane said.

Nikki agreed, but she also knew that, for better or worse, having Kathy around took the heat off her a little. It gave her relief and made her sad at the same time. No one deserved to be treated the way her mother treated Kathy, or any of them.

The pattern of abuse escalated.

One time, Kathy and Shelly were in an actual knock-down, drag-out fight on the hill by the kitchen door. Though Shelly was still pregnant with Tori, and Kathy was much larger, it was Kathy who was taking a beating. Shelly grabbed her hair and Kathy let out a scream. Next, Shelly pushed her hard and Kathy fell to the ground. Shelly started to kick her in the abdomen and Kathy went tumbling down the hill.

Kathy cried out that she was sorry for whatever she'd done to make Shelly so furious.

She promised never to do it again.

In disbelief, Nikki watched the fight from the window in her bedroom. She'd seen her mom scream at Kathy, humiliate her, play her mind games, but this was the first time she'd seen Shelly physically assault Kathy. Nikki couldn't believe it was actually happening.

But it was.

Another time, Shane and the girls watched an exchange between Shelly and Kathy from the living room. Shelly had her arms folded across her chest and was shaking her head.

If You Tell

Kathy was proclaiming her innocence. "I didn't do that," she insisted, denying whatever it was Shelly had accused her of doing.

Shelly looked concerned. "You don't remember doing it, Kathy," she corrected. "That's what you mean. You don't remember."

Kathy looked her accuser right in the eye. "I didn't do that."

Shelly shook her head and gave her friend a sad look. The kids had seen Shelly in action a million times. She had a way of twisting reality to such a degree that there were times when they'd believed what they knew couldn't possibly be true.

"Kathy," she repeated. "You know I love you."

Kathy's resolve was gone, and she started to cry.

"Yes," she said, "I know. I love you too."

"Then you need to believe me when I tell you," Shelly said. "You've been sleepwalking at night. I'm worried about it."

"But I don't remember it."

"Right," she said. "Of course you don't."

This was Understanding Shelly in full bloom.

"I would know."

"Kathy, I found the lemon meringue pie under your bed this morning."

Kathy looked confused. "I didn't put it there."

"You mean, you don't remember putting it there. The kids didn't." She swiveled her gaze to her audience. "Did you?" Nikki recognized that her mother had returned to one of her greatest hits of abuse—gaslighting. Nikki had been on the receiving end of that gambit too.

"No," they chimed in. Better to not turn Shelly's attention in their direction. But Nikki had seen her mother slide the pie under Kathy's bed. She'd also seen Shelly hide—then discover—candy wrappers.

Shelly returned her attention to her best friend. "Look, Kathy. You aren't losing weight because you are eating too much during the day and, now, I'm afraid you are doing the same thing when you are sleepwalking."

107

Kathy was confused but resolute. "But I'm not."

Shelly persisted, and over the next few weeks, she continued to make several discoveries of half-eaten food hidden under Kathy's bed or somewhere in the alcove between Nikki's and Sami's rooms. One time, her mom made Nikki hide food under Kathy's bed, so she could inform Kathy the next morning that she was "sleep-eating" and "eating all of our food at night."

"I heard you in the refrigerator last night," Shelly told Kathy during another confrontation disguised as an intervention. "You ate like a pig in the middle of the night. This has to stop!"

"I'm sorry," Kathy pleaded. "I'm trying."

Though they were young, in time the girls and Shane could see Kathy falter in her ability to stand her ground against Shelly. Just like Dave. Just like them.

✕

Nikki could see the apprehension in Kathy's eyes when Shelly confronted her.

"Last night," Shelly said, "you were sleepwalking naked in Shane's bedroom. He told me."

Kathy looked scared. "I wasn't, Shell."

"You were," Shelly said. "He *saw* you, Kathy. I know you want him, but this has to stop. I don't want that kind of thing going on around here."

Kathy stepped back a little. She was stunned by the accusation. Shelly was suggesting that Kathy, a woman now in her thirties, had been interested in having sex with an underage teen boy.

"I never would do that," she said. "I promise. I promise. I didn't."

Shelly looked at Kathy with sympathetic eyes.

"You don't know what you're doing, Kathy," she said. "You really don't. Stay here." Shelly went and got Shane.

"Tell her," she said.

Shane looked very serious and backed up Shelly's story.

"You were," he said. "Last night, Kathy. I saw you."

Kathy started to cry. She looked confused as she faced her accusers.

"I wasn't," she said. "You're both wrong."

Shane stayed firm. "You were," he persisted. "I saw you. Everything."

Kathy ran up to her room in tears.

Shane later told Nikki that the story was a lie.

"Kathy was not naked in my room," he said. "I had to go along with your mom."

Nikki understood. She had done the same thing. Two against one was Shelly's favorite mode of attack. Usually it was Shelly and Dave. On occasion, she brought her daughters in on her torment. Other times, she employed Shane—most often when it came to Kathy.

"Your mom's twisted, Nik," Shane said.

"She's psycho," Nikki agreed.

"She thinks that everyone is so stupid that they actually believe her shit."

"Kathy does."

"I don't believe anything your mom says," Shane said.

"I don't either," Nikki said. "She doesn't know how to talk without some stupid lie coming out of her mouth."

As tough as their talk was, neither had the support or the gumption to call her out on anything. They just did whatever Shelly said to do. Both teens knew why they'd participated. They were in survival mode. Going against their mother's demands meant being stripped naked and forced to wallow or maybe get beaten with an electric cord. Or other punishments she'd just made up that very day. The fear of the unknown kept them in line.

"Yeah, we do what she says but we don't believe it," Shane said. "She'd be so mad at us if she thought we didn't believe her."

Kathy had done something to piss off Shelly—though Nikki couldn't remember what it was in the same way all the kids were unable to pin down what any of them had done to deserve their punishments—and Shelly had planted her foot in Kathy's back at the top of the stairs and sent her tumbling. Kathy lay in a heap at the bottom while Shelly cursed her for being so stupid and clumsy. The kids had long since learned not to say a word; calling attention to anything their mother did only served to make them fresh targets.

Shelly started taking away Kathy's privileges. She'd been "very bad and needed to learn to do with less." That meant Kathy no longer had many of the things that she'd brought with her to Louderback. Her personal items were confiscated, starting with her pictures, her country music records, and her knitting supplies. Then Shelly started in on removing most of Kathy's clothes, leaving her a single pair of panties, a bra, and a muumuu.

Within days, the muumuu was gone too.

After that, her underwear vanished. Kathy did chores around the house nude. She was told she'd have to ask for permission to use the toilet. She could no longer bathe unless Shelly approved it in advance. In time, the bathing was done outside with a garden hose.

Seeing Kathy naked and not remarking on it just became the way things were at the Knoteks'. The kids would watch TV while Kathy would do whatever Shelly told her to do. They didn't even look up, and they certainly didn't say anything.

Sometimes their mother locked Kathy in the closet as punishment for an unknown offense. Sami overheard her mother whispering soothing words through the door as Kathy cowered inside.

"You're going to be okay," she said.

Kathy murmured something incomprehensible from the other side of the door.

"It's not okay to hurt you, Kathy. I won't let anyone hurt you. I love you, Kathy. I'll keep you safe."

Sami slipped away, wondering how it could be that her mother could punish Kathy so harshly and then act as if she would always be there to save her from any harm.

It's what Shelly did to all of them. Yet with her mother's abuse focused on Kathy, there was an aspect of it that brought relief to Sami. She was glad that it was Kathy who was getting punished instead of her siblings. A part of Sami felt grateful that Kathy stayed. If she left, Sami knew the kids would once again be their mother's favorite target.

Sami saw Kathy as a strong woman. She was larger than her mom. She was smart too.

"I kept thinking that she was a grown-up. She had a car. This wasn't her mother. She wasn't a kid. If she wanted to, she could get up and leave," Sami reflected years later. "I didn't understand everything. I was a kid. But in my mind, I thought, 'What's wrong with you? You should go!'"

Nikki felt the same way. "Something's wrong with her," she told Shane. "She should just go."

And yet, "During all of this with Kathy," Nikki recalled, "I was not getting hit hardly at all. It was kind of like they ignored me for a bit."

The pause in the abuse against the Knotek kids came with a steep price. They inhabited a world in which looking the other way kept them safe from their mother but led them to accept things that would haunt them forever.

※

Shelly showed no mercy and in time enlisted her kids to participate in some of the punishments she engineered for Kathy. Both Nikki and Sami snapped rubber bands at Kathy at their mother's insistence as the woman went down the stairs to do her chores. She was weak, and she wasn't moving fast enough for Shelly.

"Get her!" Shelly called out from the landing.

Sami, who was shaking and too afraid to ignore her mother's commands, did what she had to do.

It was Shane, however, who did most of Shelly's bidding.

When Shelly told him to kick or punch Kathy, he did. He didn't do it with gusto, but he did it, knowing how quickly Shelly could turn on him. If he didn't do what she wanted, he'd be forced to wallow or would end up duct-taped to the wall naked or made to sleep on the concrete floor without clothing or a blanket. Shane did it for another reason too. As much as he hated her for what she did to him and how she treated others around him, his aunt Shelly was the closest thing he'd ever had to a mother.

He wanted to please her, to keep her in his corner. He did what she wanted, when she wanted it done.

"Kathy was afraid of Shane," Sami recalled. "She saw him as a source of pain inflicted at Mom's request. He hit her. He kicked her. He did that because she made him do it."

Shelly worked all the angles.

One time when Kathy was running up the stairs to get away from Shane, Shelly appeared and put her arms around Kathy to protect her, suddenly becoming savior instead of victimizer.

Another time Kathy went missing, and everyone in the house looked for her. Inside. Outside.

"She has to be somewhere," Shelly said.

No one could find her, until Sami located her cowering in her mother's closet.

It turned out it had been Shelly who'd hidden her there. Sami overheard her mother talking to Kathy.

"It's going to be okay," she soothed. "I'm here to protect you. You are safe with me, Kathy. I promise. No one will hurt you. Shane won't hurt you. None of them will."

Kathy was crying and holding on to Shelly, grateful for the intervention.

"Mom acted like she didn't know where Kathy was the whole time that day. But she knew. She made her stay in that closet for hours. It was supposed to keep her from being hurt by Shane, but it wasn't. It was supposed to make her feel like Mom was on her side. She wasn't," Sami said.

Sami freed Kathy from the closet.

It wasn't the last time either.

Sometimes when people came over, Shelly would put Kathy in the closet until they left. It didn't matter how long. Hours and hours. Kathy would sit slumped on the floor, patiently waiting for a sliver of daylight.

⋇

Kathy lost weight. Her skin was bruised and scratched. Her dental work had begun to fail. And her hair—the locks that she wore so long and lovely had been chopped into oblivion by Shelly's frenzied scissors. Nikki thought of how Kathy looked at them when they were getting abused by her mom. She felt a lump in her throat as Kathy gazed at *her* with empathy.

Empathy.

Kathy, who had become the focus of her mother's need to hurt and humiliate, looked at the kids with empathy.

Kathy refused to accept a lifeline from any of the kids. She knew that if they tried to help her—tried to rescue her—they'd be their mother and father's next victims.

"I wish you could help me," Kathy said once. "But I know you can't."

It wasn't that Kathy was sacrificing herself to save them, Nikki thought. It was that she knew that in a very real way the situation was hopeless.

For her.

"I had been annoyed by Kathy telling us what to do," Nikki said many years later. "At times I really didn't like her. She'd been a pain in the ass to us kids. My mom gave her all the power and made her feel needed and important. No teenager wants a stranger to boss them around. But right then, however, I saw who she really was. She was a really good person."

CHAPTER
TWENTY-ONE

Even if the Knoteks had money for a vacation trip somewhere else, it was unlikely that any activity would hold more favor than going camping in Washington State. Dave had grown up in the thick evergreen forests and along the craggy coast of the Pacific Northwest. Shelly had too. The forests around Pacific County and nearby Grays Harbor County were dark green, drippy, and swathed in shades of gray. Muted colors, to be sure, but beautifully so. They loaded up the car with camping chairs, coolers, and the tent, and piled in for the drive up to their camping spot in Westport.

There was no room in the Knoteks' maroon Toyota with Dave, Shelly, Shane, and the girls, so Kathy rode in the trunk. Even if there had been space, Kathy still would have ridden in the trunk because that's where Shelly and Dave made her ride. Oddly, she didn't fight it.

"I don't remember a struggle," Sami said later. "I don't remember complaining. It was my mom saying, 'We're going camping, Kathy. Now, get in the trunk.'"

Within a year of moving in, Kathy occupied a strange, servile space in the family. She was included in family outings like camping, but not fully so. She lingered off to the side of the action as the kids roasted marshmallows or hot dogs. She didn't sit with Shelly or Dave when they had their coffee in the morning or a beer at the end of the day. She brought out the supplies. She set up the tent.

"It was like 'Kathy, get this' or 'Kathy, do that' and things like that. She was there to do things for my mom but not really to be part of the trip. She did whatever she was told to do," Sami recounted. "Here's the thing: at the time it didn't seem strange. We were kids. We just thought that's the way it was."

Instead of sleeping with the others in the tent the first night, Kathy slept under the car.

The next night, Shelly had another plan for Kathy's sleeping arrangement.

"It will be fun to sleep in the trunk, Kathy!" Nikki recalled her mother saying, helping her friend get inside and then partially closing the trunk lid.

"I remember my mom laughing about that," Nikki remembered. "The next morning, [Kathy] got up and fell out of the trunk. Really hard on the ground."

)(

Shelly was undeniably lazy. No one but Kathy would say otherwise. She'd let dishes stack up around wherever she was lying. Sometimes food would crust so much that plates would stick together. Laundry was another chore that piled up to Everest proportions until no one had anything clean to wear.

One time Shelly told the girls that she had something to do that day and they needed to all go to the laundromat.

"Take Kathy," she said. "We can't leave her alone today."

The girls loaded plastic garbage bags of dirty clothes into the car, and Kathy got into the trunk.

She was weaker by then, and Sami, for one, had a singular understanding that Kathy was not going to get better. She was clearly going downhill, though Shelly kept insisting that Kathy was getting better.

After they got to the laundromat and filled a half-dozen washers, Sami made trips to the car to check on Kathy. She spoke to her through the trunk because Shelly had warned the girls not to let Kathy out for any reason.

"How are you doing in there?" Sami asked.

"I'm fine," Kathy said. "How is the laundry going?"

"We're doing great, Kathy."

"What's the weather like out there?"

"Nice," Sami said. "Real nice."

Sami went back inside feeling sick and returned a little while later to check on Kathy.

"Dryers are going now," she said. "Won't be long now."

"No problem," Kathy answered, her voice muffled under the lid of the trunk. "Talk to you soon."

The conversations were just like that. Casual. Nonconfrontational. Kathy wasn't pounding her fists and fighting to get out. She didn't try to kick out a taillight. She didn't complain that it was dark inside, or that she was hot or uncomfortable. She was compliant. Calm. Waiting until they got home so she could get out and do more to help Shelly.

And even as Kathy put up with riding in the trunk, working around the house naked, and ingesting whatever pills she was handed, Shelly still found ways to ratchet up the abuse.

Simply because she could.

One time the girls watched in horror as Kathy sat outside on the porch with a bowl over her head while Shelly wielded barber's scissors, snipping off the long, wavy hair that Kathy, a stylist, had used as her calling card. Tears rolled down her cheeks. Silently. Her hair was a loose nest on the porch.

"Girls!" Shelly called after butchering Kathy's hair. "Look at Kathy's new haircut! Isn't it the cutest little bob?"

It was hard to look at it without betraying a true opinion. There was nothing cute about what their mother had done. It was, Nikki thought, the worst haircut she'd ever seen. It was so bad that it had to be intentional.

"Oh yes," Nikki said. "I love it. It looks so cute!"

Sami felt sick inside. She agreed anyway. "So cute, Kathy!"

To say anything else, they knew, would bring on something bad. Maybe for Kathy. Maybe for one of them. With their mother, there was no telling what was in store. Perhaps Shelly had gotten the idea for the ugly chop from the humiliating haircut Grandma Anna had once given her, which had really been intended to teach her stepmom, Lara, a lesson: "You can't keep her hair brushed properly, so I cut it!"

Like Lara, Nikki had also learned to keep her mouth shut. Everyone went back into the house.

"Why does Kathy let Mom do that crap to her?" Nikki asked when their mother was out of earshot.

Sami didn't know. Shane's opinion, however, was consistent.

"Your mom is fucking crazy," he said. "That's why. Kathy's scared shitless of her. Like we all are."

CHAPTER
TWENTY-TWO

It had to be the pills. Kathy had been a normal person before she'd moved in. She had opinions about things that were going on in the world. She had an identity. She was anything but a punching bag just reeling from one blow to the next.

Shane and Nikki went on a quest to find out what was happening to Kathy. They crept into their mother's room while she was away and Kathy was doing chores.

"Let's see what Mom's feeding Kathy," Shane said.

Shelly kept an array of pill bottles on the top of her dresser and on the nightstand near the bed. The medicine cabinet on the main floor was also a veritable pharmacy with dozens of prescription pill bottles, including Lorazepam, Nitroquick, Atenolol, Altace, and Paxil.

It was bewildering.

Most were drugs that neither of them had heard about before, prescribed by doctors across Pacific County, and filled at various pharmacies in Raymond, South Bend, and Aberdeen.

Prozac, in its green-and-white capsules, was the most recognizable.

"That's what she's giving Kathy all the time," Nikki said.

Shane popped a pill into his mouth and swallowed it.

"I remember like twenty minutes after he took it, he was looped," Nikki said later.

Shelly was clearly drugging Kathy.

Some would later wonder if she'd also drugged Shane or any of her girls from time to time.

〤

Nikki and Shane's bond deepened. They were pushed together by their shared abuse and the fact that they'd been singled out over Sami for repeat offenses and the humiliating and painful punishments that went along with them. Only Kathy's arrival had given them any relief.

They conspired in the way that teenagers do, fantasizing how they might end their misery and save the world from Shelly.

"The crawlspace," Shane said one time. "We should put her there."

"Or the attic?" Nikki suggested. "Anywhere where she can't get away."

"Yeah," Shane said. "But seriously. Why is your mom so fucking crazy?"

Nikki shrugged. "How would I know?"

Shane thought about it a beat. "Yeah. Some people just are. I'm getting out of here, you know."

"Me too."

"No, really I am."

Nikki wished she had the guts to do what Shane said he was going to do, but something kept her stuck in that house. She could talk a good game, yet she couldn't put her desire to break away into practice.

Shane, though, tried it a few times.

Whenever he acted on his vow to get away, Nikki would tell herself that it was for the best and inwardly rooted for him even as her mom would pile the girls into the car to search for the runaway. She never once stopped hoping he'd finally make it somewhere.

Shane had good reason to want to escape from his aunt's home. Shelly seemed to always come up with new ways to hurt him.

One time she went for the duct tape from the kitchen drawer and the Icy Hot from the medicine cabinet in the bathroom. It was the latest incarnation of punishments that started with beatings and then grew more and more bizarre. She made him undress and bound his ankles and wrists while the girls looked on. He protested, though he didn't fight her. He didn't resist.

Next, she put him in the corner by the front door and then applied Icy Hot to his penis while he yelped in pain.

"Don't ever do that again," she said.

Years later, no one could recall what the teen had done to earn that punishment. It was their mother's version of putting a child in the corner to the extreme. Shane was humiliated and angry with Shelly, but he let her do it.

※

Her mother and older sister had gone to the store, leaving Sami in charge of Shane, who had done something that made Shelly very, very angry. She'd made him strip and duct-taped his wrists and ankles and pushed him into the corner by the front door.

"Make sure he stays put," she told Sami before leaving.

The second she heard the car start, Sami did what she always did— what they *all* did—whenever their mother left the house.

She went to the bathroom.

Shelly never let the children use the toilet without permission or without the door fully open. Most times, Shelly perched next to the kids as they went about their business and watched like it was a science experiment.

When Sami finished and returned to the front room, Shane had vanished.

In a panic, she looked everywhere around the house and the yard, but no Shane. She was so angry at him for running. She was mad because she knew that her mom would make all of them pile into the car and search for Shane all day, all night. Whatever it took. Shelly was relentless that way. She was a hunter. She'd never stop until she found the boy. It didn't matter if there was school the next day and their hunting trip lasted until three in the morning.

It was dark when Sami found Shane in a neighbor's woodshed.

"You have to come home, Shane," Sami said. "Mom's mad. You know she'll find you."

Shelly didn't say a word as Shane came back inside. He was naked and freezing. He was also crying.

She gave him a hard look.

"I'm really sorry, Mom," he said. "I promise not to do it again."

Shelly finally spoke, asking the boy what he was thinking. Her tone was suddenly sweet, comforting. It was as if she'd found a lost kitten and was scooping it up to give it a home.

"We love you, Shane," she said. "Don't scare us like that. I don't know why you'd want to leave us."

Another time, when the Knoteks were going to Wild Waves Theme & Water Park just north of Tacoma, Shane went on the run again. Shelly immediately halted the trip and went on the hunt for him. Nikki and Sami knew the drill, and their hearts sank like lead weights. They'd miss the water park and their mother would search until she found their cousin.

They looked for two days. First, they looked in the Tillicum neighborhood where Shane had lived before coming to live with them in Raymond. Every tiny, ramshackle house. Behind every single run-down garage. They scoured each store in the massive Tacoma Mall. No Shane.

Shelly even stopped in at a psychic in Tacoma to see if she knew where Shane had gone.

"Mom"—Nikki braced for a hard slap to the face—"he doesn't want to be here. Let him go."

Shelly ignored Nikki and kept her eyes scanning for Shane.

All the while, Nikki was praying they'd never find him.

Please, God, let Shane get away. Mom's evil. He needs to be gone. Safe.

God didn't hear her prayers, apparently. Several hours into the search on the second day, Shelly found her wayward nephew and coaxed him back into the car with the words that meant more to him than anything.

She told him how much she loved him.

Words he had to have known by then were false.

"You really scared us, Shane," Shelly said, her voice soothing and her demeanor mimicking concern. "Don't you ever do that. You'll worry me to death. The girls too. We love you."

CHAPTER
TWENTY-THREE

After Shelly made the decision that Tori and her crib could no longer stay in her bedroom on the first floor, she told Kathy that she'd be giving up her space between Nikki's and Sami's rooms.

"I have a cozy little room for you downstairs."

By then, most of Kathy's personal items, like the bedroom furniture and clothing she'd brought when she'd moved in, had disappeared. Kathy didn't complain; it seemed she'd forgotten how to stand her ground. She was completely under Shelly's thumb.

"Cozy," it turned out, was a misnomer. Off to the right of the staircase was Kathy's new room: the oil furnace room, on the other side of the drafty basement from where Shane slept. The five-by-eight-foot space had concrete floors and unfinished walls with exposed studs. It was gritty and, even in the summer, very cold. The space was so tight it could barely accommodate a mattress.

Kathy looked a little sad about having to live down there, yet she didn't complain. She just accepted it because Shelly told her that it was better for Tori.

"You'll love it down there, Kathy."

Sami, for one, didn't love it. She felt sick about Kathy being forced to stay downstairs in that awful place. Not long after Kathy moved into the furnace room, Sami found the boxes of Kathy's things that her mother had said she'd given away because Kathy had done something that displeased her. Sami brought a few posters downstairs and put them up. Kathy started to panic when she realized what Sami was doing.

"Don't do that," Kathy said.

"It's okay."

"No," she insisted. "Please don't."

Sami went about what she was doing. "We're going to make this nicer. A better place for you."

Kathy was terrified.

"Sami, please," she begged. "Don't."

Sami couldn't comprehend the fear. She knew her mom might not like it, but this was Kathy's room and it smelled bad and looked terrible. She wanted to make it nicer. Not great. Just better.

Kathy knew Shelly better than her own daughter did.

When Shelly saw what Sami had done, she screamed at Kathy and stripped the room of the posters. When she found Sami, she told her that she was a terrible child and needed to mind her own business.

"Don't ever do that again," she said.

X

It was late one night, a few days after the freeze and thaw of a snowfall, and Kathy had done something to make Shelly angry. *Very angry.* As mad as Nikki and Sami had ever seen their mother. The girls huddled together and watched from Nikki's window while their parents instructed Kathy to climb to the top of the little hill behind the house. Shane came and watched too. Kathy was naked and freezing. It was hard to see what was in store for her at first. Nikki and Sami kept their eyes glued to the hillside as Kathy begged Dave and Shelly to let her back inside, but they weren't having any of that.

"Just do what we tell you, Kathy," Shelly yelled at her. "Do you have to make everything so hard for me?"

Dave, not saying a word, nudged Kathy from the top, and she started to slide down the hill, crying and yelping all the way down. When she got to the bottom, Shelly gave more commands.

"Get up! Go up!"

Kathy crawled upward, crying all the way.

It went on like that for what seemed like hours. Kathy was barely able to walk from the cold and the pain she was undoubtedly feeling. Over and over. Up and down. In the dim light from the kitchen window, it was clear that her bottom had been scraped raw by the icy crystals of the snow.

"I'm sorry," she repeated over and over. "I won't do it again. I'm cold. It hurts. Please, Shelly. Please!"

It was like a nightmare that wouldn't end. Shane shook his head and went to the basement. He didn't have to say a word about how messed up everything was. The sisters couldn't take it anymore either and shared Nikki's bed, holding each other until morning.

"We all went out there in the morning," Sami later said, her voice breaking. "Me, my sister, Shane . . . the snow was bloody and red all the way down the hillside. Like a big red stripe."

Tears flooded Nikki's eyes when she saw the bloody snow that morning. She didn't let them fall down her cheeks. Her mother would see. Her mother might enjoy that. Something else was at work, and the older Knotek sisters knew it. It was Kathy who was being tortured and punished, not them.

"And as long as Mom was punishing Kathy," she later said, "she was ignoring us. As sick as that was—and we knew it at the time—we were glad. We were glad Mom wasn't doing it to us."

CHAPTER
TWENTY-FOUR

Kathy's mother, Kaye, needed major heart surgery in March 1991, but her eldest daughter was nowhere to be found. They knew she was staying with Shelly Knotek, and family members had reached out to her there several times. Nothing. The phone rang and rang. Finally, when Shelly got on the line, she casually informed everyone that Kathy had moved away from the area.

"She's with her boyfriend, Rocky," she said.

"Rocky?" The name sounded vaguely familiar to Kathy's sister, Kelly, but she'd never actually met him. Neither had her brothers.

Shelly was short on specifics, but she was insistent. Then she hung up.

Kathy was gone. *But where?*

"We tried to find her," Kelly said later. "We just couldn't."

A short time later, Kelly received an envelope with a blurry photo of her sister standing in front of a semitruck. Inside was a note written in Kathy's unmistakably girly handwriting. Kathy mentioned that she was sorry that she and Kelly didn't have a close relationship, but she was fine.

"She'd talked about Rocky," Kelly said later, trying to catch a memory. "The story that was woven seemed plausible. I kept thinking I wouldn't blame her if she didn't want to be in the family and if that meant I wasn't going to see her again, that was okay. Maybe she found someone like in the romance novels. She's living the life she wants to live and not miserable at home."

A month later, on April 15, 1991, the Knoteks all piled into the car for the drive to Washaway Beach, a spot on the Washington Coast known for its rapidly eroding beach, where ghost cabins and trailers hang over the swirling ocean and surfers ride the gray waves in the distance. It was Shelly's birthday, and Washaway Beach was one of Dave's favorite surfing spots. Tori sat up front with her parents, and the three older kids filled the back seat.

Kathy, who rode in the trunk, was growing weaker by the day. Images captured by the family's camcorder that afternoon show a woman in failing health. Her front teeth had begun to decay into black nubs, and her skin sagged where it had once been full. She sat in the sun, looking blankly at the water while her friend reveled in her special day.

Shelly posed like a beach bunny on the windswept sand while Dave took her picture. Red hair lightened by the sun, blue eyes that sparkled when she laughed—no one who saw her could deny that she was strikingly beautiful at thirty-seven years old. She promised treats for the kids, and told Dave how much she loved him.

No one could see what was going on behind that pretty face and the sweet words.

Or how long she'd wear that mask.

CHAPTER
TWENTY-FIVE

Sami Knotek didn't know what her parents were thinking when they decided to buy the shingle-sided white farmhouse on Monohon Landing Road in Raymond in the summer of 1992. The house was no great shakes, and Shelly was mad about having to move there. It was a real step down from the elegance and charm of the Louderback House. It was a 1930s farmhouse that needed a ton of work. Dave was handy, but he wasn't around much because of his job.

The location wasn't terrible. Fruit trees, mostly apple, formed a small orchard on the property, and a large field ran up to the edge of a second-growth forest of fir and hemlock. Elk rutted a path through the property, and blue herons had a rookery nearby. The house was situated on a winding road that ran along the Willapa River out in the country. Way out. About the only thing Sami could think of that made Monohon Landing desirable, from her point of view, was that it sat on a main road, not tucked among towering firs off the beaten path. Maybe things would be better there, she hoped. If the property was more exposed from the road, maybe Kathy couldn't get as abused there. Maybe her mom wouldn't make her work out in the yard naked. Maybe Nikki and Shane wouldn't be forced to wallow.

But it turned out that the location was more secluded than Sami had expected. On the first or second day there, Shelly told Sami to go around the property and along the road—all vantage points—to see what a bystander or another homeowner might be able to view of their house and yard.

"Privacy," she told her middle daughter, "is very important to our family."

The almost seventh grader spent several hours doing as her mother asked. She walked up into the woods and over a recently logged area on Weyerhaeuser property. When she got home, she told her mother what she saw.

"Nothing," Sami said. "You can see part of the house, but nothing else."

The property was just shy of five acres, and mostly fenced. That was good. The Knotek household had its share of pets—mostly dogs and cats, though at the new house, the menagerie eventually grew to include horses, chickens, a cockatiel, and a rabbit named Buttercup. While Shelly professed a love for animals, in truth she only seemed to like collecting them and seldom actually cared for any.

There was also a collection of outbuildings. Most of them were small—a chicken coop, a tool shed, a dilapidated barn, a well house, and a pump house affirmed that the place was indeed a mini-farm. The largest of the structures was a pole building the size of a suburban garage, organized with a workbench, storage racks, a pantry, and a freezer. Just steps from the back door, the aluminum building provided much-needed space for all of the things that wouldn't fit in the house.

The house was too small. Sami knew it. So did the other kids.

At just over sixteen hundred square feet, with two tiny upstairs bedrooms separated by what they'd come to call the computer room and a master bedroom for her parents on the main level, there were not enough bedrooms for the three sisters, Shane, *and* Kathy.

Plus, there was only one bathroom—and it was next to their parent's bedroom. That alone made the house shrink even smaller.

Tori slept in her parents' bedroom on the first floor. Shane slept mostly in Nikki's closet, without the benefit of a mattress.

"Just a blanket," Sami said later. "That's it. The whole time he lived at Monohon Landing, Shane never had a room."

Neither did Kathy. She slept on the floor in the living room. By then, her belongings fit into a single paper bag. Almost everything she'd owned when she'd moved in with the Knoteks had vanished. Her bedroom furniture, most of her clothes, her books and other personal items—all gone. Dave parked Kathy's old Plymouth Duster in the back of the new house. After a while, it disappeared too.

Shelly immediately went to work making plans to refurbish the place—fixing the kitchen, adding a hot tub, and tearing out the junk left behind by the previous owner. For weeks, the family worked day and night, mostly at night, ripping out the carpet, gutting the kitchen. Dave would come home on weekends, exhausted from the five-hour drive from his construction job on Whidbey Island and do his best to get their home up to Shelly's standards. Nikki and Sami were given carte blanche decorating their bedrooms. Nikki asked for—and got—a black-and-white fifties checkerboard theme, while Sami picked out coral-colored carpeting.

After the house was in somewhat better shape, Shelly told Nikki that she was going to paint it barn red. When she picked up the paint, however, it was a bright red. Shelly shrugged off the color error, handed Nikki a one-inch paintbrush, and told her to get to work.

It took the teen all summer long.

Sami, for her part, was instructed to paint the pole building. To no one's particular surprise, Sami was given better painting supplies. Shane was stuck cleaning up the neglected yard and stacking wood. Shelly would check their work occasionally. Mostly she sat on the sofa watching soap operas and eating Oh Henry! bars, shoving the waxy wrappers between the cushions.

The new locale and the hard work didn't change the fundamental dynamic. Shelly continued her relentless attacks, focused mainly on Shane and Kathy.

Shelly's unpredictable abuse put everyone on high alert. Nikki flinched whenever her mother approached her. Shelly would bite her on the head. Slap her in the face. Punch her. Nikki got smacked one time because she fell asleep in the passenger seat of the car and her mother wanted her to be awake.

At the school-bus stop one time, Shelly was mad at Nikki but waited for the bus to stop in front of the house before she slapped her good and hard on the face.

"She wanted my friends to see so they could make fun of me."

Shelly showed up at Nikki's junior high in the middle of the day looking for mascara that she was convinced Nikki had stolen from her bathroom. She got her daughter's locker open and tore it apart, throwing everything on the floor while a bunch of kids looked on.

"She took it!" she yelled in front of Nikki's classmates. "She stole my mascara! That's not right. A daughter shouldn't do that! A good daughter wouldn't."

As cruel as her mother could be to Nikki, she always saved the worst for Kathy.

X

Kathy didn't bathe often before or after the Knoteks moved to Monohon Landing Road. Like the older kids, most of the time she wasn't allowed to. At first, the baths were much like the ones she'd been given at the Louderback House—the hose was turned on her while she stood naked outside on the grass behind the house. It didn't matter what time of year or how cold the weather was.

Soap was dispensed with. Instead, Shelly poured bleach on Kathy. "You're a filthy pig and this will clean you up!"

Kathy screamed as the caustic liquid splashed into open sores that mottled her skin from head to toe. When she cried out too much, or struggled to get away, either Shelly or Dave, when he was home, would duct-tape her legs and arms. When Dave wasn't there, it was Shane who was told to hold Kathy down while Shelly washed her friend with the hose.

One time Shelly put a piece of duct tape over Kathy's mouth to stop her from alerting the neighbors.

"You need to shut up! What's wrong with you? I'm helping you. You stupid pig!"

After a bath was over, invariably Shelly would switch over to a sweet, kind persona. She'd put her arms around Kathy's shoulders.

"Now, doesn't that feel a whole lot better?"

X

Dave asked Shelly about Kathy, and Shelly insisted that she was helping her get better. After a while, he saw less and less of his wife's best friend. When he came home on the weekends from work, Kathy was nowhere to be seen.

The girls told him that their mom kept Kathy in the pump house. That didn't seem right at all, so Dave confronted Shelly about it.

"Why is she in the pump house, Shell?"

Shelly seemed perfectly fine with the arrangement. After all, she had good reason for it.

"She needs to be protected," she said.

"Protected? Why?"

Shelly shook her head knowingly. "From the kids, Dave."

The kids? That didn't make sense. They were good kids. He was so tired of battling Shelly that he didn't argue with his wife—something he'd later admit that he couldn't do even if he'd had a good night's sleep.

Dave took Shelly's word as gospel. She continually insisted that it was Shane who was abusing Kathy, and that when she put her best friend in the pump house, it was only to protect her from their nephew. "One time when I came home, Shane was dragging Kathy around the yard by her feet," Dave recalled. Despite the likelihood that Shane had probably been doing so at Shelly's bidding, Dave felt certain after witnessing that incident that Shelly must have been telling the absolute truth.

CHAPTER TWENTY-SIX

"Where's Kathy?"

Shelly got up from the couch in the living room at the Monohon Landing house and started yelling. She stood there in her robe, her hair bushy and unkempt.

"She's pulling weeds," Sami said.

"She's gone," Shelly yelled, looking out the window before heading back to the bedroom to get dressed. "Go look for her in the woods. Right now!"

She didn't need to add the "right now." Everything Shelly said was a command that demanded immediate attention. Sami ran out the door and across the field to the woods behind the house. She called Kathy's name over and over as she scoured the landscape. Sami knew that her mother wouldn't be satisfied unless she looked until nightfall. The girls and Shane ran the deer trails of the forest.

"Maybe she got away," Shane said.

"I hope so," Nikki said.

Shelly drove off, and two hours later, she was back with Kathy, who carried two bags of new clothes from the Wishkah Mall in Aberdeen. Shelly said she'd found Kathy with a friend, and had been able to talk things over in the privacy of a mall bathroom. Kathy had decided to come home. She had a green outfit and a red one; both were pants sets with striped shirts to match. She was also wearing something new, which surprised Sami and Nikki. Kathy looked better than she had in ages, though some of her hair and her teeth had fallen out. She appeared clean and seemed happier.

Nikki was incredulous. She couldn't make sense of why Kathy didn't stay gone. Why Kathy hadn't used her chance to tell someone. The friend at the mall? The police?

Anyone?

"I was shocked when she came back," she said years later. "I was shocked my mom wasn't in trouble. I could not believe it. I thought it was criminal. Kathy could go to the cops and say she was abused. Why is she back here? She's just fucking crazy now. She's gone. She's mental. I thought that about my dad too. Why doesn't he divorce her?"

Years later, Sami would tear up at the thought of Kathy being happier. It was so ugly and unfair. "She got to stay inside a little while after Shelly captured her at the mall. Not very long. But some time."

A few days later, Kathy was back out in the pump house, as a punishment for running away.

No one ever saw her wear those nice new clothes again.

※

Kathy tried to escape again. And again. One time she even tried to make a run for it while naked.

A kid came up to Sami at school with a story to tell about that one.

"Ha ha!" he said. "They saw your mom from the bus. She was running around the yard naked! She looked like a big old naked bear!"

Sami wanted to curl up and die.

"I doubt it," she said, deflecting what was entirely possible.

"Erin's mom saw it."

Erin's mom was the school bus driver.

Sami tried to shake it off, but the talk went around the school like one of those steel balls in an old pinball machine. It just wouldn't let up.

Sami told her mom all about it when she got home.

"Shit," Shelly said. "It was Kathy! She was trying to run away! I caught her though."

The explanation was what she'd half expected. "It's really embarrassing, Mom," Sami said. "They think it was you."

Shelly freaked out. It was Kathy! People would wonder what was going on at their house if they'd seen Kathy run around the yard naked. She made up a plan in all of two seconds.

"Invite Erin over," she said. "You girls can use the hot tub."

Later, when Erin came over, she and Sami were in the hot tub and Shelly approached.

"Oh God," Shelly said. "I'm so embarrassed. I was in the hot tub, naked, and all of a sudden it sparked, and I jumped out and ran across the yard. I was scared! I thought I was going to die!"

The girls listened to the story and added a couple of "oh wow's" as Shelly proceeded to point to a burned spot on the hot tub walls while she explained how the wires had sparked.

"My mom was that good," Sami said later. "She burned that spot before Erin came over, so her story would seem more plausible. I don't know if Erin believed her, but I almost did."

X

Nikki heard yelling and watched through the open door of the pole building where she'd been instructed to do chores. Kathy had been let out of the pump house that day to do some weeding, and it seemed that Shelly was dissatisfied by her performance. At Shelly's direction, Dave dragged Kathy from the garden where she'd been weeding to punish her. When Nikki looked over at Kathy, she was naked and crying and lying on a slab of concrete.

"Kick her, Dave!" Shelly commanded.

Dave didn't say a word. He almost never did. He was wearing the steel-toed boots that he wore out in the woods and he kicked Kathy in the head.

"She was moaning, and she was just lying on the ground," Nikki said later. "I think it was pretty hard. And then I didn't pay attention. I just went back inside the pole building."

CHAPTER
TWENTY-SEVEN

The pump house was the smallest of the outbuildings on the property that included an old barn, a pole building, a chicken house, and a couple of storage sheds. It was dark, musty, and cold. Shelly decided it would be a good place for Kathy to think about what she'd done wrong. Nikki and Shane had also been occasional inhabitants of the four-foot-by-four-foot structure.

Kathy was forced to stay in there for days, even weeks, at a time.

Sami brought some cushions from an old brown sofa stored in the woodshed to make it more comfortable for Kathy. When Shelly found out, she made Sami remove them right away.

"We want her to get better!" Shelly said. "We don't want her to be comfortable! She has to figure all of this out and understand why she's being punished. We want her to come back inside the house, not live out here!"

Sami didn't see how it was hurting to help her friend, but she backed off. To help Kathy might incite even more violence against her.

Her mom was often a passive abuser, usually making Dave or Shane do her bidding. It was what she didn't do sometimes that showed her indifference to others.

One time Sami followed her mother and Kathy out of the house to the walkway next to the pole building, and for some reason, all of a sudden, without any warning whatsoever, Shelly gave Kathy a hard push. Kathy went flying and landed facedown on the concrete. She didn't even try to break her fall. She just fell flat. She started screaming and holding her head with her hands, writhing in agony like a hurt animal. Sami watched her mother hesitate for a beat before helping Kathy get up and putting her back into the pump house.

Nikki thought she knew why her mother had put her there. It wasn't because of some new mistake Kathy had made. It wasn't really a punishment at all. It was because her mother had grown weary of watching Kathy after she'd tried to run away. Shelly didn't say it outright, but Nikki suspected that her mother didn't trust what Kathy might say.

Like she had to Sami, her mother couched it all in something positive for Kathy. Exiling her to the pump house, for instance, was always for her own good.

"I think she'll be better off in the pump house," Shelly announced, leading Kathy by the hand out the door and across the yard. "She needs some peace and quiet."

There was always a phony reason for whatever she did to Kathy.

Now and then, Nikki helped her mom get Kathy to the pump house and put her inside. Kathy's health was deteriorating rapidly. Her mom's lie was audacious. Kathy needed medical attention. Not a stint in a dank outbuilding.

Shane and Nikki didn't need to be locked in there either, but that's where they ended up whenever Shelly tired of a beating and wanted a punishment that had a longer duration.

One that showed the magnitude of her control over everyone.

"It got us—me, Kathy, Shane—out of the way," Nikki said later, explaining the reasoning behind the banishment. "She didn't have to monitor us and worry about what we might do. Especially Shane and Kathy."

In time, however, Kathy appeared to accept her situation. The same way she'd become used to riding in the trunk.

One time, Sami was outside near the pump house when she heard the sound of Kathy's voice. "Hello?"

She went to the locked door of the pump house and leaned in. She didn't dare open it. Kathy knew better than to ask her to do so anyway. Shelly had made it clear to everyone that Kathy was there as a punishment, but also as a way to help her heal and get better.

"Is it raining out there?" Kathy asked.

"A little while ago. Not now, Kathy."

"Oh," she said, her voice a soft rasp. "I thought I could hear it rain."

※

As was usually the case, Dave was at work on Whidbey Island when Shelly needed to go into town to run errands. Before heading out, she told Shane that he was in charge of Kathy. He needed to make sure she didn't yell or call out to anyone.

"Or get away," she said. "Make sure she stays in the pump house where she belongs, Shane. We can't trust her right now. She's not right in the head."

Shane pretended to agree.

"Fuck this," he told Nikki right after Shelly drove off. "I'm letting Kathy out."

Nikki hated the idea that her mom had locked Kathy in the pump house. She knew Kathy needed a doctor. She was getting weaker by the day. Her face was swelling up, and her last few teeth were like little brown acorns looking like they were going to fall.

Shane removed the padlock and swung open the door.

Light flooded the space, and Kathy winced. She sat motionless and finally looked at him.

"Come out," he said.

She didn't move.

Nikki knew Kathy was afraid of Shane, although she had no reason to fear him when her mother wasn't around.

Shane pleaded at first, but then became irritated when she just looked at him.

"Come on, Kathy, get out. You need to get out of here."

Kathy started to cry. She was pale. Battered. Bleeding. Her hair was nearly gone. She had on a thin, tattered muumuu and nothing else.

"What's the fucking matter with you?" Shane's anger grew by the minute. "You need to go! Get the fuck out of here! This is your chance."

Kathy appeared terrified. "You're lying!" she said.

"No," Shane said. "I'm telling you the truth. You can go! Get out of here."

Kathy cowered in the small outbuilding. Finally, she spoke, her voice a rasp. "If I leave, they'll just find me. You know that. They will. She will."

Shane was beside himself. He couldn't understand why Kathy didn't run. The door was open. They were all kids and had nowhere to go. She was a grown-up.

"This is your only hope, Kathy. Don't be a fucking moron!"

Kathy begged for him to let her be.

Shane slammed the door, leaving Kathy back in the dark. "She's going to die if she doesn't get out," he said, turning to Nikki.

"I know."

Later, the two of them sat upstairs in Nikki's room for the longest time. Both had the sinking feeling that what was happening to Kathy was beyond hopeless. When Shane had unlocked the door to let her run free, it was probably her last chance. Kathy just didn't have any fight left. She'd simply given up.

PART FOUR

HUSBAND

DAVE

CHAPTER
TWENTY-EIGHT

Shelly repeatedly reminded Dave that he was a lousy husband.

"The worst ever!" she said, whittling away at his self-esteem.

She should never have married him.

She could have had her pick of any man.

He had been a terrible mistake.

Dave only agreed. He knew in his heart that Shelly was right. About everything. A good husband would be home all the time, helping with the house. Taking care of the kids. Reminding his wife that he was more than a paycheck. He was working sixteen-hour days and driving from Whidbey Island to get home for weekends during which he couldn't really do anything that needed to get done. The construction job was manual labor, and he was bone tired. All day long, he guzzled thermos after thermos of coffee and popped No-Doz and Vivarin to stay awake.

"I was running a Cat. Getting off. Getting on. Going up and down the hills to get the work done. It was physical, physical, physical," he recounted years later. "I was fighting to stay awake. It got so bad at work that I'd take those ammonia inhalants from the medicine kit. I'd crack those just to stay awake in the Cat."

More times than he could count, Dave would find that he couldn't make the drive home from Whidbey. He wondered how he never crossed the centerline and killed someone. There were times when he was driving so slowly on the highway that everyone would pass him, but he couldn't figure out why. Sometimes he'd even hear something in his head he started to call "the screaming meanies."

Whenever the meanies hit him, he'd pull over to the side of the road and nap to try to get himself together. Sometimes he'd manage to fight through the episode and get within striking distance of Raymond. Or if he made it a little closer, he'd park Old Blue, his truck, at Butte Creek, a picnic area about three miles north of home off Highway 101. Those were the times he was too tired to press the pedal any longer. Too beat. And, truly, too weak to do battle with Shelly. He needed a minute to rest, to collect himself.

To shake off the meanies.

That didn't stop his wife, however. One time, a sharp rap against the window of his truck awakened him.

It was Nikki.

"We know where you are, Dad," she said before returning to the new Jeep Shelly had purchased for herself.

Shelly hadn't bothered to get out of her vehicle or even hurl a word in Dave's direction. She'd let her eldest shame him and remind him at the same time that, no matter where he went, wherever he hid, she'd be able to track him down.

Shelly was like that. She was as relentless as a bloodhound. She had that stamina and the innate ability to find anyone.

At any time.

If Dave thought that he could grab a little respite from what was waiting at home and do so in peace, he was obviously wrong.

Lara Watson thought her son-in-law had a serious drinking problem, but it paled next to his Shelly problem. Drinking, he could quit. Shelly, it turned out, not so easily.

Lara was sure that, like Randy and Danny before him, Dave would eventually leave. While Dave would later concede that he didn't have it in him to simply leave Shelly, he always hoped that one day he'd come home and Shelly would be gone.

"Just be gone. Moved back to Vancouver or something," he recalled. "I don't know what I was hoping for. But she just kept hanging around."

As Lara weighed things from a distance, she saw the precedent that Grandma Anna had set by making her husband sleep in the shed. Shelly's first husband, Randy, had taken to sleeping in his car after rows with his wife. And now the same thing was happening to Dave.

"He didn't want to come home," Lara said. "Or she wouldn't let him. He was working day and night and then sleeping in his truck. Shelly got the big car. He got that truck, right? He was sleeping there or sneaking into the office after the people he worked for left for the night. Sleeping in the office on the floor."

※

Dave would later fasten the blame for what happened at the little red house on Monohon Landing on the fact that he'd quit his job at Weyerhaeuser. Shelly had insisted on it. Said the enormous timber company was taking advantage of him and he could make more working for someone else. But his job took him away from home, and that, he was sure, was what kept him from being an involved father and a good husband.

"Everything was okay," he claimed of life at Louderback House. "It was just me and Shell and Nikki and Sami and everything was fine. Came home every night—the way it should be. A marriage is fifty percent and after that I wasn't keeping up my end of the deal. Raising kids is a handful. You can't expect a mom to raise 'em all the time, you know, and be the disciplinarian, help with the schoolwork. I wasn't there. And when I was, I was falling asleep. I couldn't even stay awake to watch a TV show."

Shelly, as he saw it, was doing more than her fair share.

"She was one hundred percent mom and then some. I mean, those kids had birthday parties, and you know, kids come down to the barbecue pit. All of that. Shell was always going to Sami's track meets. Cuz Dad was never at Sami's school things. I really faded off being a good husband."

By trying to survive by doing the right thing, Dave was sure that he'd actually done the opposite. He'd let everyone down in the process. He'd come up short. By his estimation, way short.

"My dad provided for me, and you know, he worked very, very hard. My grandfather too. I failed my Knotek family. I let them down. It's part of me, you know, just being a failure."

Medical bills were draining their bank account. Shelly demanded Dave work harder to make ends meet. It was life and death, she insisted. Yet Dave couldn't work any harder. He was barely hanging in there, pulling in extra hours so that the avalanche of bills could be paid.

At one point, Shelly even told him that he needed to ask his family for money. Dave called his sister, whom the Knoteks considered well off, to tell her they were short on funds.

"Shell's cancer is taking us down," he pleaded.

His sister said she would help.

A few days later, Shelly returned from getting the mail. She was as angry as Dave had ever seen her.

"Thirty dollars?" she fumed. "Can you believe it? So fucking cheap! I have cancer and that's all they can do to help us?"

Dave had hated to call for money. He hated even more that his wife was complaining about the gift.

"They are helping us, Shell," he said.

"Not enough."

It was the best he could do. Dave always had her back. Asking for money. Working harder. Making excuses to his family for things Shelly did.

The pattern continued: while Shelly demeaned Dave as a lousy provider and a weak man whenever she could turn the screw, Dave used every opportunity to tell his wife that she meant the world to him.

Unlike some husbands who pull a card off the rack at the last minute, Dave was thoughtful. He never just signed his name to a sentiment written by a card writer at Hallmark. Instead, in his impeccable penmanship, he'd write messages to Shelly that were a testament to how he felt inside. Or a romanticized version of the truth.

"Remember your words to me years ago? You once said that angels take themselves lightly. I'm married to an angel. Your eyes are the kindest eyes that I have ever seen. Your soul casts shadows of kind loving warmth wherever you are . . . You love and care about everything from your children, other people, animals, plants. You are truly genuine in heart and soul."

Whether he truly believed his own words was beside the point.

His message was a wish and hope. It was what Dave needed to believe on the long drives to and from Raymond.

CHAPTER
TWENTY-NINE

Shelly wasn't a doctor . . . though she liked to play one—or so it seemed to her family. Sami remembered times as a young girl when she'd wake up and her mom would be waving a broken glass ampule in front of her face. She'd cough and nearly heave from whatever she was breathing into her lungs.

She'd seen her do the same thing to Kathy.

"Kathy would pass out from the abuse and my mom would bring her back," Sami said. "So she could do it all over again."

One time at Monohon Landing, Sami had a headache. Her mom told her they were out of Excedrin and that she had something else for her.

The pills were funny looking, unfamiliar, but she took them anyway. The next thing she knew, she was out on the porch on all fours, unable to lift up her head. Shane tried to help her. It was no use.

"Your mom gave you muscle relaxers. Fucked up shit. She did that to me too," he said.

And despite her formidable drug supply in the house, Shelly was on the hunt for something she didn't have at that time. She photocopied information extolling the benefits of the tranquilizer Haldol, a drug she was interested in procuring.

For some reason. For someone.

X

Shelly's cancer treatments dragged on so long that Lara couldn't take it anymore. The way she saw it, Shelly was putting her girls through a nightmare letting them believe that their mother was going to die at any time. Her husband should call her on it, she thought, but Dave was too gullible. *Too nice.* Lara took it upon herself to confront Shelly.

Lara called her daughter Carol, Shelly's half sister, and told her they were going to Raymond to take care of the cancer business once and for all. They weren't going to give Shelly a heads-up either. Every time in the past that they had come for a prearranged visit, Shelly would make sure no one was home at the appointed time.

Mother and daughter drove Lara's 1992 black Chevy Blazer to Shelly's house to find out what was really going on. When Shelly opened the front door, Lara could have laughed out loud if the sight wasn't so horrifically twisted.

Shelly looked like a Kabuki doll—a very unwell one at that.

"She was wearing white makeup and she'd shaved off all her eyebrows," Lara remembered. "Her face. Wow. I can see it right now. Honest to God. Unbelievable."

Shelly didn't look happy to see her stepmother or sister on her doorstep. After a moment of silence, she let them inside.

"I'm so glad you came," she said.

Lara had seen Shelly lie plenty of times, so she fibbed right back.

"We want to talk to you about what you're going through so we can do a better job of supporting you," she said.

Shelly lowered herself into a chair. "Oh, thank you."

Lara was on a mission.

"We need the name of your doctors and the clinic," she said. "This has been going on too long. We'll need to go over all your bills too."

Shelly didn't really respond. There probably wasn't a lot she actually could say.

Lara asked, "How sick are you after treatment?"

Shelly looked right at her. "Really sick."

At one point, Shelly got up and went to the bathroom. Lara and Carol exchanged looks but didn't say a word. The girls were there by then, sitting quietly and supporting their mother. There wasn't any sign of Kathy Loreno.

A few minutes later, Shelly emerged with a fistful of red hair.

"Oh, Mom," she said, dropping the clump of hair to the floor. "My hair. My hair is just falling out."

"Oh my God," Lara said. She picked up the fallen hair while everyone looked on. She studied the hair and then confronted Shelly once more.

"I've never known someone taking cancer treatment to lose their hair from the middle," Lara finally said. "Usually they lose it from the scalp. Yours is breaking off."

Lara went into the bathroom to investigate what had just happened.

"There's a wastebasket in there with some crumpled tissue on the top," she recalled, holding on to the vivid memory even years later. "I dug through the basket and there's long hair and scissors. And there is still hair in the scissors. Red hair. I walked out with the scissors. Shelly was sitting with her back to me. Carol was on the couch and she about died. The girls didn't say a word."

And still Shelly refused to tell the truth.

Back in the car for the trip home, Lara turned to her daughter.

"Oh my God, that girl is sick," she said. She didn't mean cancer.

Carol, still in shock, agreed.

Neither knew, of course, just how sick.

152

A spate of early-morning phone calls began around that time. Startled out of bed, Lara would pick up at two or three to find someone screaming in her ear. Sometimes the calls would be hang-ups. Over and over. She never doubted for a second that Shelly was behind the calls. If not her, she'd put someone up to it.

Her half sister Carol received similar calls too.

Carol was doing some print modeling for Nordstrom at the time and had mentioned it to Shelly, who seemed interested. Strangely, Carol's modeling agency had notified her to say that they'd been left an anonymous tip one night that she was a thief and that no one should hire her.

That was on-brand for Shelly. Most of her ire was fired off late at night while the world dozed.

"She was always like that," Lara recalled. "She was nocturnal. She could never sleep even when she was younger. In the mornings she'd have big circles under her eyes. We couldn't get her out of bed. And if she had to go somewhere it was a fight every single day. It was a knock down drag out fight no matter what it was."

Shelly was livid. She'd found out that there was a spaghetti dinner to raise money for one of Nikki's high school classmate's parents who had cancer.

"Why didn't you do that for me?" Shelly asked. "You don't love me at all."

You don't have cancer, Mom, Nikki thought.

"I'm sorry, Mom," she said instead.

Shelly shook her head in bitter disgust. "I don't know why I bother with you at all, Nikki. All you do is disappoint me. What a fucking disappointment you are."

CHAPTER THIRTY

At almost sixteen, Shane Watson was exhausted. He went to school, worked in the yard until dark, and slept in his cousin Nikki's closet. He was physically and mentally exhausted. None of what was happening around him, the things Shelly and Dave forced on them, was right or normal. He hated it. He wanted out. Ultimately, however, Shane knew he was just as trapped as Kathy was. It would have been ironic if it weren't so horrific. The Knoteks had been his backup plan, his great hope. They were the ones who had rescued him from a life on the streets, but for what?

The way Shane saw it, Shelly was beyond a piece of work, but Dave was no better. Maybe worse. Dave was a grown man, and it seemed incomprehensible that he'd do whatever Shelly told him to do. Naked exercises for Shane and Nikki. Jumping jacks outside in the winter. Trips around the house in the middle of the night until they'd collapse. As he got older, and bigger, Shane would push back and let everyone know just what he was thinking. How fucked up everything had become before and after Kathy. He and Dave got into it more than once while Shelly lurked nearby telling her husband to teach Shane a lesson.

"For his own good, Dave!"

A few times at Monohon Landing, things escalated to physical altercations.

One time Shane hit Dave during an argument in the laundry room. Years later, it would escape Dave's mind what had transpired between him and his nephew and led them to come to blows that evening. It might have been something that Shelly reported to him about how Shane had disrespected her.

"He was getting more opinionated on his own," Dave recalled. "He kept running away. He's just a boy unto himself. He'd challenge anybody."

And yet Dave liked Shane.

"He'd call Shell Mom and me Dad," he said later. "He worked hard. Tried to learn in school. Shell tried to help him cuz everybody disregarded him, and he was her nephew. Her blood. It was a struggle because Shane was hard. He always got in trouble at school."

Shane's falling grades had everything to do with what was happening at home. But Dave couldn't see that because he was never around.

Shane wrote in some schoolwork what alluded to a crack in the façade that Shelly and Dave had tried to create in their home.

"Well man is becoming more civilized but at the same time he is becoming more barbaric . . . well it is probably because I don't like it hear [sic] and because I don't like the people hear [sic]."

In another class assignment, Shane made a list of the things that mattered to him most.

"Put everyone in my family before me.

"Do not do drugs or alcohol.

"Never tell on or snitch."

Shane understood his role in the family. One time, he kicked Kathy with a boot because Shelly commanded him to do it. He'd watched Kathy struggle to get up, like an animal that had been bounced off the hood of a car on the road in front of the house. She was crying and screaming and begging for mercy.

"Kick her again, Shane!"

And so he did. Yet it wasn't who he was. While he loved pushing Tori on the swing, or playing games with Sami, Shane's closest confidant continued to be Nikki. When they weren't talking about how much they hated Shelly or how they'd like to toss a hair dryer or radio into her bath, they plotted their escape. Shane was firm that no matter how dysfunctional his family life had been before moving in with the Knoteks, it was far better than what was going on there.

"Anything would be better," he told Nikki. "I need to get the fuck out of here. We all do."

Nikki wanted to get away too, but she only had a couple of years of high school to get through.

"I need to graduate, then go to college," she said.

Shane shook his head. "I can't wait for that."

"If you go," she said, "please don't leave me."

Shane always promised. "Right. We're out of here together. But if I have to go really fast, I'll be sure to come back for you."

"You better."

In her heart, Nikki doubted she'd ever really be able to leave. She had her sisters to think about. She knew that her mother had a strange, ironclad hold on her. She also knew that no matter where she went, or how far away, her mom would track her down. She'd found Kathy at the mall. She'd even managed to track Shane in the middle of Tacoma.

Her mom was a hunter.

CHAPTER
THIRTY-ONE

Dave Knotek was a willing participant in the abuse of Nikki and Shane, but Shelly had insisted the kids were out of control and needed the harsh discipline to ensure that they'd be on the right path in adulthood. In some ways, that made a little sense to Dave. Kids did need a firm hand.

He didn't blame his dad for hitting him with the razor strap.

But Kathy? Dave had a harder time defending what was happening to her. She was an adult, not a kid. Besides, she did what she was asked to do. She did the laundry. Cleaned the house. Fed the animals. She didn't always do things the way Shelly wanted her to, but she was trying.

Dave sat in his truck at the river landing. He was scared, tired—a leaf on the surface of a river—and felt unable to end what was happening to Kathy. It wasn't that he looked the other way—really, there was no other way to look. He simply didn't have it in him to fight Shell or even to tell her to knock it off.

When Shelly blamed Kathy for bringing her state of affairs on herself or belittled her friend's efforts to pull herself up by her bootstraps, Dave never flipped it back at his wife and pointed out how what was happening was Shelly's doing. When Shelly blamed Shane for the cognitive issues Kathy was having, Dave didn't call her out. He didn't retort that Shelly was the one who forced Shane to kick Kathy.

Dave could see where things were headed, and what his part in all of it had been. Kathy's physical decline was escalating, and it was obvious to him that, if things continued, she might die. He pulled Shelly aside on one of his trips home to Raymond and offered a solution he thought might work.

"Let me take her somewhere," he said.

Shelly didn't understand. "What?"

"I could take her to Oregon or somewhere and just drop her off."

Shelly didn't think that was a good idea. For one, Kathy might tell someone what had been going on. Besides, she was going to recover.

"Don't worry," Shelly said. "She's going to get better."

Dave didn't believe it, but as usual, he didn't contradict Shelly. Still, he worried about what was going to happen.

Besides following Shelly's orders, worry was all Dave seemed to do.

※

When it came to manifesting anger, Shelly Knotek was a kind of jack-in-the-box. She could be in a dead sleep in the middle of the night, then bolt from bed with an angry scream at one of the girls or Shane. She was like the villain in a slasher flick. She went zero to sixty, from calm to rage, in less than five seconds.

Years later, her daughters would also say that, while there likely was no other person on the planet as lazy as their mom—she'd often lie on the sofa all day with her eyes riveted to a book or the TV—if something spurred her into action, then suddenly she was like a cat seeing a mouse run across the floor.

It wasn't a mouse one day.

It was Tupperware.

Shelly was curled up on the living room sofa when she looked over to the kitchen and saw a Tupperware container of feces on the kitchen floor. Shelly ran to the kitchen and grabbed an appliance cord from the counter. Kathy, who had been let into the house that day to work in the kitchen, cowered and tried to get away. Shelly was immediately on top of her, lashing her with the cord. Kathy started crying and begging Shelly to stop hurting her, but she wouldn't let up.

Shelly was Cujo. Freddy Krueger. The freaky clown, Pennywise, from *It*.

"Goddamn you, Kathy!"

Kathy was the girl in the shower. The woman trapped in the car. She was the victim that begs for one more chance before her attacker finishes her off.

"I'll never do it again," Kathy said.

Shelly kept at it and started to pull Kathy's hair and drag her about the kitchen. Kathy had lost considerable weight, yet she was still a large woman. Shelly moved her about like a rag doll. Rage gave her superhuman strength.

Shane and the girls had seen that before. Adrenaline.

"I don't ever want to see anything like that in my kitchen ever. Ever! Do you understand? You are filthy, Kathy. That's what you are!"

The fact that Shelly had revoked Kathy's bathroom privileges made no difference. That Shelly had to give her permission to urinate or defecate was beside the point. The fact that Shelly had been asleep, and Kathy didn't dare wake her to ask permission to use the toilet, didn't factor into any of it.

It was time to think up something new. A punishment that would make Kathy understand once and for all that she needed to follow the rules of the house.

Shelly told Dave when he came home what Kathy had done.

"Tupperware full of shit in our kitchen, Dave! What in the fuck is that about? She's really done it this time and you need to do something."

Dave agreed that what Kathy had done was beyond gross; however, he didn't have any suggestions on what they could do beyond isolating her in the pump house.

He liked Kathy. They all did. Yes, she'd misbehaved, but he didn't want to beat her, kick her. It was pointless and—though he never said it out loud—*crazy*.

Shelly already had an idea on what they should do to break Kathy of her bad habits.

"Waterboard her."

She instructed her husband to build a seesaw device with a wide plank over a metal fulcrum made of an old tank from the pole building. Without saying a word, Dave went about it as Shelly barked orders. This was what they needed to punish Kathy. A bucket of water was placed at one end of the board.

"You two stand watch," Shelly told Nikki and Shane. Shane quietly muttered to Nikki that, while he didn't think any of the abuse being inflicted on Kathy could be worse, this was "a whole new level of fucked up."

Shelly brought Kathy, now naked, from the pump house. Shelly helped her walk, because by that time Kathy was having a difficult time moving. She'd lost a lot of weight, and the sight of her made Nikki nearly gag. She was black and blue, and her skin hung in soft red folds.

"I'm sorry," Kathy repeated. "Please don't do this."

"Shut the fuck up," Shelly snapped. "You are a no-good piece of shit and you're going to listen to me!"

Kathy begged and pleaded. She looked at Nikki and Shane with an expression Nikki read as, *Won't anyone help me?*

Dave put Kathy on the sheet of plywood facedown. She tried to fight him, but she was too weak. He pinned her down and ran duct tape over her body to hold her like a mummy on a stick.

Shelly gave her husband a signal, and he lowered Kathy's face and head into the bucket of water. He continued to hold her down for a moment. It wasn't meant to drown her. Just to get her to follow Shelly's orders.

To be a better person.

Once it got going, Shelly told Nikki to watch the road from the front deck, and she immediately went there. Shane was directed to the driveway to make sure that the family across the road didn't hear Kathy's screams. Sami was positioned in the yard to stand watch.

They could hear their mother laughing at Kathy. Calling her stupid. Fat. Ugly.

"You're worthless, Kathy! You need to shape up!"

Nikki tried to shut out the sounds of Kathy's cries as the woman's head was lifted and submerged into the water. Kathy's voice was on the lower register, and it was more of a gurgling than a true scream as she fought for air and begged for mercy. Nikki stood at her post while her mom barked orders and her dad did the dunking. The scene was shocking, a horror show, and incongruous with the pretty bucolic setting of the country. Apple trees. Horses in the pasture. And a naked woman bound to a board and being dunked repeatedly.

The waterboarding didn't go on long. Maybe ten minutes or so. Long enough to freeze the image of Kathy, naked, duct-taped, and screaming for help, in Nikki's memory forever.

Later, Shelly would characterize the waterboarding punishment as a "shower" or "bath." Her best friend hadn't been keeping herself clean, so Shelly and Dave had employed the technique as a way to wash her.

None who witnessed it saw it that way, of course. It had nothing to do with bathing Kathy.

"My mom enjoyed doing that to Kathy," Nikki recalled one afternoon from her Seattle-area home while her children played outside, and she took herself back to that time when she was a teenager in Raymond. "I don't see how or know why, but she really did. It only happened that one time. The contraption was put away. We never saw it again."

Beatings. Waterboarding. Endless days in the pump house. Shelly was on overdrive when it came to harassing and torturing Kathy. It was as if Kathy wasn't even a human being anymore. Shelly seemed to treat her like a sadist's worst pet. She fed her rotten food from the refrigerator that she'd whirl around in the blender.

"Drink this smoothie, Kathy."

Kathy's hands trembled as she took the glass and looked at its brown and gray contents.

Shelly kept her eyes fixed on Kathy. "Isn't it good?"

Kathy drank the concoction of far-beyond-pull-date hamburger and spoiled produce.

"Delicious," she said. "Thank you, Shelly."

Another time, Nikki watched her mother fill a kiddie cup of Morton Salt from the kitchen cabinet. She couldn't understand what her mom was going to do, but she was morbidly curious. Shelly had enlisted Shane to be a part of whatever her plan was, and he did as he was told. Nikki followed the two of them out to the pump house. She didn't go the entire distance, however, instead choosing to linger back and watch as her mother unlocked the door.

Shelly handed the cup to Kathy, who by this point could barely stand without assistance.

"Eat the fucking salt."

Kathy squinted into the bright light of day. "No."

Shelly said that the salt was good for her. "It will help your swollen feet."

"Obviously I wasn't a doctor, but I think anyone would probably know that there was no way that salt was going to do anything good for Kathy," Nikki recalled. "My mom acted like it was a big treatment. She always had a reason for all the shit she did to us and Kathy."

Kathy tried to resist, which was unusual. She was always so compliant.

"I don't want to."

Shelly wasn't having any of that.

"Eat it!" she yelled. "Eat the whole thing, Kathy!"

Kathy resisted somewhat. Like always, she was no match for Shelly's indomitable will.

Nikki couldn't see Kathy from her vantage point all the time, but she could hear her refusing the salt as her mother and Shane screamed at her.

"Eat the fucking salt! I don't have all day!"

Nikki heard the sound of Kathy spitting as she ate the cup of salt. Her mother and Shane kept at her until she finished every last granule.

"Eat it all!"

After that was done, Shelly gave Kathy some pills and told her to take those too. Then they locked the door and left.

CHAPTER THIRTY-TWO

No one seemed to notice what was happening in the little red farmhouse on Monohon Landing Road. Some people would later say that they thought something odd might be going on over there, but other than a neighbor who called the authorities about the horses being neglected, nothing was ever reported. Even after the kids on the bus saw a naked woman running in the yard, Shelly's quick thinking about the hot tub mishap had proved a winning cover story.

No one heard Kathy scream as she was kicked or waterboarded in the yard.

No one noticed the patches of sodden earth where Shane and Nikki had wallowed.

No one.

And yet inside the house was an overwhelming feeling of foreboding. It was heavy, like one of those lead aprons dentists use when taking x-rays. Teenagers Nikki and Shane talked about it when they shared a smoke out in the woods behind the house. They were allies more than ever, bonded over what Shelly had done to them.

And even more over what they'd witnessed Shelly doing to Kathy.

It was bad.

"She needs to go," Shane said of Kathy.

"She can't go," Nikki said.

And she was right.

Kathy's breathing was labored now even when she sat. Forget standing. She could barely do that under her own power. Her eyes seemed somewhat cloudy, and her skin was a map of swollen red tributaries with spots of blue. Every mark told a story of how Kathy had made Shelly angry. Shelly told Sami that they were going to bring Kathy inside from the pump house for a bath or a shower.

"It will do her good," Shelly insisted.

Sami was glad Kathy was coming inside. The woodstove was always going. Its radiant heat would help her, she was sure. Kathy had been suffering in isolation in the pump house for weeks. Maybe months. It was hard for the girl to keep an exact time frame on the things her mother did. The abuse was erratic—a moving target that kept everyone on edge.

"Okay, Mom."

Kathy moaned with each step as they helped her across the lawn, then into the house, through the living room to the bathroom, adjacent to the master bedroom. Hideous bruising marked her body, and her skin hung in folds from extreme weight loss. She'd lost more than a hundred pounds since she'd moved in with the Knoteks. Gone were the comments from Shelly about how "terrific" Kathy looked now that she was slimmer.

Shelly acted as if the shower was a big treat, which it was. Kathy hadn't been allowed to use indoor plumbing in months. Her "baths" had been bleach straight from the bottle and water from the hose.

"This is going to be nice, Kathy," Shelly told her friend. "Warm water will make you feel better."

Kathy made some unintelligible responses. In a strange way, it seemed to Sami that she was grateful for the shower. When it became obvious that she wasn't going to be able to stand, Shelly switched tactics and changed plans for a bath. She started the water.

As they tried to get Kathy into the tub, she slipped, and the glass shower door came unhinged and fell from the track, crashing to the floor. Glittery pieces of tempered glass scattered. Kathy was crying, and Sami tried to keep her from getting hurt, but she'd rolled around into the glass and cut her abdomen and legs.

Long after, the memory of what she saw that day brought tears to Sami's eyes.

"It's hard," she said, going back in time. "I just try not to picture her, but I see her. It's hard. So many bruises everywhere. All from my mom. She was just a big, giant bruise."

Sami felt the vibe in the room shift. By then Nikki had joined the three of them. Shelly was piling on the kind words and the loving touch of a good friend.

"Everything is going to be okay, Kathy," she said, her eyes meeting her daughter's.

Sami could tell that at that moment her mom was scared. Shelly was carrying on as if trying to convince Kathy that all would be fine when she knew full well there was no turning back. Kathy needed to go to the hospital, though Shelly insisted that she could help her.

Cure her.

Save her.

"We're going to keep you in the house now, Kathy," Shelly said. "You'd like that, wouldn't you?"

Kathy slurred her speech. It seemed that she agreed with Shelly.

The three of them helped Kathy to the toilet, where they tried to stop the bleeding with towels and toilet tissue.

Nikki left in tears, shaken to her bones. The next time she saw Kathy, her mother had done what she could to stop the bleeding. Some of the cuts still needed medical attention.

"My mom had wrapped a thick bandage around her. I don't think she was bleeding a lot, but she should have been taken to the hospital and had stitches."

Nikki told Shane what had happened, and Shane flipped out.

"She needs to go to a hospital," he said. "This isn't right. We all know it."

✕

Dave had been working on an extension of the laundry room at the back of the house. It was a small space, unfinished. Unlike the pump house, it was heated and dry. Shelly set up a twin mattress with a pillow and some blankets. She tucked Kathy into the bed and told her that everything was going to be fine.

It was a lie. Sami thought she could detect a look in Kathy's eyes. Fear. Disbelief. Confusion.

Not long after the Knoteks moved Kathy into the laundry room, the girls and Shane helped her into the living room to watch TV. She was unsteady on her feet, and it took a kid on each side to help. They sat her on the couch while Tori's cartoons played on the TV. Kathy was awake, though not lucid. Sami gave her one of Tori's toys, a small plastic telephone with two cords that snapped together. Kathy held the cords with her bruised fingertips but couldn't manage what a three or four year-old was proficient at doing. She tried over and over, never able to connect the pieces. The kids took it all in. They knew at that moment that there was something wrong with Kathy's brain.

Later, Sami found a two-by-four plank to put across the bed at waist height so Kathy could grasp something and pull herself up. She nailed it to the room's exposed studs on either side of the bed. Almost immediately, Shelly told her to take it down.

"Why?" she asked. "It helps her."

Shelly gave Sami a look.

"You don't understand," she said, treating Sami's act of kindness as some kind of silly mistake. "Kathy is lazy, and she needs to get stronger.

You're enabling her, Sami. We want Kathy better, right? She needs to get better on her own."

Sami didn't argue with her mother. She knew Kathy was extremely ill, not lazy. "She couldn't walk. She'd fall down, stand back up, and then fall down. Her equilibrium was all messed up. She had no teeth. Her hair had fallen out."

One day after school, Sami waited until her mother wasn't looking and went into the laundry room. She knelt next to the bed and put her hand on Kathy's hand. It felt cool.

"Kathy," Sami whispered, "I came to see if you are doing okay."

Sami pulled up the blanket and adjusted Kathy's pillow. Kathy gurgled but didn't really respond. Her eyes looked at Sami's and seemed to track her. Other than that, nothing.

"Kathy," she repeated. "Can you hear me?"

Kathy nodded and her eyes rolled backward.

Sami started to cry.

Something's really wrong here. Kathy needs help.

CHAPTER
THIRTY-THREE

Dave Knotek had been driving for God knew how long to get home from Whidbey Island. A ferry. The freeway. Seattle traffic. The 101. It had taken forever. He was wired on a gallon of coffee and a fistful of No-Doz. His mind was in that foggy state where things didn't always make sense. He was more stressed out than ever. Shelly had renewed her complaints about money and how hard it was for her to manage the kids and Kathy.

And Kathy.

Dave knew about the bath incident that had lacerated Kathy's abdomen and legs. Shelly said she'd fixed her up and that she'd be as good as new. He doubted that.

As he arrived home after the long drive in July 1994, he heard a sound coming from the laundry room that was like nothing Dave had ever heard in his life. He knew it wasn't an animal, but it didn't sound entirely human either. It was a soft moaning punctuated by a peculiar gurgling sound.

"What's that noise?" he asked.

Shelly, who was getting ready to go pick up Nikki from the Sea Star Restaurant in Grayland where she worked washing dishes, seemed unconcerned.

"Oh, it's Kathy. She's fine. She's resting."

"She doesn't sound fine."

Shelly ignored Dave's remark and called out to the girls. "Sami! Tori! Let's go!"

"What's going on around here?" Dave asked. On his last visit home, he'd remarked to his wife about the decline in Kathy's condition. One side of her face had started to droop a little. She was also bruised. It didn't appear that she was tracking what he was saying or even able to hold his gaze. He'd put his finger in front of her face, but her eyes had failed to follow the trajectory of his movements. She'd needed help standing up, and even staying standing. Her balance was off.

"She's getting better," Shelly had insisted.

Now, Shelly and the girls left to get Nikki, leaving Dave standing there baffled. Shane did dishes in the kitchen.

More guttural sounds from the laundry room brought Dave to Kathy, who was lying in the makeshift bed Shelly had fashioned earlier that summer. The hot July air filled the small room.

Dave leaned in close to Kathy. She had vomited, and the sounds coming from her indicated she was choking. The smell was nauseating too, and Dave's heart pounded so hard he was all but sure he'd have a heart attack. Kathy's eyes rolled back into their sockets. She was struggling to breathe. She was mostly motionless, slumped over, emitting pitiful little noises.

"What's wrong with her?" he called out to Shane, grabbing Kathy by the shoulders and shaking her. She was listless.

Shane stood statuelike, terrified. "I don't know."

"Jesus," Dave said, looking up at the boy. "This is bad."

And it was. Very bad.

"Kathy?" Dave raised his voice a little. "Are you okay? Kathy, answer me."

Kathy gurgled some more, and Dave started to panic.

"She's not breathing, Shane!"

Dave dropped to his knees and somehow managed to get Kathy on her side. He started to clear the vomit from her mouth. There was vomit in her nose too. He scooped it out with his fingers.

"She's not breathing!"

Dave was shaking as he tried to perform CPR. He worked on her for a long time, maybe as long as five minutes. He did chest compressions too. But nothing helped.

Later, he'd recall what he was thinking at the time.

"I know I should have called 911, but with everything that had been going on I didn't want the cops there. I didn't want Shell in trouble. Or the kids to go through that trauma . . . I didn't want this to ruin their lives or our family. I just freaked out. I really did. I didn't know what to do."

Kathy remained unresponsive. Dave struggled to lift her, but she was too heavy. Somehow, he managed to attempt a Heimlich maneuver. Nothing worked. He didn't know how long he tried to save her, but it was futile. Shane became agitated by then, talking about how fucked up all of this was. He and Dave locked eyes and then they just sat there in a stupor, not really knowing how to handle the situation.

Everything had indicated an ending like this was possible, but in the moment, it didn't seem real.

Kathy Loreno was dead.

Dave called the Sea Star to see if he could catch Nikki or Shelly at the restaurant, but they already were in the parking lot. The kid who took the call got Shelly to come back inside.

The girls remembered Shelly looked white when she came back to the car.

"Is Kathy okay?" Sami recalled asking her mother over and over on the drive home. Shelly stayed unusually quiet and wouldn't even look in the direction of her middle girl. She kept her eyes on the road. "She's fine."

Nikki knew something terrible had happened.

She just didn't know what.

When they got home, Dave immediately yanked Shelly aside, telling the kids to give their parents a moment to discuss something very important. The girls and Shane lingered in the living room for only a second before, in a firmer tone, he told them to go upstairs and watch TV.

"She's gone," he told Shelly when the kids left the room.

"What do you mean 'gone'?"

Dave pulled her closer. Shelly needed to grasp what he was telling her.

"She's not here no more! Shelly, Kathy's dead. Go look."

Shelly pulled back. With an exasperated and perplexed expression on her face, she made her way to where Kathy's body lay on the mattress in the airless laundry room. It was as if she didn't have any idea why Kathy might have died.

※

The kids huddled in Nikki's room. They could hear something going on downstairs—arguing, yelling. None could hear exactly what their parents were saying.

"You stay here with Tori," Nikki finally said to Sami. "Shane and I are going to find out what's happening."

Sami was crying by then. Something was really wrong.

Nikki and Shane snuck down the stairs and through the living room. Dave and Shelly were outside arguing in the yard, so they went into the little room where Kathy had been staying. It was dark, and they didn't turn on the light.

Although Shane knew what was going on, he didn't say anything to Nikki at the time. They called out Kathy's name, but she didn't answer. Shane pushed her foot, but nothing. Finally, he picked up her arm and dropped it. Her face was still. Puffy. Bruised. Completely lifeless.

"Yeah, she's dead," he said. "She's really dead. Holy fuck."

Nikki was terrified. She was shaking when she and Shane crept back upstairs and told Sami.

"Sami started freaking out," Nikki remembered. "Really. She loved Kathy so much."

Shelly, hearing the commotion, went to comfort Sami and then returned downstairs. A minute later, she was back.

"She came back and said, you know, get in the car . . . my mom was actually being nice at that time, telling us that it would be okay. And we can't let anyone break our family apart," Nikki recalled.

"We need to call an ambulance," Shane said.

"We aren't going to do that." Shelly's eyes narrowed. "There's no point. She's gone."

The house was in complete turmoil. The kids were hysterical. Shelly was crying too. She alternated between letting everyone know that everything would be all right and sobbing her eyes out. Dave was bawling as well. His nerves were beyond frayed, and his chest thumped like a jackhammer.

It ran through his mind just then that he should have put his foot down.

But he hadn't. And he didn't now.

Instead, Shelly packed up the girls for a motel near Westport.

It was after ten when Shelly checked in on the girls, gave them money and some snacks, and promised she'd be back later with Shane. In the meantime, she told them not to talk to anyone. Not a single person. Not about anything that had happened at home. It was confusing,

Shelly said. She was going to get some answers to see what happened. Things needed to get sorted out.

You killed Kathy, Mom, Nikki thought at the time. There was nothing to sort out. None of this was confusing. It was messed up beyond belief.

Shelly and Shane arrived around midnight.

The next morning, Shane went swimming with Tori and Sami in the motel's heated pool. At any other time, swimming there would have been the highlight of summer vacation. As they splashed around, no one would have known why they were there or what was going on back in Raymond.

When Shelly arrived later that morning to pick up the kids, she made Nikki call the Sea Star.

"Tell them you can't come in today," she said. "Family emergency."

CHAPTER THIRTY-FOUR

Dave Knotek went over the grim details of the situation at hand.

It played in his mind that what was happening wasn't real at all. He told himself that he and Shelly were normal people caught up in a tragedy that would undo their family if someone took things the wrong way.

Kathy's death had been an accident. Natural causes. No one's fault.

He was going to have to get rid of her body.

Shelly was by his side, telling him what to do and how to do it.

Dave would later recall that he burned Kathy Loreno's body during "graveyard hours," without seeming to grasp the irony of his own statement. The house on Monohon Landing sat close to the road, and the firepit was only a few steps from the back of the pole building. Burning there wasn't unusual. It's where they burned the trash.

Dave retrofitted the firepit with sheets of heavy-gauge tin and steel "to hold the heat in" as it started to blaze. The air was a little damp that night, and it was completely dark outside. Planks from the old barn provided the wood. Though he'd never done it before, Dave knew he needed a very hot fire for cremation. Dave and Shane carried Kathy's body to the fire, set her down, and then piled more wood on top of her. He topped the pyre with old tires and diesel fuel. Dave would later recall that he felt what he was doing had been for "humanitarian" reasons, which might've been the only thing that kept him on task. It was a ghoulish and horrific process. It took more than five hours to make Kathy vanish by the faint light of daybreak.

When morning light came, Dave looked down on the ash and bone. When it all cooled, he loaded up some Home Depot buckets and drove out to Washaway Beach, where he carried Kathy's remains to the ocean. Knowledge he'd gleaned surfing came in handy; he knew the tides and knew that her ashes would be carried out to sea. Gone forever. He didn't say a prayer for her; he couldn't think of what to say. He returned to Washaway three more times. He also took some of the ashes and dirt from the firepit to Long Beach and disposed of them there.

Shelly, for her part, loaded up Kathy's clothes and had Dave burn those too. She retrieved other things she'd taken from Kathy—personal papers and jewelry—and tossed those in the firepit. Very little of Kathy had been left for anyone to find.

※

The scent that permeated the air was thick and unmistakable. When the Knotek sisters and Shane returned from the motel the next day, the yard still carried the acrid smell of burning tires and diesel oil.

And the odor of something else that had burned with it.

Nikki only glanced in the direction of where her dad had set the fire.

"I didn't go back there behind the pole building," Nikki said later. "Shane told me what happened. We had a bunch of tires, but they were all gone now too."

The kids went inside. Sami was still in tears over Kathy. Tori was too young to really know what happened, and the older kids focused on her. Shelly paced around the house and Dave sat slumped in a chair at the kitchen table. Bags hung heavy under his eyes. He drank coffee and smoked cigarette after cigarette.

Kathy's death, and what he'd done to get rid of her body, was an anvil pitched on Dave's shoulders. He knew he could never erase what he'd done. He thought of how Kathy's family would always wonder where she'd gone, and if she was happy. He didn't know how he'd react when he saw Kathy's mom, Kaye, around town. What would he say when she asked about her daughter? Because of what he and Shelly had done, Kathy's family might never have closure. It was something he thought about every second from the moment he'd begun to carry Kathy's body to the firepit.

Shelly told him she felt the same way, that she was devastated by the loss of her best friend—but she seemed much more pragmatic about it, telling him what was done was done and they needed to pull themselves together.

Shelly told the older kids that they needed to stay in lockstep from now on.

"All of us will be in jail," she warned, "if anyone finds out what happened to Kathy."

She sent up a trial balloon the day they returned from the motel.

"She committed suicide and we didn't want her family to know," Shelly pretended to speculate.

No one said anything. They simply let Shelly's ridiculous musing fade away. Nikki and Shane didn't see how anyone would believe that story. *Suicide?* Nikki doubted it. *No one takes a five-year route to kill herself.*

Kathy had been beaten, starved, and tortured to death.

With Dave back at work on Whidbey Island, Shelly had a chore for Shane and Nikki a few days after the fire had cooled. She led the pair outside to the pole building and handed them a Home Depot bucket.

"Dad burned some insulation in the burn pile and I need you to find the bits and pieces and put them in here," she said.

They both knew that wasn't what Shelly was looking for at all.

Shelly went back inside the house, and they walked over to the burn pile. It was a gruesome task, and they poked through the dirt without saying much at all.

"You think that's something?" Shane asked, pointing his stick at a tiny shard of white.

Nikki looked at it.

"Yeah," she said, feeling sick inside. "It's part of Kathy."

Shane found quite a few pieces of what they both knew were fragments of bone, not insulation. He found some melted jewelry too. Nikki, who could barely keep her mind on the task, also found a couple of fragments. They gave Shelly the bucket at the end of the day. Shelly put the particles in a plastic bag.

She made Shane look in the burn pile a second and third time over the next few days.

On one of his next trips home, Dave managed to get his hands on a backhoe. He drove it over to the old burn pile and scraped off the top, down a foot or two into the clean earth. He drove the dirt out to a remote logging road up Ward Creek and dumped it on a fresh road the loggers had cut so that the soil would blend together.

"Later," he said, some years after the fact of the old burn pit in the backyard, "we planted a garden in that spot."

CHAPTER THIRTY-FIVE

Kathy Loreno's disappearance needed a cover story.

Suicide was a no-go. After all, there was no body.

Shelly, whose mood had brightened considerably since the first few days following Kathy's backyard cremation, practiced her concept first on Dave. It was like she was spinning a tale from one of the thriller potboilers she loved to read. She was excited. Buoyant. It was as if she was lifting the curtain on some kind of big reveal and was waiting for the audience to gasp and nod in enthusiasm.

"We'll continue telling everyone that she ran off with Rocky. I introduced them and the two of them hit it off. She wanted to start over somewhere and, really, she didn't have any boyfriends so Rocky would be really important to her," Shelly said, testing out her story.

Dave went along with the story, but he wasn't sure anyone else would buy it. Kathy hadn't really dated anyone they knew about. That she would run off with a guy—especially in her weakened condition—was far-fetched, to say the least.

"I don't know if anyone will really believe it."

"We'll make them," Shelly said.

Next, Shelly held a family meeting with all the kids. She brought them all into the living room and sat them on the couch. Dave didn't say much. He sat next to his wife and nodded in agreement at what she was proposing.

"Remember my friend Rocky? Remember how he was so interested in Kathy? Wanted to date her?"

None of the kids remembered anything of the kind. None of them had even met him, though they vaguely remembered having heard their mother mention the name back at the Louderback House.

"You all liked him."

It was typical of their mother, however, to suggest a shared memory as if it were something that could be planted and made to become real.

Shelly went on with her plan. "It's very important that we stick together on this, okay? I need all of you to understand and know that Kathy went off with Rocky."

"But she didn't," Shane said.

Shelly shot Shane a harsh look. She had a way of burrowing her gaze into another's eyes as if she was willing them to believe what she was saying, simply because she was saying it.

"You don't know that, Shane," she said. "You don't know that at all."

Shane did, of course. He'd helped Dave start the pyre and drag Kathy's body to the firepit. Nevertheless, he backed down.

"Okay, if you say so, Mom."

Nikki knew her mom was full of crap too. But, somehow, Shane's support of the Rocky story gave Sami a little hope. It made her think that somehow, maybe, she'd been wrong after all.

Maybe Kathy *was* alive.

Maybe what she thought had happened had only been a bad dream.

A story needs details to make it persuasive. Shelly had one item already in her arsenal—a blurry photo of a woman standing outside a semi-truck. Only if someone was *told* that the woman was Kathy could anyone imagine it was. Next, Shelly had Nikki forge cards and letters with Kathy's signature to make the Rocky love-on-the-run tale even more convincing. She sat Nikki at the kitchen table with practice paper, cards, and a box of Ziploc bags.

"Close, Nikki. Do another one."

And so that's just what Nikki did. The messages were brief, extolling how much fun she was having on the road. She was in Canada. Mexico. California. She was happy and never coming back to Raymond.

Nikki was thinking the same thing. She couldn't wait for high school to be over so she could leave the craziness of Raymond too.

Shelly studied every signature and praised her oldest daughter when she considered it work well done.

"Mom never touched the letters," Nikki remembered. "She actually wiped down each card and put them into the plastic bags. She was putting to use all of her forensic knowledge, I guess. Or thought she was."

When the missives met her approval, Shelly handed them off to her husband to mail to Kathy's family.

"She made me go all the way to Canada to mail the card to Kathy's mom's house in South Bend. So that's what I did," Dave later said.

That wasn't the strangest part of Shelly's plan. Even though she'd made Nikki forge them and Dave mail them, she changed her mind about Kathy's mom actually getting all of the messages, and on one occasion she instructed Dave to hurry back to South Bend, use the mailbox key that she'd taken from Kathy's belongings, and steal a card back before Kaye got it.

Dave did just that. He waited like a cop on surveillance, and when the card was delivered, he retrieved it and returned it to Shelly. She put the card in a Ziploc bag and squirreled it away.

"I really don't know what she was thinking," he recounted. "An alibi? A diversion? It didn't make any sense to me, but I was in such a panic over what happened to Kathy that I did what Shell told me to do."

※

Even as the Rocky plan was in full swing, Shelly shifted gears. She got quiet and worried. She didn't say that she doubted her plan would work. She simply thought she needed a backup plan too. She mulled it over for a couple of weeks. The older kids and Dave could see that Shelly, who lived to be in control, was sputtering a bit. Maybe she'd seen something on television in which a perpetrator was caught through the skills of an FBI forgery expert? Or maybe an episode with a cadaver dog?

Her plan needed adjusting. Shelly's eyes landed on Shane during one of their family meetings.

"If you tell anyone," she said, "we'll pin it all on you, Shane."

The kids looked at each other, mouths open.

Shane stood up. "That's bullshit," he said. "I didn't do anything."

Shelly stayed on the teenager. "That's what we'll do, Shane. We'll say you killed her. You killed Kathy."

"That's a lie," he insisted. "I'm not going to say anything. I would never say something against my family."

Shelly burrowed her gaze deep into his eyes.

"That's good," she said. "I need to believe you."

"You can," he said. "You can."

"I sure hope so."

Later, Nikki and Shane discussed their mother's surprise threat. It really shouldn't have been a surprise. They knew she was a survivor—a selfish one at that. She'd do whatever it took to save herself. Everything that had happened to Kathy—the bloody snow, the waterboarding, the long stretch of time in the dark of the pump house—had been Kathy's fault. Shelly had been forced to punish her friend. It was daunting and tragic, but everything she'd done was out of love for Kathy.

Despite his promises to keep his mouth shut, Shane was smart enough to know that in time Shelly would turn on him. Someone someday would figure out everything and come knocking on the door.

"We should tell," he said. "We should have taken her to the hospital that night."

Nikki agreed with him, though she was too scared to say or do anything.

"What can we do now?" she asked instead.

Shane didn't know, but he was thinking.

Shelly wasn't exactly discreet when it came to her doubts about her nephew either. She brought it up all the time to Dave, and within earshot of Nikki and Sami.

"Shane's going to tell," Shelly said whenever her nephew wasn't around. "He's going to bring us all down."

Shane knew it was only a matter of time. He had two choices—tell someone or run away.

Both options were on the table.

CHAPTER THIRTY-SIX

Shelly continued to juggle her lies and conspiracy theories about what had happened to Kathy, and how blaming Shane might be the answer. In the weeks following Kathy's death, Shelly told Dave that she thought it would be a good idea to gauge whether Kathy's family would even look for her. After all, they'd barely registered any interest in Kathy throughout the nearly five years she had lived with the Knoteks.

"I'm going to call Kaye," Shelly said. "Tell her that Kathy wants to see her and see if she'll come over."

Dave was alarmed and almost didn't know what to say.

Invite her mother over there? To the place where her daughter died and had been burned?

"Why do that?" he asked.

"I want to see what her reaction is," she explained.

Dave thought Shelly was playing with fire, but he backed down and watched as she dialed Kaye at her little house in South Bend. The call lasted barely a minute.

Shelly turned to Dave. She had a satisfied smile on her face. Her instincts had been correct.

As usual.

"Shelly said that Kaye was pretty abrupt," Dave recalled. "Didn't want to talk with Kathy at all." He played that moment back in his mind later. In a way, it was a willful version of chicken, a concept that Shelly was a master at.

Shelly had proven her point.

They had nothing to worry about. Kathy's family had disowned her. They wouldn't be a threat whatsoever. The Loreno family out of the way, Shelly suddenly shifted her concerns to the neighbors across the street from their house on Monohon Landing Road.

"I wonder if they know anything," she told the oldest kids. "They might have heard or smelled something."

Nikki doubted it. She thought that if anyone had heard or seen anything that night, they would have called the sheriff.

"We need to find out for sure," Shelly said. "They could tear this family apart, you know."

Nikki understood what her mother was getting at. There was always the threat that if the sheriff figured out what happened to Kathy, her parents would likely get arrested and sent to jail. She and Shane would be homeless. Sami and Tori would end up in foster care. Their family would be gone forever.

The neighbors in question had three little boys and were in a financial world of hurt. They were on public assistance and trying as hard as they could to try to keep afloat. Their yard was cluttered with toys and the house needed major repair, and since they couldn't afford garbage service, they loaded up garbage behind and under their house. But no one who knew them could say they weren't trying. The boys were clean, well fed, and happy.

Shelly kept saying that she was sure the family was going to do something against them.

"We need to find out what's going on over there," she said. "You need to go over there and listen."

"What do you mean?" Nikki asked. "Go over there and ask them or spy on them?"

The scenario was crazy. The teenagers could only imagine such a conversation.

"Hey, did you guys hear anything? Any screams? Did you smell a burning human being?"

Shelly indicated they should spy on them.

"Don't get caught, whatever you do."

Nikki and Shane went off on the bizarre reconnaissance effort.

"Your mom is fucking paranoid, Nikki."

Nikki didn't know what to think. Her mom could seem so convincing. So smart about things. There were times when she and Sami thought their mom was psychic because she just *knew* things.

"But what if she's right?" she finally asked.

Shane didn't see how the family across the road was a threat of any kind.

The two of them snuck over anyway and looked around and tried to listen in the window. When they returned hours later, Shelly wanted to know what they'd found.

"Nothing," Shane said.

"Yeah, Mom," Nikki said. "They seem fine."

Shelly pushed for specifics and details. "What did you see?"

Nikki told her mother about the lay of the land there, the garbage in the back, the freezer on the porch, and how she couldn't hear anything coming from the window while she hunkered down.

"Crawlspace," Shelly repeated, letting the word hang in the air. "You need to go into the crawlspace and listen. This is important, Nikki. Our family depends on you. We need to stay together."

"The fucking crawlspace?" Shane couldn't believe it. "I'm not doing that."

"She says it's important, Shane."

Shane thought it was crazy.

"I'm not doing it."

That summer, Nikki spent her days in the neighbor's crawlspace, against the garbage, looking up between slits in the floorboards as the family that lived there went about their daily lives. She could hear only a few words here and there. She stayed frozen, terrified she'd be discovered, unsure of the point of it all.

"I let my mom think I could hear them," Nikki said later. "I told her over and over that they didn't know anything."

Shelly could never quite be convinced.

"You need to follow them the next time they leave," she said.

That's just what Nikki did. She tailed the family to the grocery store, to the post office, to the welfare office in South Bend. She watched as they did the mundane things that people do. Then she reported back to her mother.

"Mom," she said, almost pleadingly, "they don't know anything."

"You don't know that for a fact, Nikki."

She didn't. Her mom was always good at making people question facts. Nikki *knew* Kathy was dead, yet there would be times when she hoped that maybe Kathy *had* run off with Rocky.

If Sami could believe that, why can't I? Nikki thought.

Her mom had Shane steal the neighbor's food a few times too. He also put pepper spray on their door handles.

"I think my mom had it in her mind that she could run them out of town. She was messing with them," Nikki said later. "Trying whatever she could to get them away from here."

After the pepper spray and the constant requests to hassle the neighbors, Shane once more said he wanted to get out of there.

"Your mom is off her rocker," he said. "I'm going. Are you staying or leaving?"

Nikki wanted to leave. She dreamed of leaving every day. All day.

She couldn't quite get there. Her mom was a monster, but she was the only mom she'd ever had.

"I can't," she finally told Shane. "I just can't."

※

For more than a year after Kathy's death, Shelly burrowed in with her paranoid thoughts and bizarre edicts to the family. She tested the kids about the Rocky story. Sami wanted to believe it so badly that, in time, she allowed the tale to replace what she knew to be true. Shelly had Nikki follow the neighbors. Throughout all this, Dave stayed up on Whidbey Island—working as many hours as he could, partly because Shelly needed the money, but also to stay away from Raymond. With Kathy gone, she ramped up the punishments on the two oldest kids in the house, Nikki and Shane. The wallowing had subsided some, though the midnight hunts for shoes, homework, and hairbrushes continued.

Sami lived in another world. She was popular. Wore nice clothes. She hated what her mom did to Shane and Nikki, and she knew they didn't deserve it.

But it wasn't her.

Nikki went to class and did her best to blend in. She was quiet. She didn't invite anyone over. She didn't have a boyfriend. She didn't see how she could mix her school and social life with the craziness of what was happening at home the way Sami could.

Shane had reached his limit. He wanted to finish high school, but he was ready to bolt the first chance he had. One more night in the pump house or being forced to run around the yard naked, and he'd be out of there.

All the while, Shelly beat the drum.

Shane is going to tell.

Dave fought her on that.

"He's blood. He's family. He's not going to do that."

Dave had talked to Shane. Although he was angry at what had happened, Shane wasn't going to squeal on his parents and send his cousins to foster care.

Shelly wouldn't hear of it.

"I don't trust him, Dave."

"He's okay," Dave insisted, though part of him wasn't completely confident. He could imagine an older Shane getting loaded in a bar and spilling the beans.

"No shit. You think your family is fucked up? Mine killed a lady and burned her in the backyard!"

Whenever Dave came home, Shelly would start up again. She wouldn't stop. She kept pushing at Dave in an unrelenting, nagging manner like some kind of vocal tinnitus. Her words pointing the finger at Shane rang in his ears even when she wasn't around.

When Shelly didn't get her way, she manufactured the evidence—the way she had with her hair loss because of the supposed cancer, the bruises when she claimed to have been raped by the intruder when she was married to Randy, or the forged cards to Kathy's family.

Proof was important to Shelly. Proof was undeniable.

One time when Dave came home, Shelly met him at the door. He was exhausted from the drive, but his wife's expression gave him the jolt of a thousand cups of coffee. Shelly's face was red, and it seemed that she might have been crying. She was so angry that she was shaking.

"I found them in the woodshed, Dave!" she said, holding up a pair of bloody panties. "Shane must have hidden them there."

Dave knew what Shelly was insinuating right away.

"No," he said. "Can't be."

Shelly was as angry as she'd ever been.

"They're Tori's," she said flatly. "Shane's abusing our baby! You have to do something!"

Neither Nikki nor Sami believed a single word of it. They knew Shane, and they knew their mother. They were positive that she'd planted the underwear to get Shane in trouble. It was a game to her. Shane denied it with everything he had. He'd never hurt Tori. The idea that Shelly would even think it hurt him to the core. He wasn't like that.

Nevertheless, with Shelly egging him on, Dave beat Shane that night.

The next morning, Shane, swollen and battered, renewed his vow to run away. He told Nikki that if she didn't go with him, he'd go on his own. He'd had enough.

Hadn't she?

CHAPTER THIRTY-SEVEN

Suddenly, Shane was gone.

Shelly and Dave gathered the girls in the living room to tell them that their cousin had run away. It was February 1995, just a couple of weeks before Nikki's twentieth birthday.

"He'll turn up," Dave said.

"He always does," Shelly added. "We'll look for him."

"You kids hear anything last night?" Dave asked.

None had.

"Any noises at all?" Shelly asked.

Neither Sami nor Tori had heard a peep. Though Nikki remembered that when she'd gone to bed, Shane was not in the closet where he usually slept.

"Nikki, did you hear him come in last night?"

"No, Mom."

Later, Shelly came into the kitchen holding a small wooden birdhouse, which the girls recognized as something Shane had built for a school project. On one side, he'd painted a little dog as a decoration. Their mother was misty eyed when she put it on the table. She said Shane had left her the birdhouse as a gift.

"He left me a note too. He said, 'I love you, Mom.'"

No one ever saw the note.

Nikki, for one, was skeptical.

"Shane hated Mom," she told Sami after their mom made a show of the birdhouse. "There's no way he'd leave her a note like that."

Sami didn't buy a cozy relationship between Shane and their mom either, but she didn't want to think that the whole story was some big lie.

"Shane's always running away," she reminded Nikki.

Nikki didn't answer. Something about the birdhouse bothered her; she knew he would never have left Shelly a gift, or a loving note. Yet Nikki didn't want to think that anything had happened to the boy she considered her brother.

Shelly and the older girls got into the car later that day and went looking for Shane, though the excursion was brief.

Oddly so.

"Usually Mom made us look for hours and hours. This time I doubt we drove around more than an hour," Nikki said later. "I don't think we looked for Shane more than a couple of times."

A few days later, Nikki was out feeding the horses and for a fleeting moment she thought she heard Shane's voice. She spun around, but he wasn't there. She went to her mother later and told her.

"Mom, Shane's still around. I think I heard him."

Shelly looked concerned. "What are you talking about?"

Nikki loved Shane. She wanted him to come back, like he always did. "Maybe he didn't run away?"

Shelly held her daughter's stare for a second but didn't say anything more.

About a week later, Shelly packed up the girls for a getaway weekend at a motel in Aberdeen. It was a spur-of-the-moment vacation. They swam in the pool and ate at the nearby Denny's. The older girls talked about Shane and hoped that he was doing all right.

Wherever he'd gone, it had to be better than home.

✖

Finally, they got some answers. Their mother told them that their cousin was fishing on Kodiak Island.

He called when you were at school.

You just missed him.

He's doing great! He misses all of us.

Shelly said that she'd also received a number of hang-up calls.

"I got another one last night," she announced with complete conviction. "I'm pretty sure it was Shane."

Nikki didn't ask why Shane would call and then hang up. Or why only their mother would receive these calls only when no one else was around. Neither she nor Sami ever picked up the phone and heard only the click of a disconnected line. She didn't think there was any point to challenging her mother on that particular lie.

Shelly also reminded her daughters that if anyone inquired about Kathy, they needed to provide the party line.

"What would you say if the police came and asked about Kathy?"

"That she went away with her boyfriend," Nikki answered.

"What was his name?"

"Rocky."

"What did he do for a living?"

"He was a trucker."

"Where did they go?"

"Far away?"

Shelly made a face. She was annoyed.

"Think, Nikki. Be specific."

"California or Alaska."

"California. Why don't you ever listen? Shane's in Alaska."

Nikki could only hope he really was.

CHAPTER
THIRTY-EIGHT

Nikki attempted to twist the knob of the front door. *Locked.* With Kathy and Shane gone, she was on the outs again. Literally. She'd become her mother's favorite target. She stood by the door and knocked softly. Too loud of a knock would make her mom even angrier. She rapped just enough to make sure her mother knew she was there, as if there was any doubt about it.

"Please, Mom. Let me in."

No answer.

"Please, Mom. I'm freezing out here. I'll be good. I promise."

Shelly ignored her and stayed on the couch watching TV.

It became almost a daily occurrence. One time Shelly handed her daughter a blanket. Usually, she got nothing at all. Once, Nikki stashed a sleeping bag and some matches under the old dilapidated barn. The next time she was banished from the house and went to retrieve them, they'd vanished.

Her mother, she knew, had a knack for finding things.

On some nights, Nikki slept in one of the outbuildings, but most often, she was out in the woods up behind the house trying to stay warm, wishing the night away. Wondering how she was going to get out of the mess she was in. She could see the headlights of a car as Sami's friends brought her home from wherever they'd been. She would see the glow of the light in Tori's bedroom window. She loved her sisters more than anything, though she also wondered why her mother saw her so differently, treated her with such hatred. Why she told her over and over that she was garbage, a bitch, a loser, a whore, any nasty name that came to mind as she rattled off insult and epithet.

"No one will ever love you, Nikki. No one!"

Every now and then, Shelly would let her inside. It wouldn't be the result of any of Nikki's quiet begging or promising. It would just happen. Shelly would fix her something hot to eat and tell her daughter how much she loved her.

"It would be good for a while," Nikki recalled many years later. "Maybe a day or two. I didn't trust her, but I always hoped it would last longer."

Then, without warning, back outside. Often naked. Sometimes with a change of clothes. Always with hurled insults and anger.

The violence escalated too.

One time when Nikki was outside working in her underwear, her mother came at her with a knife. Shelly was mad for some reason. It might have been because Nikki had been unable to get a new job after she lost her dishwashing job at Sea Star, or maybe she hadn't been doing a good enough job with her chores. Whatever the reason, Nikki ran outside, then past the pole building into the field, with her mother on her heels screaming at her to stop.

"God damn you, Nikki! Do not defy me!"

She lunged and pinned Nikki down and sliced her leg with the knife. Blood oozed from the wound. Shelly looked at what she'd done, then let her go. Nikki ran for the woods, blood dripping down her leg from the two-inch gash that almost certainly needed stitches, though she knew she couldn't seek medical attention for the same reason Kathy couldn't.

Then someone would know.

Nikki slept in the woods that night. When she came back inside the house the next morning, cold and dirty but no longer bleeding, her mother said nothing about the violent altercation.

It was like it never happened.

Around that time, the chicken house became a hiding place for the sisters. Mostly for themselves, but also sometimes for things like blankets and coats, since they never knew when they'd be forced outside in freezing weather.

One afternoon Sami was doing her chores—feeding the dogs tethered to the trees, then the rabbits, which were kept in the chicken house. When she went inside, she found Nikki sitting on a hay bale, laughing and crying at the same time.

"I tried to kill myself," she told Sami.

Nikki pointed to some twine from the hay bales she'd fashioned into a noose that she'd hung over a beam. It had snapped when she'd jumped from a bale to the chicken shed floor.

"I can't even do that right," she added. Despite the circumstances, both sisters laughed.

Sami didn't blame Nikki for trying to end her life. She tried the same thing later. She'd stayed out late with friends, and when she came home her mother refused to let her in.

"You're sleeping outside tonight."

It was fall and the air was chilly, and she'd had it. She was sick of her mother's games and saw no way out, so she ran into the woods and found a bush with red berries that she knew were poisonous and she ate them. First one, then another, then a handful. She was crying, and it was dark and hard to see. She didn't care. She just kept putting the berries into her mouth and swallowing.

The berries, however, were a failure.

"I came home after eating all those berries and my mom acts like nothing happened," she said later. "It was past midnight and she wasn't even looking for me. She knew I would come back. I was trying to make a statement by eating those berries and she didn't even care."

She vomited and had diarrhea for more than a week. If she had hoped to make a statement living a real-life nightmare, no one picked up on it.

)(

In mid-September 1996, more than two years after Kathy Loreno vanished, Shelly applied for a teacher's aide position with the South Bend School District. Despite the dreadful state of the Knoteks' own finances, she boasted that she'd been a self-employed tax preparer but was now ready to return to her first love, caring for children.

"I have spent a good part of my life raising my children, helping with their schoolwork, their school activities, volunteering at their school and even helping their friends from time to time."

She felt she had the necessary "patience" to work with special-needs children.

CHAPTER THIRTY-NINE

While Nikki found herself banished to do yard work all day, the two youngest Knotek sisters went to school and acted just like the other kids. Tori was a quiet little girl who'd really been too young to see what their mother had done to Kathy, and she'd been shielded from the harsh punishments given to Nikki and Shane. Sami was a social queen bee who used her sense of humor as a cover for life with her mother. She didn't cry about it. Humor was the curtain she put around everything. Her friends knew that her mom was a royal bitch with nonsensical rules and punishments that went far beyond any real or perceived transgressions. Because of that, they were also persistent. When Sami's friends came to pick her up and there was no answer, they'd just wait. Nikki's friends weren't like that; if they came for Nikki and she wasn't there, they figured she'd changed her mind or was off somewhere else. Sami's friends knew that her mother was a weirdo who was holding Sami captive.

So they'd knock.

They'd wait.

As long as they needed.

Sometimes they'd go to McDonald's in Raymond, then come back and wait some more. The teenagers could outlast and annoy Shelly, so that's just what they did.

"Go. Get out of here," Shelly would finally call upstairs to Sami when the constant knocking and hovering on the front porch interfered with whatever TV show she'd been watching.

Sami knew how to handle that. She knew that her mom wouldn't want to be seen as anything other than wonderful. She'd go outside and tell her friends the same made-up story.

"My mom didn't know you were here," Sami would lie. "She just heard you now."

And then the biggest lie of all:

"She feels so bad."

Shelly never felt bad about anything. At least not when it came to other people's feelings. The girls noticed she'd shed a torrent of tears for dead pets, but never for another person.

※

Shelly assessed the relationship between her older girls. Tori was no threat, of course. She was young enough to be either clueless or easily scared by mere intimidation.

Those other two? They were getting big. They were mouthy. They were spending too much time together. Just as she had at the Louderback House, Shelly told Nikki and Sami that she didn't want them talking behind her back.

She put it mostly on Nikki's shoulders.

"Sami, your sister is a bad influence."

Bad influence? The idea was laughable. Nikki worked in the yard from sunup to sundown. She didn't drink or use drugs. She'd smoked cigarettes a few times with Shane, but she hadn't even liked it.

Looking back, Sami struggled to remember a single time when she and Nikki hung out in each other's bedrooms after they'd moved to Monohon Landing. Their mother didn't approve of them spending time together alone. The only contact they had was when they did chores. Over time, even those connecting moments decreased.

After Kathy died and Shane disappeared, they stopped altogether.

"Nikki was always outside," Sami recalled. "She was out doing chores. Until late. Dark. I had my friends and was busy in school and I just remember my sister just not being there. She was there, but not around. In my heart of hearts, I think she was being groomed by my mom not to be here anymore."

None of Sami's friends even knew Nikki lived there.

One time when the girls were doing the dishes, their mother came in and literally pulled them apart.

"No talking!" she said.

"We weren't talking about anything," Sami said.

"None," she insisted. "No talking."

Sami left her sister to finish the dishes alone.

"Most of the time we *were* talking shit about her," Sami recalled. "We weren't talking about homework, that's for sure."

✕

Shelly started to put more emphasis on her appearance, which was a welcome distraction. She'd gained some weight over the past couple of years. As Dave continued to send his paycheck home, Shelly decided that it was her turn for a little fun. She slimmed down, colored her hair, and went out to the bars a few times. One time she told the girls that she'd met a new friend.

"He's an airline pilot," she said. "And girls, we're just friends. Nothing more. I've invited him over to visit."

Sami had other plans and Tori would be content to be in her room during the time Shelly would be entertaining her new friend.

Shelly turned to Nikki.

"You need to stay outside and make yourself scarce."

Nikki promised she would.

She saw the man's car later, a new Geo Storm. *Can't be much of a big-time pilot if he drives one of those,* she thought. He stayed a couple of hours and then left.

"I don't know what happened," Nikki recalled. "I think she was teetering on the idea of an affair. Or maybe she had one and it didn't go anywhere."

CHAPTER FORTY

Lara Watson figured her grandson Shane was being a typical teenager whenever she reached out to talk to him. In addition, her timing must have been seriously off because he never made it to the phone.

"Just missed him," Shelly frequently moaned, claiming he was off hanging out with some high school buddies. A couple of times, however, Shelly played the victim and said she was at her wit's end because Shane had run away.

"Don't worry," she said, making a show of putting on a brave face. "He always comes back, or we'll find him and bring him home."

During those exchanges, Lara would thank her lucky stars that Shelly was looking out for Shane. He'd be running on the streets of Tacoma if not for Shelly and Dave. Though she had initially been skeptical about the rough-around-the-edges boy's potential impact on the girls, she was happy that he had a life that included school, chores, and family time like trips to the coast. Shane had never let on to Lara what was really going on at the Knotek place, with Kathy, or the things that Shelly made him do. Not even a whiff of it. He didn't tell her how he slept on a concrete floor in a cold basement, or in Nikki's closet, or, at times, in an outbuilding at Monohon Landing.

When the teenager with the big smile and eager sense of humor vanished, Shelly didn't tell her stepmother about it for the longest time.

In fact, whenever Lara sent a check for Christmas or his birthday, it got cashed immediately—endorsed by Shane.

"Can I talk to him?" Lara asked Shelly, who adeptly pushed the request aside with an excuse.

Shelly sighed as if she understood the disappointment. "He's not home."

"He's never home," Lara grumbled.

"Teenagers," Shelly shot back with a short laugh. "What can you do?"

Every time that happened, Shane's grandmother would hang up, somehow placated by her stepdaughter's insistence that Shane was doing fine, doing just what kids do. Later, it would eat at her as to why she put up with it. She should have pushed Shelly a lot harder. But she'd allowed herself to accept what Shelly was saying.

Teenagers!

"I have no doubts that Shane would have been happy to call me back," Lara said, many years later.

Except he never did.

Finally, after a series of similar exchanges, Shelly finally divulged to her stepmother that Shane wasn't coming back to Raymond anytime soon.

"He's up in Alaska," she said with a sigh. "He's working on a fishing boat up there. You know that he's been wanting to do that for a long time."

Shelly's story was plausible yet still not quite right. He would have told his grandmother his plans.

"I just talked to him," Shelly went on. "He's doing great. He loves it up there. It's his dream come true. I'll tell him to call you the next time we talk."

"He never said that to me," Lara said, pushing back a little.

Shelly seemed miffed. "What?"

Lara pushed a little harder. "That fishing was his dream."

"You aren't close to him like we are."

"I've known him since he was born," Lara countered. "He said he wanted to finish school, Shelly. You know that."

"He changed his mind."

"I don't understand."

"Look," Shelly said, "Shane was all about making money. That's why he left. He'll be back. I know it."

But, just like before, Shane never called his grandmother.

He never called anyone except Shelly.

CHAPTER FORTY-ONE

After graduating from Willapa Valley High in 1993, Nikki set her sights on two things: getting a college diploma and moving the hell away from her parents and everything she'd ever known. Or seen. She'd enrolled in Grays Harbor community college with the plan of earning a degree in criminal justice. She'd even managed to arrange for financial assistance in the form of a student grant. She'd been beaten down by things beyond her control, but still had a measure of genuine optimism. Yes, she was lonely and almost didn't dare to hope for a future that involved happiness and love and freedom. But she did hope. She knew she deserved better.

And then, like the drip, drip, drip of a leaky kitchen faucet, her mom went after her dreams.

First the clothes Nikki wore to class disappeared. All she had to wear were the sweatpants she used when working in the yard. They were dirty and torn. To show up on campus looking like that would chip away at whatever personal pride she'd been able to grow by being away from Monohon Landing during the day.

Next, Shelly told Nikki that she no longer had a bedroom upstairs.

She pointed to a spot in the living room. "You'll be sleeping down here on the floor."

It was the same place she'd made Kathy sleep.

Something was happening, and Nikki knew it.

Then Shelly took away the money and transportation to class.

"We are cutting you off, Nikki. You don't deserve anything we've done for you. You are selfish. Ungrateful. Dad and I mean it this time."

Nikki could cry. She could argue. Any reaction would have been expected, but she didn't fall into her mother's trap just then. She had no car, and no money for bus fare. No clothes to wear to class. That meant no more school. No more being in the world to get the hell out of Raymond.

There was nothing she could do.

Nikki was trapped.

Shelly put her to work in the yard, digging out the garden, moving wood from one place to the next. Doing random tasks that never seemed to go anywhere. Her mom insisted that she make a new flowerbed, but she had no intent—or none that Nikki could see—to do anything with the space. She'd get up early and be told to get out the door and not come back in until nighttime.

Her mother would come out every once in a while and harangue her for not doing a good job.

"Is that all you did today? You lazy bitch!"

At night—on those occasions when she was allowed inside the house—Nikki slept on the living room floor with a sofa cushion for her pillow.

When Dave would come home, he'd join Shelly in a barrage of insults, berating Nikki for being lazy and worthless and needing to get a job.

Tears would come, and both of her parents would push it even harder.

Shelly seemed to enjoy her daughter's tears.

"You need to get a job!" she'd rail over and over. "You worthless piece of shit!"

Seriously, Nikki thought. *Really? How could I get a job? I have no transportation. No money. I shower outside with the hose!*

She was technically living in her family's home, but she was homeless in nearly every way.

Finally, she spoke up. It took everything she had, but it felt good. Very good.

"I can't get a job! Look at me! I have nothing to wear! No way to get anywhere!"

"I was yelling at her and him"—Nikki remembered trying to defend herself—"and my mom would put on an innocent act and say, 'You should have told me you needed a car! I had no idea that was your problem.'"

※

Nikki was getting stronger. Her mental resolve had gone from rubber to titanium. One time when she refused to acquiesce to a demand, her mom came chasing after her. Nikki ran from the house to the chicken coop and tried to lock it before her mom got there, but her mom was too fast.

"My mom had the adrenaline of a frickin' linebacker and the strength too," Nikki said later. "But I didn't care anymore."

Shelly got on top of Nikki and started screaming at her and pulling her hair, and Nikki fought back. Her mother fell to the ground. She looked startled. Shocked, even. No one ever fought back.

I'm almost as big as you, Nikki thought. *I don't need to be treated like this.*

"Fuck off, Mom! Don't you ever touch me!"

And then she got up and ran with Shelly right behind her.

Nikki made it into the house and saw Sami.

"I just told Mom to fuck off!" she yelled, but kept running, this time out the other door and into the woods, where she slept that night.

It felt good. Scary. But good.

A few days after the shoving match in the chicken coop, Shelly approached Nikki. She wore a weary mask of concern. Her voice stayed oddly calm, almost sad.

"Sami doesn't want you here anymore," she said in a tone of heavy disclosure, "fighting with her mother the way you've been doing. I'm sending you to Aunt Trish's."

That came out of the blue. Nikki didn't know what was happening. Trish was Dave's sister. She was nearly a stranger to Nikki, who'd only seen her a couple of times in her life. She lived four hours away in Hope, British Columbia, on a reservation. Shelly gave her daughter some clothes, fifty dollars in cash, and drove her to the Greyhound bus station in Olympia.

This was sweet and understanding Shelly the whole way. She was going to miss Nikki so much, but it was for the best.

"Ten days," she said. "Then you'll come back home, all right?"

Nikki was just out of her teens, but had never been anywhere by herself, and was worried about the trip, and whether fifty dollars would go far enough.

As it turned out, however, the stay with Aunt Trish in Hope turned out to be the best thing that had happened to Nikki in a long time.

"Bad things happen at home," Nikki told her aunt, choosing words that she thought got the message across but weren't specific enough to escalate blame. "Please don't make me go back."

The days turned into weeks, then a couple of months. Trish cleaned churches and houses and enlisted Nikki to help. On weekends, she learned to tie fishing nets. Nikki didn't mind the work. She enjoyed it. No one yelled at her. No one told her she was worthless.

Nikki never wanted to leave.

◊

Sami understood the reasons behind Nikki's absence, of course. Tori, however, felt abandoned. She was just a little girl, fourteen years younger than Nikki, and she idolized her oldest sister, who'd been like a second mother to her. Nikki was beautiful, and kind, and she always made time for Tori. The night her big sister left for Canada, Tori asked Jesus to please bring her back. She had no idea where Nikki had gone, but she suspected that she'd left because their mother had been so cruel to her. Tori wrote a note to that effect and put it on her windowsill and went to bed.

Early the next morning, she woke to her mom punching and slapping her in the face.

"What's this?!" Shelly waved the note as she screamed.

Tori, then six, started to cry.

"You think I'm mean to your sister?" Shelly hit her again. "Is that what you think, Tori? Really?"

It was exactly what Tori thought, but she told her mom no and that she was sorry. The truth was she was frightened—Shelly had never acted like this toward her before.

"I think that may have been, like, the first time my mom, like, hit me in the face," Tori recalled. "It was very scary."

Not long after, a few gifts arrived. There must have been something in Shelly that understood the impact of Nikki's departure on her youngest.

"This is from your sister," she'd say.

"Why can't I see her?" Tori asked.

"She just left this. She didn't stay."

"But why?"

Shelly never really had a good answer. In time, she started to do her best to end the relationship between the two of them.

"She's no good," she told Tori over and over about Nikki. "She doesn't love you."

And then, just like that, Nikki no longer existed. Shelly never brought her up. Neither did Dave. It was like she was a ghost that had faded away somewhere never to return.

Sami never brought Nikki up either. She didn't dare. She didn't want her family to know that she was still in touch with her sister.

⋈

Trish tried to keep her niece in British Columbia, but like just about everyone else, she was no match for Shelly. Eventually Nikki headed back to Washington.

But she didn't go home.

Shelly told Nikki that she had some thinking to do and was not a good role model for the other girls. She couldn't come back to Raymond after all. At least not yet. Instead, Nikki moved into a tent adjacent to her stepfather's jobsite on Whidbey Island. It was far from ideal, but it was an eye-opener. Nikki saw that, despite working full time, Dave Knotek lived like he was destitute. He literally had zero money in his wallet. The two of them got groceries from a charity food pantry. They showered every morning at the state park not too far from the jobsite. Nikki remained justifiably bitter about the punishments her stepdad had forced on her, but mostly she now saw him as pathetic, a loser.

She had no respect for him.

"Why are you living like this?" she asked. "Why are you still with Mom?"

Dave didn't even blink. "You," he said. "You girls."

A couple of weeks later, Nikki and Dave temporarily moved into an Everett condo to be near a job he was working near Paine Field. *Hot running water,* she thought at the time, *is an amazing thing.* Almost every weekend, they'd make the trip to Raymond for a night or two.

Each visit home was the same. Her mother would treat Nikki as though the exile to Canada and then Whidbey Island had been a learning experience.

"Do you think you are ready to come home? To pull your weight around here, Nikki?"

"Do you think I am?" Nikki asked, knowing there was no way she was ever coming back.

Shelly shifted her tone. She was irritated. "I can see someone needs more time to think about things," she said.

It was the kind of response for which Nikki had prayed.

I'd rather be homeless, she thought.

She and Dave moved back into the tent after the condo. It was cold and drafty, and by then Nikki had been looking for a way out. She got a job in Oak Harbor at Baskin-Robbins and then a second one cleaning motel rooms. The motel owner gave her the use of a single-wide trailer. It was a shabby dump, but she was grateful for it. All in all, she thought things were looking pretty good.

She felt free.

CHAPTER
FORTY-TWO

Sami Jo Knotek knew not only how to hide her bruises, but the importance of doing so.

Having someone see the marks left by her mother or father might have sparked a conversation that no one wanted to have. Or even worse, it might have led to something as dire as the ruin of her family. Even on the crazy train, there is a place where the world is shut out and things go on feeling as though they are normal or even worth fighting for.

On the outside, Sami was blonde, pretty, popular. She was homecoming-court material. She was smart, and funny too—the kind of girl who got the attention of the boys with a funny quip. Yet by her senior year, Sami was taking a "fuck it" approach to life. She'd grown tired of covering up what her mom had been doing to her and her older sister. She'd learned from Nikki's experience that not rocking the boat didn't stop bad things from happening. It only allowed them to continue.

"You're late with your homework," the teacher said.

"My mom threw away my paper," Sami said.

And so it went. Time and again.

"You are late to class."

"My mom made me sleep outside last night and only let me in this morning to get dressed."

"You're going to be charged for missing library books."

"Fine," Sami said. "My mom burned my books in the fireplace."

And so on.

Not long after, Sami was called in front of the school counselor.

"We've been listening," the counselor said. "You have a little sister at home and we're concerned about her too. We're going to report what you told us."

Sami sat there with mixed feelings. They believed her—that part was good. But now shit was going to hit the fan.

Big time.

As that dawned on her, she grew frightened. The elated feeling of calling her mother out for being a cruel, chronic abuser was fading. Fast.

"We're going to make arrangements to have your sister removed from the home," the counselor said. "We are going to call your mom now."

As the counselor reached for the phone, Sami panicked.

Years later, it would be difficult for her to articulate why she backed down at that point, but that's exactly what she did.

"All of a sudden," she said, "I don't know. The truth became scary. I took it all back. I said that I'd made everything up. I said I was lying. I guess I didn't want them to make my mother mad."

X

Sami and her high school boyfriend, Kaley Hanson, had been out late to a party. Sami knew what her boyfriend would do. He'd keep his headlights on and wait for his girlfriend to get inside safely. If she'd been locked out—as had been known to happen—he'd ratchet up his duty by honking the horn a few times to let Shelly know that someone needed to get into the house.

Shelly would let her inside . . . until Kaley's car disappeared. Then Sami would be sent back outside to sleep on the porch.

One night, Shelly stood there with a big glass of water and told her daughter to get out.

"You're sleeping outside."

"I'm not. It's cold and you aren't going to make me."

With that, Shelly threw the glass of water at Sami and shoved her outside. Sami immediately started running to Kaley's house. She'd had it. She wasn't going to take it anymore. It was more than a mile, but Sami was a track star; she'd lettered in the four-hundred-meter run and the mile relay.

Every time headlights cut through the darkness, she threw herself into a ditch, sure that her mother would hunt her down and bring her home. But Sami kept going and finally got to Cemetery Road where Kaley lived.

Sure enough, her mother's car, hot on her trail, went by like a shark searching in the dark. Sami was terrified, but she let herself into the Hansons' garage.

She stayed there for a while, dodging her mother and hoping she hadn't made things worse.

Dave Knotek would later say that he wasn't at the Monohon Landing house all that much, so he really didn't have a clue about how bad things actually were. He insisted that Shelly would never, ever hurt Sami or Tori. He loved his girls, but he stood by his wife. Sami, he thought at the time, was a storyteller, and he'd "have to raise an eyebrow" about what she said. Indeed, nothing would convince him that anything abusive was going on.

"There's no way Shell's going to sit there and beat Sam or Tori," he said years later. "She'd spank Nikki. I've spanked Nikki, okay? That's it. Those kids didn't suffer no abuse like that."

Even after his own world had disintegrated, Dave just couldn't find fault with Shelly. He turned a blind eye to physical evidence too. The day Sami graduated from high school, she was badly bruised from injuries inflicted by her mother in one of her tirades—the reason behind it so minor, no one could even remember later what the transgression was. *Not doing the dishes to her satisfaction? Not watering the animals? Loaning a jacket or sweater to a friend?* But Dave attributed those graduation-day bruises to Sami's own side of the scorecard, saying that she'd been a daredevil and risk-taker and had injured herself in a fall.

Pressed further, he came up with a story.

"Shell lent Sam some money for something and Sam had to paint the pole building. She came home from school and she was really, really tired you know, but she went out and painted anyway. She was complaining how sore she was, this and that, and Shell was telling me that's from a bad fall. I don't know. I never seen it on Sam."

CHAPTER
FORTY-THREE

Sami Knotek was in turmoil. It was the summer of 1997, and she didn't know how to take the next step forward. Through her mother's devious sabotage over admission forms, she'd missed the enrollment period for Evergreen State College. College had been a dream that she'd had for as long as she could remember. There was something special about imagining that she'd be the first person in her family to earn a college degree. She loved her boyfriend, but she didn't want to get married. She didn't want to get a job in town like some of the other locals, stuck in the glue of their parents' footsteps. Sami wanted more. Anything. Something bigger. She even mused about seeing what kind of work she could get in Hollywood.

She planned her getaway on two occasions.

The first had been back in April. The plan wasn't fully baked. Plus, Sami wanted to go to a dance because she'd made a beautiful new dress and didn't want to miss the chance to wear it—so she'd returned home a couple of days later.

But Sami carefully planned her great escape in the last months of her senior year. It was hard knowing that she'd be leaving her little sister, Tori, behind, but she convinced herself everything would be all right.

Her older sister was gone. Her little sister didn't seem to be a target of their mother. None of the weird stuff had been happening for some time. The only people Sami let in on her plan were her friends Lauren and Leah—and she knew they could be trusted. Just before she, her mom, and her little sister left for a shopping trip to Aberdeen, Sami filled five black plastic garbage bags with everything she owned. All of her clothes, her boots, and the knickknacks that meant so much to her.

"I was very materialistic," she conceded years later. "I refused to leave one sweater behind."

The plan called for Lauren to break into the house, get Sami's stuff while they were away, and meet up at Lauren's house.

Sami wanted to give Tori a vague heads-up.

"If I don't come back later today," she told her sister, "I will leave a little note for you—just for you—under my pillow."

That was the only information Sami would provide. She trusted Tori, but knew their mother would stop at nothing to worm details out of the little girl, then eight. She'd threaten. She'd promise. She'd cajole. Shelly was never one to let go, and Sami didn't want her mother to know where she was going.

When they returned from Aberdeen, Sami went upstairs. All of her stuff was gone. The plan was now a reality.

"Mom, Lauren ran out of gas and I need to go pick her up," Sami lied.

"All right," Shelly said. "Fine."

Sami got into her little white car, looked up at the house one more time, and left for Lauren's, where she hid for a day. Then she went to her boyfriend's house for a night. She knew that Shelly was searching high and low for her, and the thought of her mother coming to get her made Sami sick inside.

Even so, the hold her family had on her was like a leg trap and she was some animal out in the woods. Sami wrote a letter to her mother.

"I thought of all the reasons why I couldn't leave you because I love you so much. And because I love you so much, I wouldn't want to hurt you. I started thinking about hurt and life and how much I hurt and how much hurt I cause. So then I thought it would be good for me to leave. Things would be quieter. Things got quieter when Nikki left and with me gone everything would be OK."

She closed the letter by saying she thought living in her car was an option.

"It will be OK. If this is how it was meant to be, then this is how it was meant to be. I just wish you understood, but I know now you never will."

Sami had no idea where she'd go until she talked to Nikki. Her sister told her that she'd been in touch with their grandmother, Lara, and planned to see her too.

"Call Nana," she said.

Which is exactly what Sami did, and Lara gladly invited her to her home, now located in Bellingham at the northern end of the state.

Sami had heard that her dad was on the lookout for the car, that her mom had reported it stolen. She needed another way to Bellingham. Kaley's mother, Barb Hanson, offered to take her. She'd never thought much of Shelly anyway, having been awakened once in the middle of the night with questions about how much money she and her husband made.

"I told her I didn't appreciate the call at that hour and it was none of her business," Barb said later.

Barb drove Sami to Bellingham the next day. On the way, Sami shared bits and pieces of what her mother had done to her and her sister. Later, when Barb was dropping Sami off, Lara told them additional disturbing details about things Shelly had done during her childhood and young adulthood.

"She told me that my mom tried to set fire to the house," Sami recalled. "Things she did to her sister. How she thought my mom poisoned us with Ipecac to stop her from taking us places. [Barb] sat there and took it all in. It made me feel better that it just wasn't me saying what my mom had done, that there was someone else who backed me up. Someone who knew even more than I did."

Sami stayed with Lara all of summer 1997.

Like Nikki's experience in Canada, it was one of the happiest times of Sami's life.

CHAPTER
FORTY-FOUR

Nikki had struggled with her sisters' absence from her life. Although she didn't regret leaving, and felt she had saved herself, she missed her sisters. When she heard Tori had been ill, she sent a card.

"I hope you are feeling better, kiddo. I hear there's snow on the way. I bet that will make you a little happier. Are you taking good care of Mommy and Sami? Well, when you're not sick?"

Tori never received the message.

Shelly tried to keep in touch with Nikki during that time, but her oldest daughter refused to return her calls. Nikki didn't want a thing to do with her crazy mother. She didn't care if she ever saw either of her parents again. Then Shelly showed up unannounced. She was all sweet and concerned and told Nikki that she should come home. She could live at home. Go to college. Nikki knew it was a big lie. Everything her mother said had been a lie. Another time, an Island County sheriff came to the trailer and asked Nikki if she was okay.

"Your mom is very worried about you," the deputy said.

"I'm fine," she said.

"You need to call her."

She said she would, but she had no plan to do so. It was clear that her mother and father were unnerved by her newfound state of independence. Nikki knew the reason why.

Fear. They were afraid she would talk.

When a brick was thrown through the window of the ice-cream shop where she worked, it was followed up with a call that Nikki had been involved somehow.

"I know my dad did it," she said later. "He did it because my mom told him to. She wanted me to lose my job and move back home where they could keep an eye on me."

Not long after the brick incident, Nikki called Lara with the idea that she could maybe leave Oak Harbor and get a job with her at the nursing facility in Bellingham.

Lara was thrilled at the prospect. She also had some very happy news.

"It's funny that you should call just now, Nikki," Lara said, her voice full of excitement. "Sami's here too."

Nikki could barely contain herself. She left for Bellingham on the next Greyhound.

Tears came immediately to Sami's eyes when she saw Nikki. It had been almost a year since the sisters had seen one another face-to-face. Sami thought Nikki had never looked prettier or happier. She had on fitted Gap jeans and a purple tank top. She was wearing makeup. Her hair, which their mother had always chopped off in the most cruel and unflattering ways, was long, slightly curly.

"She was beautiful." Sami remembered that reunion. "More than anything, she was confident. Until then I never pictured my sister out in the real world. Just as she'd been at home, in her holey sweatpants out in the yard all the time. She had no friends. She never had a boyfriend. Never, until she escaped from our house when she was twenty-two. She had nothing."

✕

Nikki got the job as a nurse's aide at a division of the care center where Lara worked. The work was tough, but the pay was better than the motel or the ice-cream store. Even better, she was free of her parents and everything that had happened back in Pacific County.

"I was changing colostomy bags," she recalled. "But I didn't mind it one bit. I was away."

Not long after she started working there, her administrators at the facility started getting anonymous complaints that Nikki was unkind to elderly patients or incompetent when it came to giving them the care they needed. The state came in to investigate. Each time, Nikki and Lara would be dumbfounded as to why anyone would complain. The staff, patients, and their families all liked her.

The anonymous calls hadn't been the worst of it.

Dave Knotek started to show up in the parking lot of the facility. Sometimes he'd be in his truck; sometimes he'd be standing in the bushes. He didn't call out, but he wanted Nikki to see him. She saw it as a kind of implied threat. And she began to worry that he'd try to abduct her. Maybe he and her mom had plans for her.

Like what had happened to Kathy.

A few times Dave even followed Nikki as she drove home from her shift. Scared to death, Nikki took long, circuitous routes all over Bellingham to lose her stepdad on the way home.

"I wondered if he was going to try to grab me," she recalled. "I didn't know for sure. I am almost positive . . . that they would try to grab me. I can just see Mom hounding him about me." Given everything she learned later on, Nikki says, "I'm lucky to still be here. My sister thinks the same thing."

CHAPTER
FORTY-FIVE

It was more than halfway through the summer of 1997. Dave Knotek had been under increasing pressure from Shelly to find out where their wayward middle daughter had gone—and who she was with. Shelly had her ways, of course, and somehow, she'd heard that Sami was up in Bellingham with Lara and Nikki. The idea of the three of them together made her angrier than ever. The betrayal made Sami's vanishing act all the more painful. It also made it more crucial that Shelly get her and bring her home.

"They might tell someone, Dave."

"They wouldn't."

"We don't know that."

Dave was sick of Shelly's drama. He said he wanted to let the girls grow up and be on their own, but Shelly kept calling him at the job on Whidbey Island with every lead she could uncover.

But, as always, he did his wife's bidding, and followed up on every one of them.

Shelly learned there was an open day at Camp Firwood, a church camp on the shores of Lake Whatcom that she'd heard Sami and Kaley were attending.

It turned out to be a good bet.

As Sami was making her way through the camp counselors and attendees, she caught a glimpse of a familiar face.

Her dad!

Startled, she almost did a double take because he was wearing an obvious disguise. He had on a pair of sunglasses unlike any he normally wore. A baseball cap and a hoodie completed his ridiculous charade.

Oh my God, thought Sami. She felt sick. She loved her dad, but she knew he was there for a reason. He was there, she was sure, to bring her back home. Dave came up to her.

"Sami," he said, his voice muted and full of concern. "Your mom is worried sick. We need you to come home."

She didn't say anything right away. What could she say? Her mom was a monster, and Sami was justifiably distrustful of her.

Instead, she led him past a rope swing down a secluded path and they took a seat. No one said anything at first.

After a beat of silence, Sami finally told him why she'd left. A lot of what she said centered on Kathy.

"I know she's dead, Dad. I saw her."

Dave just sat there, looking beaten. He said nothing.

She also launched into her thoughts about her mom's dubious cancer diagnosis, a disease that had required constant medical attention for her entire childhood.

"You don't have cancer that long," she said. "Mom would have been dead by now."

Dave refuted that one. "She has it," he said. "I know it."

"Look, Dad," Sami said. "She doesn't. Have you gone to her appointments?"

"I've dropped her off."

"Have you ever gone in? Have you ever gotten a doctor bill?"

The questions she asked were the same ones Lara had asked years earlier.

When he finally answered Sami, it was with that same kind, understanding demeanor. He didn't specifically deny or confirm.

"I'm sorry, Sami. I know. I know."

They cried, and they talked for a long time. Sami could see that her father was a broken man. That was obvious. She could tell that her mom's hold on him was the same one she'd had on Kathy. No one who knew Dave Knotek would say a bad word about him. Town locals all thought he was the quintessential nice guy. He was a timberman's kid. He was one of them.

But that woman he was married to? She was not only an interloper, she was something else. They even had a nickname for her.

Crazy Shelly.

Or, for those who preferred a little alliteration with their coffee and smear, *Psycho Shelly.*

"I'll come home, Dad. But there's something I want. Mom screwed it up. I want her to fix it. I want her to get the paperwork done for college."

"I don't know about that," Dave said.

But Sami, like her older sister, had found her voice. If attending college to pursue a teaching degree meant making a deal with the devil, she decided she was willing to do just that.

After her dad left Firwood, Sami called her mother to say she was considering coming back home if she could get some financial support for school. Shelly balked, and ran through a litany of excuses. Money was in short supply, as always. Marital discord between her and Dave had also escalated to the point Shelly confided that a divorce was imminent. And if that wasn't enough, she wasn't feeling well either. The cancer was back, Shelly said.

Sami hoped her parents *would* get divorced. She'd heard from Nikki how their dad lived while he was working. A goddamn tent and trips to a food bank when he worked all kinds of hours making his body old before its time!

As far as the cancer went, Sami never considered the disease anything to joke or laugh about, but honestly? Her mom was a freak to carry on like that for so long.

Sami ignored all of that. She went for what she wanted—college.

"You said I could go," she said. "You sabotaged me, Mom. You know it and so do I."

"I don't know what you are talking about."

Really, Mom? Are we still going to play that game?

"You do," Sami said, letting the space between them fall silent.

The long pause was one of her mom's favorite techniques. She was like a predator that way . . . content to wait until the weaker party caved and gave up what she wanted.

"I won't tell anyone anything about what happened," Sami finally said.

There was a stillness on the line for a beat. "What?"

Sami was on a roll. "You know." She could imagine her mother's face. The red coming. The eyes so angry.

Shelly Knotek hated being called out, and if she was, it was only that one time. No one wanted a second helping of Shelly's wrath.

Sami hadn't been explicit. She didn't need to be. It was a clever blackmailing technique, and it worked. Before she returned home to Monohon Landing at the end of the summer, her mother had not only filled out the paperwork, she'd turned it in.

⋇

That same summer, Sami celebrated her nineteenth birthday with a surprise party at Planet Hollywood in Seattle. It was the best birthday she'd ever had. She felt happy and free, and hopeful. She'd been in touch with her mom and knew things were moving along the way they needed to. She and Nikki remained close, a relationship they kept secret from

Shelly. The secrecy was needed. Shelly had it in for Nikki, and both girls were unsure how far their mother would go to get even.

When Sami and her boyfriend, Kaley, got to the door at the Monohon Landing house, Shelly met them with a frightened and panicked look on her face. She'd shaved off her eyebrows and applied the same white powder she'd used when Lara and her daughter Carol had visited.

She shook her head sadly. "The cancer's back."

Kaley and Sami looked at each other. It was all they could do to keep from laughing. It was ridiculous and embarrassing at the same time.

"Why does she do crap like this?" Kaley asked Sami later.

"I have no idea. She likes the attention, I guess."

There were better ways to get attention than claiming cancer, both Kaley and Sami thought.

When Kaley left, Shelly pounced and read Sami the riot act.

"Your dad said you don't think I have cancer! Well, look at me, Sami! Look! I am losing my hair!"

Sami pushed back. Hard. She had a new sense of confidence that she'd never had before.

"I know you are lying," she said. Shelly just fumed. "I know Kathy is dead. I know you killed her. I was there, Mom. I was on top of her. She was dead."

Shelly waved her finger. "She choked on her own vomit."

"Because you abused her, Mom."

"It wasn't like that."

"It was. You killed her, Mom. You did it."

Suddenly, Shelly became really quiet. "I'm sorry," she said. "I'm sorry."

Sami saw it as an admission.

"Sorry?" she asked, as though repeating the word of a foreigner just to make sure it was understood.

Shelly nodded. "Things got out of control. I couldn't stop it, Sami. I tried."

Part of what she said was true, and Sami knew it. Things did get way out of control. But no, Shelly hadn't tried to stop it. She had made all of it happen.

Five minutes later, the wind suddenly shifted.

Shelly took back her words. She reeled back every single thing she'd said.

"You took everything the wrong way, Sami. I never said anything like that at all," Shelly backtracked.

"She acted like she'd never admitted anything to me," Sami said later. "It was just like, whatever. Like I was crazy that I would even think she'd confessed to anything."

Sami didn't care. She was enrolled in Evergreen. She was gone too.

CHAPTER
FORTY-SIX

The Knotek finances continued to tumble downward. College expenses didn't help, and they had debts all over town too. Stan the Hot Water Man was owed for work he'd done. The phone company threatened to terminate service. Shelly stayed fast on her feet with excuses to hold things at bay until some money came in. She told the water company that a family emergency had transpired and she'd be unable to resolve the bill anytime soon. Her husband, she wrote, had suffered a major heart attack.

"He is doing fine now . . . I am at his side constantly and am trying to do so many other things, it's really overwhelming . . ."

In another missive to a lender, she pinned her tardiness on different fictional family diseases.

"My life has been very hard this year. My eldest daughter has been fighting MS and my father is very ill."

Shelly would play the illness card whenever she thought it might help. When making excuses for a moving violation in South Bend, Shelly wrote traffic court that she was under a lot of stress and that her transgression—which had led to her car being impounded—should be forgiven.

"This has been a hard year for me. My daughter has cancer. I need to take her in for treatment in Olympia twice weekly. I left my job to be with her. My daughter is everything to me and she depends on me. I am not a criminal."

The Washington State Patrol granted her hardship.

While Dave was barely functioning at work, cracking ammonia vials so he could stay awake to run the machinery and sleeping in his car because that was the best he could do, back home Shelly was on a perpetual spending spree at the little mall in Aberdeen. Dave had no way of knowing, of course. She had removed him as a signatory on the couple's checking account. Dave never saw what happened to his paycheck.

Not that his paycheck was enough. Not for Shelly.

She also managed to procure more than $36,000 in personal loans behind Dave's back—a testament to her persuasive nature with the Raymond branch of Bank of America. It was quite a feat. The couple had zero collateral. The house on Monohon Landing had been refinanced to the hilt, and their credit rating would have been abysmal.

Yet Shelly, persistent and ever resourceful, always found a way. And once she got the hefty credit line, she immediately went to work at whittling the balance down. She did it in a frenzy too. It was as though spending money had become a drug. Or maybe a replacement for one. Shelly wrote as many as thirty checks a day at stores at the mall in Aberdeen. One afternoon, she wrote nine at a Target store, moving from one red-smocked checker to the next as the day wore on. None of the purchases were large; most were only five or ten dollars. That could have been strategic on Shelly's part. She might have been thinking that smaller checks would be more likely to go unchallenged. It wasn't that she was lavishing on herself. She mostly purchased things for Sami and Tori and, occasionally, some little knickknacks for the house. Some of Shelly's sprees were inexplicable not only for how many checks she was writing at a single place each day, but because the sprees repeated themselves over the course of a week. Every day. She'd return to Aberdeen and spend whatever she had—and some of whatever she didn't.

She'd take a single day off, then start up again.

It didn't matter that everything could implode around her at any time; she just bought until her reserves ran dry.

And when they did, the checks would bounce all over town.

Some months, Shelly was stuck with more than $250 in fees for overdrawing her checking account. When the balance became too thin, she'd simply go to another branch and open a new account. When it reached the point where she was spinning without a retail lifeline and no one would give her money at the moment, Shelly would drive to the branch in Raymond and withdraw money from her daughters' bank accounts.

"That's Raymond for you," Nikki said later. "Such a small town that someone's mom can go to the bank and empty out an account that she's not even on."

To apply for a loan or a security deposit—really anything in which a Social Security number was required—Shelly Knotek had surefire advice for everyone with money troubles.

Sami called her mom from school once, and told her that her Social Security number didn't work.

"Just keep changing the last number until you get one that works," her mother said.

Sami said she didn't feel comfortable doing that.

"Then use your sister's," Shelly advised, as though that was perfectly acceptable advice. "Tori's is clean at the moment."

Sami refused to do that too.

Shelly's alchemy with other people's money and Social Security numbers went on for a very long time. Some years later, when Sami tried to get an apartment, her application was rejected because she had

Gregg Olsen

bad credit. There was a debt of $36,000 associated with her Social Security number. It wasn't her name on the account, however.

It was her mother's. Shelly Knotek had presented Sami's number as her own.

Shelly tried to explain it away. She told her daughter that there had been a mix-up at the bank. Sami knew better. Dave, however, continued to stand by his wife.

"Sami and Shell shared the same account. Our name had been screwed up in the account and it was the bank's fault. There was a rift about that between Sami, Shell, and me, but it all got worked out," he said.

For his part, Dave would scratch his head years later when confronted with what his wife was doing behind his back with their always-on-the-brink, completely chaotic finances. For a couple of years, he foolishly believed Shelly's spendthrift ways were long gone. They had to be. They didn't have any money to spare. It had been a problem early in their marriage that he believed he'd solved with a combination of tough love and a dose of reality.

"I had to curb [the spending] but she'd gotten better over the years. And, there'd be just stuff and it was for the house. She was buying a lot for Sami too."

In reality, Dave, who had grown up dirt poor on the banks of Elk Creek, had never wanted the girls to go without. Arguments with Shelly over money never entered into the territory of depriving Nikki, Sami, or Tori of anything they might desire. Dance and drama lessons, sports, new clothes, birthday parties, and a menagerie of pets were all fine with him.

Yet Dave could never fathom where all the money went.

"Where the hell did that money go? I mean Shell obviously would have bought herself a car or something like that. Something nice. You know we drove around in junkers for years."

CHAPTER FORTY-SEVEN

All alone in the house now, Tori had been tagged *you're it.*

Shelly had turned her attention to Tori shortly after Sami went away to college. She'd reverted to some of her old favorite bits before Sami was completely gone, but they were subtle. As early as elementary school and into middle school, Tori would often wonder if she was losing her mind because she kept misplacing her homework.

"Mom, have you seen my paper?"

Shelly hadn't.

"I know I put it away, but I can't find it."

Shelly would give her a look. "You'll just have to do it again."

Mom was weird, she thought. *But Mom was Mom.*

Some of Tori's greatest difficulties came from how badly she missed her father. He was tired when he came home, but he spent time with her and they laughed and did things together. Later in life, she'd hold dozens of good memories of time with her dad—even if it was just small stuff, like watching TV or fishing in the river. Sometimes, however, it felt almost a little easier having him away. It wasn't that she didn't want him around. It was simply because whenever he was home, her mother would pick a fight.

Screaming and yelling would fill the air. Things would get thrown. Threats would be made. Shelly would call Dave every ugly name under the sun.

No kid wants to hear that.

"I remember being so excited for Dad to come home when I was little," Tori said later, "but after a while I, like, got to the point where I was older, and I was, like, more of a teenager where I, like, didn't care as much because he'd come home, they'd just fight . . . There were a couple of times where it was a good time, like we'd play video games. I think he had the ability to be a great dad when I was younger, but it was just a toxic situation. I know he loved me a lot."

On no occasion could she remember the fights being her father's fault. Shelly was always the instigator.

"Where's your goddamn paycheck, Dave?" Tori remembered Shelly yelling into the phone. "You fucking hick! You said I'd have it today!"

Tori could only imagine her father on the other end of the line, likely insisting that he'd sent it. She couldn't picture him delaying it or keeping it to himself. He gave Shelly everything she wanted.

"It wasn't in the fucking PO box. I checked. I'm so fucking tired of you."

And finally: "I should just divorce you. I should never have married such an idiot."

When he came home, Dave slept on the floor next to the couch.

All of it was heartbreaking and confusing. "My dad seemed unhappy all of the time," Tori said. "He looked really bummed, like he didn't want to be home. I remember feeling bad in general that he was married to my mom because he looked so sad."

In time, Tori could see that she was in the middle of a war between her parents. It was a knock-down, drag-out, and she was all but certain to be collateral damage.

There would be others, of course. Her mother's first stealth attack against Tori came in the darkness of the night. The house was empty. And Shelly, who only slept when Tori was at school during the day, jumped on her daughter and pulled away the bedcovers.

Tori's eyes popped open and she gasped. She didn't know what was wrong. Maybe the house was on fire? Maybe her mom was having a heart attack?

It was sudden. Scary. And it came from nowhere.

"Would you ever consider killing yourself?" Shelly demanded.

"No, Mom," Tori said.

Shelly stayed put for what felt like a very long time. Maybe she was looking for more of a response. Maybe a different response? Tori didn't know. She stayed silent. She was too scared to engage with her mother.

Finally, Shelly left the room.

Tori couldn't sleep. All sorts of things ran through her mind. One stayed at the forefront.

Oh my God, is she going to kill me and make it look like I killed myself?

※

The Knoteks kept a large ham radio tucked in under the breakfast bar of the kitchen. It was Dave's and he was the only one who really messed around with it. Since he was never home, it just sat there. One day Shelly blew her top about something that Tori, then eight, had done and shoved her hard into the radio.

Tori was in shock. She knew her mother shouldn't have done that. She couldn't imagine her mom doing anything like that. Not to her. She touched the side of her head. It was wet.

Blood.

She started to cry. Instead of apologizing or helping her, her mother just stood there, frozen, with a look of complete disdain.

"You pussy!" Shelly screamed. "Get up!"

The incident had a profound impact on the girl. After that, whenever her mom commanded her to do something that she knew was embarrassing or wrong, she thought of the time her mom had cut her head open. She knew that, no matter what, if her mom wanted to, she could really hurt her.

X

Shelly's voice scared the hell out of her youngest daughter. At the beginning of the TV show *Fear Factor*, there was the sound of a woman's terrified scream, and every time that intro came on—even though she knew it was coming—Tori would cringe, thinking it was her mother downstairs screaming at the top of her lungs.

At her.

Oh my God, I'm going to get it tonight, she'd think.

Shelly found a new use for one of Dave's fishing poles when Tori made her angry by telling a friend that her mother had hit her with a wooden spoon. The other girl's mom confronted Shelly about the beating at school, and Shelly later responded by striking her youngest daughter so hard the pole actually broke.

"You're no good! You're ungrateful. I wish I'd aborted you!"

Tori's lower back and bottom were lashed in ugly red streaks. She was going swimming later that week and was worried that the marks would show and she'd have to make up some excuse.

"But the marks were gone by the time I had to go swimming," she said later. "My mom made sure they went away."

As was usual for Shelly, some punishments were less about physical pain and more about humiliation.

Shelly made Tori wear the same outfit to school every day for a week when she came home with a less-than-stellar grade on her schoolwork. It was a dirty pair of Winnie the Pooh denim overalls and a striped Tweety Bird top. No coat.

"I was really cold, and I remember hating her for that. People were noticing, asking me why I was doing that. I told them that I didn't do the laundry or something," Tori said later. "After about the third or fourth day, I just stopped saying anything."

She wondered what, if anything, any observers of the goings-on relating to her mother were thinking at the time. Like her sister Sami, Tori was a girl who'd always dressed nicely. Always had new clothes. But now here she was, walking around in the same outfit every day. Did anyone think something strange was going on?

"I know it sounds like a very small thing," she said years later. "But it felt like a big deal, because at school, you know, it *is* a big deal."

When Tori hit puberty, Shelly instigated a new and very awkward routine. Once a month, she'd call Tori into the living room.

"Oh, Tori! It's time now. Time to see your progress."

If Tori didn't answer the call right away, she'd be subjected to that awful *Fear Factor* scream of her mom's.

"Take off your top," Shelly ordered.

Tori was embarrassed and didn't want to do it.

Shelly pooh-poohed her concerns. This was something very normal. Very natural.

"I need to see how you're developing," she said. "All moms do this."

Okay, Tori thought, *that's so not true.*

None of her friends ever talked about their mothers doing anything like what her mother forced her to do.

"I don't want to, Mom."

Shelly had that steely look. It was a look that often came before the belt or a punch.

"Look," she said. "You do what I tell you to do when I tell you. I'm the mom. You're the kid. Off with your top, Tori."

"I don't want to, Mom."

"Why is that, Tori? Do you think I'm perverted or something?"

Tori knew it was an unwinnable impasse. Like all of them. She removed her shirt and stood motionless while her mother examined her.

"Okay," Shelly finally said. "Looks fine."

It went on and on.

Sometimes Shelly would tell Tori to remove her panties too, so she could examine her vagina.

That was even worse than showing her developing breasts, but Tori did it anyway.

And one time she made a bizarre and humiliating demand.

"Tori, I need a lock of your pubic hair for your baby book."

Tori didn't want to do it. It was too far.

"That's crazy," she finally said. "No one does that, Mom."

Shelly shrugged and looked disappointed. Even a little hurt.

"Your sisters did it for me," she said. "Why do you have to be so difficult?"

"I'm not being difficult, Mom," she said. "It's weird. It feels creepy."

First disappointment. Then hurt. Now complete indignance.

"Creepy?" Shelly asked. "There's nothing wrong with the human body, and if you think there is, there's something seriously wrong with you."

With that, she handed Tori a pair of scissors.

"Sami and Nikki did this too?" Tori asked.

"That's right," Shelly said. "Even Nikki, who was nothing but trouble, did it."

Tori took the scissors and went to the bathroom and emerged a minute later with the hair her mother requested. "Here." She held it out.

Shelly looked her right in the eyes and started to laugh. "I don't want that."

Tori was in tears, embarrassed, and thoroughly humiliated.

"What?"

"I just wanted to see if I could make you do it," Shelly said.

Tori felt completely alone. During that time, she lived for the weekends when Sami would come home from college. She'd stopped wishing for Nikki to come back. Her mother had waged a campaign to make her fear, and then hate, her oldest sister.

"That girl was a monster," she said on more than one occasion. "Thank God for you and Sami."

Tori didn't have to ask for specifics. Her mom freely shared those.

"She beat on me, Tori. Can you imagine a girl beating up her own mother?"

Shelly also trashed Lara, calling Tori's grandmother a mean, destructive woman.

"She used to treat me like dirt when I was a girl," Shelly claimed.

Tori took it all in. She absorbed the message: she had the best mom in the world, and Nikki and Lara were her sworn enemies.

CHAPTER FORTY-EIGHT

The connection between each of the sisters was at once broken and convoluted. The middle sister, Sami, was the one in contact with both Nikki and Tori. While Nikki, who was working on starting a life of her own, missed her little sister and asked about her all the time, it was not a two-way street. Tori had learned to stop asking about Nikki, which at least meant that Sami didn't have to lie to her little sister and risk the fallout from her mother, who would surely consider contact with Nikki a betrayal of the highest order.

Even once Sami went to college, Shelly's incredible reach remained indisputable. Her need to control every aspect of her middle daughter's life brought eye rolls from the other girls in her dorm at Evergreen. She'd call at ten or eleven nearly every night, and if Sami didn't answer, she'd go through the roof and phone the resident aide or Sami's boyfriend, Kaley.

The best calls came at three in the morning.

"Is she there?" Shelly would ask.

Kaley would say she wasn't, but then turn to Sami after hanging up. All they had to do was exchange a look.

Sami had made a deal with her mom, but that didn't mean she'd stopped continuing to confront her. She wrote a four-page letter reminding her that while Shelly claimed memory lapses about what happened at the Knoteks' house, Sami hadn't suffered the same fate.

"I can't forget and, no, I am not talking about Kathy . . . I might have been younger, but I remember what went on and I'm sorry to tell you this, Mom, but I think you forgot everything about that and conveniently remember just what you want to remember just like a lot of things. Like what you did to Nikki and Shane, wallowing and hot baths. You forgot, I guess. I will say that I was treated the best."

And while Nikki had moved on and put as much space between her mother and herself as possible—and Tori, as far as the older sisters knew, didn't know the depths of their mother's depravity—Sami kept coming back for more. What happened in their family was a burden on all of the sisters, but the one who always found a way to set things aside with humor was the one who was always in the middle.

She continued to call her mother out.

"I know what goes on in other people's homes. Maybe not everything. And I know what is right and what is wrong. I have been living a lie my whole life and you cannot like me for saying that, but it is true. I know the truth about everything."

As Sami questioned her past, and her mother's actions, Shelly thought of new ways to bring her back in line.

"Honey, I've been diagnosed with lupus," she said one time over the phone. "It's really bad."

"Oh God, Mom," Sami said. "I'm so sorry."

Sami didn't know much about the disease, but she knew it was serious. Her mother filled her in about the treatment she would require. And if that weren't bad enough, she also indicated another major health concern.

"I have a massive ovarian cyst, honey," she added. "Going to need major surgery."

241

Sami thought her mother's cancer had been some kind of a game, a ruse, but for some odd reason, she didn't think the latest medical issues were a lie.

They were.

"The funny thing is," Sami said later, "I don't think Mom ever mentioned the lupus again."

X

Her mom was a liar and Sami knew it. Yet she wanted proof. She *needed* proof. Sami decided to poke around her mother's bedroom when she wasn't at home, just to see what she could find. It was like turning over rocks to see what might crawl out. She was careful not to disturb things. Her mom had a talent for knowing if any item in her room had been moved even the slightest. Or turned. Sometimes it seemed she knew if one of the girls even *looked* at something.

Under the bed, Sami discovered a small garbage bag.

When she looked inside, at first she wasn't sure what she was seeing. *Dirt? Shells?*

She peered closer and shifted the contents toward the light.

It was a bag of bones mixed with ash.

Human bones.

She knew they must've belonged to Kathy Loreno.

Who else could they be?

X

Dave Knotek had not been back home to Raymond in a very long time. There were plenty of reasons for that too. His job was far away, of course. Other than his girls, there was nothing pushing him in the direction of home. Certainly not his wife. Shelly had threatened divorce off and on but for some reason—likely the steady paycheck—never took action. Dave sent his money home to Shelly, which seemed to be all she wanted anyway.

It was a call from his father-in-law's new wife that finally nudged Dave in the right direction, when she questioned why he hadn't seen Tori in over a year.

Dave immediately pushed back, making excuses for something for which there was nothing even remotely acceptable. He couldn't put his finger on why he wouldn't go home. It wasn't that it wasn't on his mind. His boss asked him every Friday if he was heading home, but Dave always deflected by saying he was needed up at the jobsite the next day.

"Bullshit," the boss would say.

"He'd seen it in my eyes that I wanted to go home," Dave said later.

After the call, he sat there for a long time, thinking. He finally asked God for help.

You gotta give me an answer, he recalled thinking. *You gotta help me. What do I do?*

He was penniless, and he had no car at the time. Still, God answered him. Dave said God told him that he needed to live up to his vows and go home. His boss, a family man himself, loaned him an old Cadillac. It was a gas-guzzler of the highest order, but it was an answer to Dave's prayers.

"I'd get off work at five on Friday night. Bad traffic. Drive all the way from Sedro-Woolley to Oak Harbor in the company rig. From there I'd drive all the way back because I'd miss the ferries. All the way down I-5. I'd get home Friday night, midnight, one in the morning. Shell had dinner waiting for me. Tori's up too. Everything was going good. Tori's happy. Shell was happy. I was happy."

Everyone was happy. Or seemed happy.

Until he'd leave town again.

PART FIVE

SCAPEGOAT

RON

CHAPTER FORTY-NINE

Sami first heard about Ron Woodworth when her mother called her college dorm and mentioned a "new friend" who was helping out an elderly woman who owned dozens of cats but was being evicted from her home in the Riverview neighborhood not far from the local campus of Grays Harbor community college. Shelly had finally landed a job, as a caseworker for Olympic Area Agency on Aging in Raymond. She met Ron through Habitat for Humanity on the case of the woman with all the cats.

"I brought all of her stuff to the pole building. I've asked her to move in, but she wants her own place."

Good, Sami thought. That was a huge relief. She didn't want anyone moving in with her mother.

"Ron," Shelly went on, "helped find homes for most of her cats. She had something like eighty of them."

Sami thought the idea of eighty cats in a small house was beyond gross.

"Ron sounds like a good guy," she said.

"Yeah, he loves cats."

Indeed, Ron also had several cats of his own. Around that time, Tori began visiting Ron's trailer after school, and noticed how his cats had made a mess of his trailer. The place stank, but Ron, like a lot of people who live with more cats than they can handle, didn't notice the smell at all.

He wasn't a large man, but when Sami first met Ron Woodworth a short time later, she noticed he had quite a belly; it hung over his belt like a fleshy fanny pack. His hair was thinning on top, but he kept it long in a ponytail that he secured with a rubber band. He wore earrings and other jewelry and appeared proud of his appearance. A former copy editor at the local paper and a licensed caregiver, Ron was "going through some things" at that time and was unemployed.

He was quick, sarcastic, and Sami liked him right away.

During her after-school visits to Ron's trailer, Tori looked through his books on Egyptology, a keen interest of his, and they talked about the gods and the mythology of that time in history. It fascinated him more than anything. He told her about the importance of life and the role of the hereafter.

Later, when her mom would insist that Ron could be suicidal, Tori would transport herself to that visit.

"He would never do that," she claimed.

Tori grew to love Ron. Sometimes he let her win at playing cards or checkers. She started calling him Uncle Ron. He was a friend, and she hoped, though she didn't ever say so, an ally.

※

Ron Woodworth had followed Gary Neilson, his partner of seventeen years, to South Bend in the late summer of 1992. Gary's sister was already in the area, and in 1995, Ron's parents, Catherine and William, also moved up the coast from California at Ron's insistence, as his father was in ill health at the time.

In a very real way, the relocation to Pacific County was a bit of a fresh start for Ron and Gary, who had been feeling some pressure and discord in their relationship. In fact, when Gary broached the subject of relocating, he told Ron to take it or leave it. No second thoughts came from Ron. Gary was the love of his life and there was no way he was going to let him go.

But after his father's death in June 1996, Ron's behavior changed. Drastically so. He suddenly became unable to hold down his job as a caregiver or even carry on a conversation without becoming distracted. He'd been outgoing most of his life, but suddenly he was sullen and introverted. While Gary had sympathy for his partner's loss, he could not take living with Ron anymore, and by 1997 he knew the relationship was over.

Ron didn't take the breakup well. He was both grief-stricken and volatile. When Gary returned to their trailer one day after work shortly after their split, the locks had been changed and Ron refused to let him inside.

"He wanted to bargain with me for my property," Gary said later. "I told him if he wanted it that bad he could keep it."

The next day, Gary returned to collect a few things Ron had secured in a shed for the purpose of handing them over. The two of them never spoke again—not face-to-face or even over the telephone. A month after that, Ron sent his ex a letter stating that neither he nor his mother ever wanted to see Gary again.

After he found himself suddenly single, Ron Woodworth's downward spiral began to spark concern among his small circle of friends. One of those friends was Sandra Broderick, who'd known Ron since their days in the supply department at McClellan Air Force Base in Sacramento, California, in the early nineties. After Ron moved to the Pacific Northwest, Sandra eventually did the same. Geography played a role in keeping their friendship intact, but there was also a genuine fondness between the pair.

While Ron made some veiled threats post-breakup that he had "nothing to live for," he didn't explicitly threaten suicide. Besides, like Tori, Sandra figured Ron's staunch beliefs in ancient Egyptian traditions prevented him from ever contemplating suicide, no matter how bad things were going.

Even so, by 1999, Sandra could see that Ron was still having problems, so she offered to have him—and his mother—move into a five-bedroom house she owned in Tacoma. Ron was polite about the offer and even made a visit to check it out. He told Sandra that he preferred staying put for the time being, though he certainly wasn't going to stay in Raymond or South Bend. Gary was living in Aberdeen, and Ron didn't want to run into him around town. He told Sandra that he expected to move in with his friends Shelly and Dave Knotek, who he told Sandra were going to buy a house in Oak Harbor.

And yet by July 2000, there still was no house in Oak Harbor, and Sandra heard once again from her military buddy. Ron was in financial trouble. He needed money to pay back overdue rental fees on his space at a trailer park in Willapa. She gave him $500 so he wouldn't end up homeless.

Later, she heard from another friend that Ron had borrowed $2,000 to retain a lawyer in his continuing quest to keep from losing his mobile home.

Sandra called him the minute she learned the news.

Ron acted as if things were under control.

"He told me that he had given $1,000 to Shelly Knotek to get a lawyer," she said later.

Sandra was suspicious, so she asked Ron for the lawyer's name.

"He said that he would have to get it from Shell, because she had hired him. I never learned if an attorney was hired or not."

A little later, Sandra made the trip to Raymond to visit with Ron and his mother in her trailer at the Timberland Recreational Vehicle Park.

Unexpectedly, Shelly also showed up, and the visit petered to an end.

Those who knew her would later remark on Shelly's propensity for marking her territory.

CHAPTER FIFTY

In his midfifties, it was late in the game for Ron's do-over. He had lost his home, his father, his partner. He was also estranged from his mother, with whom he had lived after the foreclosure of his trailer in 1999. Worst of all, he had lost his cats. Shelly told Tori that they were going to take Ron in, to help him get back on his feet. Tori didn't know that this was one of the same lines Shelly had once used to sell Dave on bringing Kathy Loreno into their lives.

"To help her," Shelly had told Dave about Kathy. "And she can help us at the same time."

Shelly put out the welcome mat for Ron and set him up in Sami's old room. He had a bed, a dresser, and a nightstand with a bedside lamp. He brought along a bunch of his books and personal things that he'd been able to gather from his mother's place.

Dave hadn't heard much about Ron Woodworth, or if he did, it had gone in one ear and seeped out the other. There was good reason for that. He was still working in Oak Harbor on Whidbey Island and was almost never at home; whatever was going on there eluded his attention. He only discovered that Ron had moved in when he returned to the Monohon Landing house one day.

Shelly was sweet and excited when she made the introduction.

"This is my friend Ron," she said, quickly adding, "He's gay. He's been evicted from his place and he's going to work around here."

Frankly, Dave didn't care at all. He wouldn't have cared if Ron was interested in Shelly. In fact, it would have been great if he were. Dave wanted out. He couldn't handle the stress of being in Shelly's life with all the stories they had to juggle.

And secrets to hide.

"I was waiting for Tori to grow up, so I could leave," he admitted later. "I only had to hang in there for three or four years or whatever and then I could leave."

Shelly went on to say that Ron had babysat Tori a few times and was very loyal and trustworthy.

Ron shook Dave's hand. He was a short man with thick glasses. His ears were pierced, and he wore a number of gold necklaces coiled around his neck, including an ankh pendant.

"He seemed nice. I just wanted out of the stress," Dave said. "Just didn't get out of there in time."

⪥

Oh shit!

Those words popped into Sami's mind when she heard Ron had moved in with her mother and sister. *This isn't a good fit,* she thought before reeling it all back inside. It was what she had done her entire life. She was smart enough to see what was right in front of her, but survival mode gave Sami the singular ability to shove it all aside.

She told herself that despite everything she knew of her mother, there was no way that history could truly repeat itself. She'd seen her in action with Kathy, her father, and other people. Shelly was all about Shelly, and that meant that she needed to be front and center. Always in control. Everyone else existed only to serve her needs. Shelly was the boss. But Ron was Ron. He wasn't Kathy. He wasn't Dave. Sami was sure Ron could hold his own.

That thought. That wish. That prayer. It was tenuous at best. There were warning signs that Sami was wrong almost immediately.

On her first visits home at that time, Ron and her mother were what Sami would later describe as "lovey dovey." Still, she noticed how Ron waited on Shelly and did whatever she asked.

"Yes, Shelly Dear," he'd answer to any request.

Shelly would either give him a big hug and thank him for being so good to her, or she'd chide him for not doing something that she wanted done, but in a gentle tone that mimicked the way a mother might reprimand a small child who didn't understand what had been requested or the importance of getting it done.

At dinnertime, she'd call him to the table.

"Ron, come and get your dinner!"

"Oooh," he'd say. "It looks so good, Shelly Dear."

It didn't matter what was on the plate. To Ron, it was a gourmet meal made by a contender on *Top Chef* or some other TV show.

Shelly's initial warm welcome cooled quickly.

Around his second week there, things started to change. Tori noticed how Ron seemed to irritate her mom.

"I saw you roll your eyes," she snapped at him. "I don't appreciate that at all."

"I'm sorry, Shelly Dear," he said.

"Did you mean to insult me with that tone?"

Ron backed down. "I'm sorry, dear."

Soon epithets were mixed into her dialogue.

It was jarring and mean. Tori couldn't believe her mom was talking to her friend like that.

"I don't want a useless fag like you talking to me," Shelly said. "You disgust me, Ron. Get out of my sight and stay away from my little girl. You're a bad influence."

And then it got worse.

A whole lot worse.

The truth was, things got easier for Tori once Ron moved in. Her mother's attention moved swiftly to the newest member of the household on Monohon Landing Road. Where Tori had once been the object of abuse for any minor transgression, now Ron was the victim.

"She'd just get this horrible look in her eyes and then she'd end up hitting him or taking him out back, and I don't know what happened because I was told to go up to my room."

It was a scenario that played out every night.

And every day too. Ron was no longer allowed to eat any meals with Tori and her mother. Shelly served him toast and water. Twice a day, she'd feed him a handful of pills.

"What are those pills you keep giving him?" Tori asked more than one time.

"Sleeping pills," Shelly replied. "To calm him down."

Ron changed almost immediately once Shelly started abusing—and drugging—him.

"Ron was one of the smartest people I knew [but] after he lived here, he didn't know anything," Tori recalled. "He just wasn't himself anymore. It was like he wasn't even there."

※

Shelly evicted Ron from the bedroom upstairs. It was done unceremoniously and quickly, like a tablecloth yanked from under a set of dishes by a magician. She took away almost everything he owned and told him that he'd be sleeping on the floor of the computer room. For some reason, Ron didn't resist anything Shelly told him. He was barely inside the house anymore anyway. She'd given him a laundry list of chores to do and he spent most of his time in the yard.

Then it was Shelly's next go-to move: restricting access to the bathroom. Shelly said Ron needed her permission to use the bathroom. With his room upstairs and the bathroom and the couch that she commanded all night downstairs, there was no getting around asking permission.

"Shelly Dear, can I go to the bathroom?" he asked.

The answer was no, right away.

Again, the magician's tablecloth.

"Not the one in the house," she said.

"Dear, where do you want me to go?"

"You need to do your business outside. I won't have a fag using my bathroom."

And that's the way it was.

When Ron needed to urinate at night, he'd pee into a Windex bottle and try to hide it all day.

One morning, Tori was using the computer, and Ron hadn't made it out the door yet for his chores. She'd seen his bottle of pee, and he'd noticed. She wondered why he didn't know better. When Shelly found it—and there was never any doubt she would—he'd be punished. *Why would he disobey Mom? He knows what will happen to him.* It made her so angry that he had done that.

Tori's tone was accusatory. "Why do you keep doing this?"

Ron looked flustered. "I'm sorry, Tori," he said. "I'm sorry."

Later, Tori would replay that moment and feel sick about it. She'd come off as cross, when that's not how she'd felt at all. She just didn't want him to get yelled at or beat up.

Though she didn't tell Ron, Tori did the same thing. She didn't want to wake her mother with the creak of the stairs in the middle of the night and risk a tirade, so she peed into a container too. She'd dump hers out her window in the morning.

She just wished Ron would be smarter about it.

Every once in a while, Shelly would ask her youngest if she remembered Kathy. She'd seen pictures of Kathy taken with her when she was a baby. She knew Kathy had been a part of her life, but didn't really know how Kathy fit into the family. She couldn't quite understand why her mom kept bringing her up.

"Has anyone asked you about Kathy?"

"No, Mom."

"Someone at school? A neighbor?"

Tori shook her head.

"No one. I promise."

CHAPTER
FIFTY-ONE

The office staff at Olympic Area Agency on Aging wondered how Shelly Knotek managed to get—and keep—a job there as a case aide, given her defiant and erratic behavior. A caseworker? Seriously? She was completely inappropriate in her dealings with clients, often switching between being overly involved or indifferent. Her boss wrote her up in early December 2000 for two incidents. She'd told one client that she didn't need to take her medication, which led some staff members to worry that Shelly's interference with doctors' orders could lead to tragic and irrevocable outcomes. Another episode concerned a low-income client who complained that Shelly had absconded with a valuable hand-crafted tablecloth. Shelly was ready with an excuse on that one, insisting that the tablecloth had been a gift for her help in getting the client settled in a new place after being evicted. The client disagreed.

Shelly started lying directly to her coworkers. About small things at first, then larger as time passed. She fabricated comp time. She was chronically late, sometimes claiming it was because she'd been out seeing a client, though no one at Olympic could think of any reason why a case aide would need to make such early calls. She told a coworker she'd sent out the agency's Christmas cards, but no one ever received them.

When it was time to go to the company Christmas party in Aberdeen, Shelly said that was the first she'd heard of it. And though it was during office hours, she said she couldn't make it as she was doing something with Dave at that time. She was also caught listening to office messages from home and deleting them without relaying the information to the respective parties.

During a performance evaluation meeting in late January 2001, Shelly agreed that she could be doing things better. She promised to be a superior employee, but over the next few months, her performance continued to decline.

The manager wrote of the feelings of a coworker.

"[She] is unable to trust Michelle. She said Michelle lies and backpedals. [She] feels that she's been compromised in the community."

When a male coworker refused to tell Shelly his birthday, she went behind his back and got the date by calling his wife at home. Next, she turned a pre-arranged lunch date into a surprise birthday party, cake and balloons and all.

She invited everyone except the woman in the office who'd complained about her sloppy work. It was a well-aimed knife in the back. Shelly and the woman had once been friends. There weren't many—any, really—women in town that Shelly could call a friend. It had been a huge betrayal. She told others that she had once loved the woman. Their kids had played together.

She didn't care. She'd been slighted and she was at war. Sometimes, Shelly said, you just never know how far someone will go to get what he or she wants.

Following Shelly's poor performance evaluation, on January 20, 2001, Ron Woodworth wrote a letter to Shelly's director, praising her care of his mother. The first part of the well-written letter of commendation was directed at Shelly's supervisor, indicating how helpful and courteous he'd been, but Ron's greatest words of support were all about Shelly.

She was, by his estimation, one in a million.

"Most employees in a bureaucracy quickly learn to do only the absolute minimum necessary to keep a job. And no more! Which is nothing less than an absolute shame, and clearly not the right thing to do! Mrs. Knotek, however, knows (and absolutely believes) that a true public servant must be willing to go the extra mile to help clients cope with their many problems. I have heard stories from around Raymond of Mrs. Knotek's willingness to help clients rectify their many problems. Mrs. Knotek helped my mother when a visitor to her neighborhood accidentally struck the skirting of her mobile home with their car."

He signed his name and then forged his mother's signature.

It was a nice try. But decidedly too little, too late. On March 27, 2001, Shelly was given a written warning: shape up or face termination. She argued each point with her supervisor before agreeing that the list was a fair representation of what had been going on. Neither her performance nor her reputation improved subsequent to that meeting.

". . . MK got argumentative and defensive. MK told me she did not want to 'be put in a corner again.'"

Later that spring several calls came into the office praising Shelly and her astonishingly excellent work. The staff was sure that Shelly was soliciting each one in order to save her job. It was a campaign that was destined for failure.

On May 9, 2001, Shelly was summarily put on probation by her supervisor. It was a move that made her blood pressure rise. She said so at the time. And in true Shelly fashion, she again challenged every point in a written statement. She insisted she would appeal.

Her supervisor wrote of the encounter:

"She said I did not like her. She said I was mean. She said I was like a police officer. She cried. She told me her blood pressure was 180 over 120. She told me she was separated from her husband and needs a job."

A few weeks later, Shelly's conduct moved further in the wrong direction. The office was now a "hostile" workplace. She became more and more erratic, while at the same time promising to improve the way she did things.

"MK said she is being picked on . . ." her boss wrote. *"She said I'm not listening to her and that she is being spied on."*

During that time, her boss questioned her about anonymous phone calls directing complaints against another employee.

"Is Ron Woodworth a friend of yours?" he asked.

"Not really," she hedged.

The boss didn't tell Shelly that when the 800-number calls came in, all were traced to Ron. Nor did he mention to her that the employee who noted the complaint said that Shelly's daughter Tori called him Uncle Ron and, in 1998, he had identified Shelly as his "sister." Or that a coworker had seen a sign at Shelly's house advertising "Uncle Ron's Parking Spot."

The manager told Shelly about the complaints, vague in nature as they were. He didn't mention that the coworker felt unsafe because of the calls and had taken to locking her office door during the day to protect "my job, my files, and integrity."

Shelly hesitated before answering.

"Well, Ron hasn't been in here," she said before she shifted her ground slightly. "Ron hasn't been in here for a long time."

At 3:30 a.m. on May 31, Shelly left a voice message on the company's answering machine. She indicated there was a family emergency and she would not be in. It was the beginning of a drawn-out end of her employment.

Less than three weeks later, on June 19, 2001, Olympic Area Agency on Aging cut her a severance check for $4,849 and some change. In a touch of irony, Shelly was also terminated from the Health and Safety Officer Team of which she had been a "valued" member. Shelly didn't take the news well. She stormed out.

Later that morning, she and Ron drove past the office windows, and Ron gave the finger to a woman Shelly had insisted had it in for her.

CHAPTER
FIFTY-TWO

In the summer of 2001, Ron's friend from the service, Sandra Broderick, moved from the Tacoma area to Copalis Beach on the Washington Coast, a little more than an hour from Raymond. She wanted to reconnect with Ron, who was living with the Knoteks. She'd called several times, but each time Shelly said Ron was out in the yard or away. He never got on the phone.

It was both tiresome and concerning.

The next time Shelly answered and coolly told Sandra that she had no knowledge about where Ron was, Sandra wasn't about to let it go. She'd had enough of what she was sure was some game.

"You better have him call me ASAP or I'll call the police, Shelly. I will. Don't think I won't."

"Well, I don't know where he is," Shelly said.

"I'm filing a missing person's report," Sandra said. "The police will go to your house."

Less than twenty-four hours later, Sandra's phone rang. It was Ron calling. He seemed nervous, upset. He confided that his money troubles had accelerated. In turn, there were legal issues.

"I'm hiding from the police," he told her. "Staying in Shelly's attic. They have a warrant out for me."

Sandra heard a noise. Someone was breathing into the receiver.

"Shelly! I know you are on the other line," she said. "You better hang up right now!"

The phone suddenly went click.

Angry but determined to help, Sandra offered Ron a job working at the restaurant she then owned.

"And you can live with me."

Ron flatly refused and he did so in a New York minute.

"No," he told Sandra. "Shell is helping me find a new job. Housesitting in Seattle."

They talked a little more, but the call—and the offer for help—was clearly going nowhere.

Sandra was worried but wasn't sure what she should do. Ron was a grown man. He claimed to be in trouble with the police and she couldn't do any more than she already had.

A week later, Shelly phoned.

"You're stressing Ron out," she said. "You're no good for him. Stay out of Ron's life, Sandra."

"I will not," Sandra said. "Ron needs someone to take care of him. You're not doing it, Shelly."

Then the line went dead.

Sandra was right, of course. Ron had been sinking lower by the minute. He didn't tell her, but in his quest to prove that Shelly was the best caregiver in the world, he'd crossed more than one line. Indeed, that summer, a lawyer for a Seattle firm representing the Olympic Area Agency on Aging dispatched a letter advising him to stay off the agency's premises in Raymond because employees there felt harassed and unsafe. He was instructed that no contact would be allowed, including written and by phone.

"Employees will call the police and request that you be arrested for trespass."

Since Shelly Knotek came into his life, Ron's world was now a black hole of money trouble, legal trouble, and family trouble. And Shelly was right there, stirring the pot, making things worse and worse.

CHAPTER
FIFTY-THREE

At fifty-six, Ron was beside himself over the discord he was facing with his mother, Catherine Woodworth.

And as it turned out, his new friend Shelly Knotek would be right there to help exacerbate things.

Catherine had complained to other family members that the level of care her son was providing was subpar at best. Ron was indignant. Shelly pushed the issue, telling him that he'd been turned in to the authorities for neglecting his mother. It would be embarrassing and ruin him in town. Even before any charges could be filed, Shelly convinced him to put together a rebuttal.

With Shelly hovering over his shoulder, Ron made a point-by-point list to counter what he insisted had been an unfair characterization of his duty as a son. The most substantive complaint centered on the cleanliness of her trailer, most notably the infestation of fleas that she'd told a reporting agency had been the by-product of Ron's cats.

I kept her house up to her standards. Anytime my mother wanted me to clean the house, I would do so immediately. My cats were indoor animals completely and had no fleas when I moved them into my mother's home.

Ron blamed a neighbor's outdoor and indoor dogs for the infestation.

"When I moved out of my mother's house in late September 2000, she had very few flea bites on her—the complaints about the sudden infestation occurred after I moved out and before my mother unilaterally kicked my cats out of her house."

)(

Unbeknownst to Ron, Shelly was also driving a wedge as deeply as she could between Ron and the rest of his family. She'd done it with Kathy. She'd done it with Dave too. In fact, Shelly seemed buoyed at the possibility of being both Ron's benefactor *and* his antagonist. She cozied up to Catherine, and fanned the flames with Ron's family back in Michigan. Shelly made calls to the Woodworths, lamenting over what was going on with Ron, painting herself as Catherine's number-one advocate.

"I lost my own mother at two," she told Ron's younger brother, Jeff Woodworth, during one of many phone calls she made behind Ron's back; it was a bit of an exaggeration, as Sharon had died when Shelly was thirteen. "Your mom is like the mom I never had."

She went on to say how her husband, Dave, adored Catherine too.

"She made him a pie for his birthday and he thought that was so great."

Shelly insisted that Ron could stay with them until he got back on his feet.

"And in return for staying there," Jeff recalled, "she quite bluntly told him what he was expected to do around there—feed the dogs, cats, and horse. Nothing major."

Later, Ron would complain about his duties at the Knotek house in letters to his family. For her part, Shelly told Ron's family about a time when she gave Ron specific instructions regarding leaving two of her cats outside when she was away. When she returned home after picking up Sami, she was stunned to see that he'd disobeyed her.

"I asked you to leave them outside," she said.

Ron piped up. "It's okay. They're with me. I'm watching them."

Shelly became angry, telling Ron she didn't want the cats in the house because of her cockatiel.

Ron pushed back a little. "I told you I was watching them."

"You're not listening to me," Shelly said. "I don't want them in my house!"

"I made a mistake! I apologize," Ron finally answered.

Just then, Sami came into the room. "Why are you yelling at my mom?"

Ron didn't answer. He didn't say anything at all. He just stormed outside.

)X(

On October 1, 2001, while Shelly looked on, Ron wrote a scathing letter to his mother. He'd regretted doing anything to help her.

"When I brought you and father up here, I did not expect you of all people to stab me in the back. We both know that father would be very saddened by your heartless cruelty to me and my cats. Father could not be cruel to an animal if his life depended on it."

He told his mom that not only couldn't he stand the sight of her, he considered her his murderer.

"On June 8, 1997, Gary Neilson heartlessly killed me as a man when he abandoned me; well, congratulations, on October 1, 2001, you finished the murder by destroying my pride in being a Woodworth."

He closed his acid-soaked missive by saying he no longer had a mother.

"She died the day she killed my cats."

Two days later, Ron wrote what he promised would be his last letter to Gary.

"You have shown no compassion for me since you murdered me in June of '97. You were greedy, selfish, uncaring, dishonest . . ."

Ron sent a second letter just four days after the previous one. This time he called his mother "Madam" in the salutation. Again, he railed more about her betrayal over the cats and told her that he was moving to Seattle, *"where (maybe) I can forget my traitorous mother."*

That same day, Ron sent a three-page letter to his brother and sister in the Midwest. Once more, he recounted all that their mother had done to him, the unspeakable cruelty of *"kicking my beloved cats out into the cold."* Because of that, he noted, he could no longer watch over her. After all, he couldn't trust her and couldn't stand the sight of her. He indicated that it had all happened when he'd moved in with Shelly and she couldn't take his cats and their mother promised they could stay with her for a week. However, *"within three days"* she'd let them out.

"For my own peace of mind, I therefore must wash my hands of any and all responsibility for her or her care. I am, in fact, so mad and furious with her that I will within the next few months formally and legally change my name."

He told them he was moving to Seattle where he'd live under a new name—one that he would tell them, but they were forbidden to disclose it to their mother.

He provided Shelly's phone number if they needed to reach him.

"For my emotional stability, we will for the foreseeable future be communicating through Michelle's good graces. Michelle really regrets being in the middle of this since she cares about both of us. So I don't blame her for anything. As always, I have to carry all the blame for everything."

One line caught everyone's attention.

"My heart aches, but I need to do this, or I could do something far more serious, and right now, that I do not want to do."

Ron's siblings—and ever-helpful Shelly—saw it not as a suicide threat but as a threat to Catherine's safety.

Ron wrote a handwritten letter to his mother on October 9, 2001.

> Madam,
>
> *This is to inform you that I am giving Mrs. Michelle Knotek permission to remove all my personal property from your home and storage building. What she does with it is none of your business. Once she has removed everything, you will receive no more communication from me. I pray that you will live for one hundred years in perfect health, both physically and mentally; and that for every day of the rest of your life you will remember the cruelty of what you did to me. You are now their responsibility, not mine.*
>
> *I was once your loving son.*

Ron was alone. He didn't have anyone in his life.

Just Shelly.

CHAPTER
FIFTY-FOUR

By 2001, Lara Watson had retired from a career setting up operations for hospitals and nursing facilities and she wanted a new project. When she came across the opportunity to refurbish an old monastery in Sandy, Oregon, into a bed-and-breakfast and wedding venue, she jumped at the chance. She hadn't spoken to Shelly in quite some time, and that was just fine with her. Every time they talked—about the cancer, her marriage to Dave, what was going on with Shane in Alaska—Shelly would offer up a one-sided conversation that went nowhere. Every call to Shelly seemed to end up with a sputtering monologue and a hang-up.

It was in early July 2001 when Nikki called to say she was thinking of heading down to Oregon also to see about finding a new job. Lara was thrilled, of course. The connection between Lara and her granddaughter was powerful. Nikki was the baby she had nurtured years ago when Shelly had abandoned her. Lara remained close with the two older Knotek sisters. Sami was thriving in college, and Nikki was in Bellingham. Both of them were on the right path, which brought Lara a lot of solace.

Nikki landed a job on her first day in Oregon, and it seemed like an echo of their happy time together up north in Bellingham. But things shifted, tectonically so, later that first night, when she and Lara were watching a crime show on cable TV.

Nikki had always been fascinated by crime; she wanted to understand why bad people did the things they did. Before she dropped out of Grays Harbor, she'd even had aspirations for a career in law enforcement. Her mom, she knew, was the same way—though Nikki figured Shelly was less interested in figuring out how to catch the killer, and more in how to stay ahead of the police.

Then again, Shelly could surprise her. One time when they were watching *Mommie Dearest,* Shelly turned to her girls with a stunned expression on her face. "I can't believe that a mother would do that to her kids!"

Nikki and Sami had exchanged incredulous looks. Had their mom forgotten about the duct tape? The Icy Hot? The wallowing?

That night, while they watched TV at Lara's, Nikki suddenly got very quiet in a way that felt strange to Lara, though she didn't say anything at the time.

Maybe Nikki was tired from the long drive from Washington?

The next morning, Nikki found her grandmother in her office sorting through paperwork.

"I have something to tell you," she began. Lara could tell she'd been up all night. Nikki's eyes were wet and red. She'd obviously been crying.

"What is it, honey?" She put her arms around her granddaughter. A long pause filled the small office.

"Mom and Dad killed Kathy," Nikki said finally.

The word nearly stuck in her throat when Lara repeated it. "Killed?" Nikki nodded. "Murdered."

Both started to cry, harder than they might ever have cried before. Between the sobs that stopped and started her story, Nikki told Lara what had happened first at the Louderback House and then Monohon Landing Road.

Lara was tough and had heard plenty of things in her day; this time, however, she could scarcely believe her ears. And yet, she knew of no reason why her granddaughter would fabricate such a tale. Nikki, she knew, wasn't a liar.

Shelly, however, always had been.

Lara pulled herself together and came up with a plan.

"We have to tell," she said.

Next, Lara phoned the local chief of police there in Sandy, Oregon. When he came over, Nikki shared what she knew, and he called the sheriff's office with the jurisdiction over Raymond, South Bend, and Old Willapa—Pacific County, Washington. He got Pacific County sheriff's deputy Jim Bergstrom on the phone and reported back to Lara.

"He told me to write everything down and gave me his fax number," Lara said later. "So that's what Nikki and I did. We sent everything down to Pacific County."

On July 11, 2001, Lara Watson faxed three pages to Jim Bergstrom. She marked the cover sheet "urgent" and expected a response.

She didn't get one.

In the fax, she wrote how Nikki had come forward with her story of what had happened at Monohon Landing and in the house in Willapa. She included a copy of Nikki's original statement:

"Long time ago, when I think I was about 16 when Mom did it. Mom was always mad at Kathy. She treated Kathy really mean. She would hit Kathy with steel-toed logging boots of Dad's. She would give Kathy all kinds of drugs and Kathy was acting weird. This one night, us kids heard all kinds of things, so we peeked in Kathy's room and saw Dad doing something to Kathy, 'cause [a] lot of white foaming stuff was coming out of Kathy's mouth. I think Mom poisoned her. Or caused Kathy so much brain damage from hitting her in the head. But Kathy wasn't moving. I think she was dead. We had to run back away from the room 'cause we are not allowed to be downstairs and we didn't want Mom to know what we saw. She would beat us or do bad things to us if she knew what we saw."

Nikki had written how she and her siblings had been taken to a motel while their parents disposed of Kathy's body in the burn pile on the Monohon Landing property.

"We drove home. We smelled something really bad and rubber burning. Dad was outside throwing all of Kathy's stuff on top of the tires. He kept the burn pile burning."

Finally, Nikki closed by pointing out the fear she had in telling on her parents.

"Mom's going to do something really bad if she knows I told. Or she's going to blame Dad. I hope Dad doesn't commit suicide because of me."

CHAPTER
FIFTY-FIVE

Telling her grandmother, Lara, what had happened to Kathy Loreno and the subsequent talks with the police were, Nikki knew, the right thing to do. She felt in her bones that Kathy's family had been owed the truth for a very long time.

That didn't mean, however, that she wasn't terrified. That her mother and father might be brought to justice had propelled her to disclose her story, but she knew it was no guarantee. What if they didn't have to pay for what they had done? It niggled at her. What if they continued to get away with it? What would happen to Tori? Would Shelly take it out on her little sister?

It scared Nikki so much that she didn't show up for her new job, and instead returned to Bellingham, where the more than two-hundred-mile distance from Raymond would keep her safe.

Once she'd started talking, however, Nikki found her voice to tell the story again. This time, after a few drinks had loosened her tongue, she confided the story to her boyfriend, Chad. She was a ball of nerves and felt like she was going to throw up when she told him everything.

She told him that her grandmother had it all handled. That she'd faxed a statement to the authorities in Pacific County. Chad thought what he was hearing was complete bullshit. It wasn't that he didn't believe Nikki but that it sounded to him like dropping a bomb and running away, which wasn't the right way to get a murderer arrested.

Even if the murderer was her mother.

"You need to tell them in person," he said.

"I can't do that," Nikki said. She was too scared. "I can't go back down there and just tell."

"Look," he said, "either you tell the police, or I will."

"I don't think I can tell."

"You can," he said. "And you will."

The next day, they got into his Yukon and started for Raymond. Nikki's stomach didn't feel any better. She knew they were doing the right thing, but the idea that they'd be within close proximity of her mother was almost more than she could take.

As they drove south, it passed through her mind that she had, in fact, taken a lot. And now, her tormentor, her jailer, the woman who'd poisoned her as a child, who'd shoved her naked into the snow or through a plate-glass door, was about to get hers.

The tables were going to turn. Shelly was going to pay for what she'd done to Kathy.

Around Mount Vernon, a few miles south of Bellingham, Chad's phone rang. He didn't recognize the number when he answered the call. A second later he turned to Nikki.

"It's your mom," he said.

Nikki couldn't believe it. Somehow her mom had gotten Chad's number. *How? Maybe from Sami?*

Her mom had that bizarre power, it seemed. She just knew things.

Chad pulled over, and the truck idled while Nikki spoke on the phone, her heart pounding like a sledgehammer.

"I'm planning a trip to Disneyland," Shelly announced, completely out of the blue and in a kind of casual way that suggested there had been no estrangement.

But there had been one. A long one. A separation that had given Nikki a chance to make a life.

"You girls and me and Dad," Shelly said. "Won't that be wonderful?"

Nikki's hand was shaking. "Yeah," she said. "Sounds great."

Shelly went on about the trip, and Nikki made up a quick excuse that she needed to get off Chad's phone, and ended the call.

"I was freaking out," she said later. "It was almost that she knew what was going on and she was trying to reel me back in. I was in shock. I was heading toward Raymond to tell on her."

Nikki phoned Sami next and told her that she was on her way to tell the police about Kathy. She also dropped a bomb.

"I think Mom had Shane killed."

It was the first time she'd ever said it to her sister.

Sami didn't know what to make of it. She'd been sixteen when Shane had disappeared. She'd accepted her mom's story of the birdhouse and the note and the phone calls.

"Shane would never leave Mom a letter, Sami."

"I guess not."

"We barely looked for him . . . Not like all the other times he ran away. Why do you think that was?"

Sami didn't know.

✕

Chad waited outside while Nikki told Pacific County sheriff's deputy Jim Bergstrom what she knew about Kathy. Bergstrom told her that he'd been out to the Monohon Landing house a few times in recent months, making inquiries to Shelly about Kathy and her disappearance at the request of Kathy's family. After the interview, Chad took Nikki back to Bellingham.

They broke up not too long after that.

"Too much baggage, I guess," Nikki acknowledged. "He was a good guy. And I'm grateful that he helped get me where I needed to go in terms of telling what happened."

Nikki felt sure she had started something big. She felt she'd started an earthquake.

Yet nothing happened. Nothing at all. As far as Nikki knew, the deputy never followed up. Never spoke to Sami. Never searched the house.

"He never even brought Mom in for questioning," she said. "He should have done that."

CHAPTER
FIFTY-SIX

The Pacific County sheriff's deputy had, in fact, tried to reach Sami, with whom he needed to verify what Nikki had told him. Sami got all of the messages but pointedly declined to call him back.

She figured that Nikki and her grandmother had told the police everything they needed to know. And while Sami believed that what Shelly had done to Kathy was beyond forgiveness, Shelly was still her mother, and she didn't want to be the one to put her and her dad in jail.

She told herself that if her mom got picked up, she'd talk then. Not before.

She also hedged her bets that her mom might get arrested, so she told her supervisor at the preschool where she worked that her mother was a little crazy, though she wasn't specific.

"My mom might get in trouble for something," she told her boss. "It could be big."

Part of Sami's fear of talking to the police was stoked by the reaction she'd received from the one person with whom she'd shared the truth—her on-again, off-again boyfriend, Kaley Hanson.

Sami and Kaley had been drinking beer in her dorm at Evergreen, talking about everything and nothing.

Sami leaned into Kaley. "What's the worst thing you've ever done?"

He disclosed something she considered somewhat dark, yet it paled next to a million things Sami could share from her childhood.

She decided not to mess around. She went for the biggest skeleton in the Knotek closest.

"My mom killed somebody," she told him. "Her friend Kathy. She moved her into our house and Mom tortured her until she died."

If it was a game like "never have I ever" or "truth or dare," Sami was the winner.

Kaley's face went white, and he jumped up and ran for the door. Sami hadn't expected that kind of reaction. She'd never told anyone before what her mother had done. She'd felt safe with Kaley. She'd lived with it so long that she'd nearly made it seem like a story, something that's mostly true but not completely so. She thought of it so often—and lived through such craziness—that she said the words as though they needed no preamble. No "are you sitting down" cues that something big was coming.

What did she just do?

She chased after him and brought him back into the dorm. He was in shock and had been sick. Too much beer.

Too much of a real-life horror show.

"I was just joking," she said, trying to walk it back.

"Joking?" he repeated. "That's seriously fucked up, Sami. That you would even joke about something like that."

That reset button had failed. It made things even worse.

"Okay, I wasn't lying," she blurted. "It's true. I'm not lying."

She went on to tell Kaley everything she could remember. She provided all the context she could, including how much she'd loved Kathy and how trapped she was.

How trapped they all were.

After Kaley took it all in and tried to process it and left her a second time, Sami sat there in the dark, thinking over and over that telling someone was not a good idea. It hadn't felt good. It hadn't freed her from anything. Instead, it had made her sick to her stomach, angry, confused. It didn't matter that she trusted Kaley. It was his reaction that had sucker punched her. She'd been a part of something so terrible that, even though she'd been a child, it felt like a huge, ugly mark against her.

Against the family. Against her sisters.

What would Kaley do with that information? Would he tell someone?

It wasn't until years later that it would occur to Sami to consider what passing the burden of that secret onto Kaley might've done to him.

"I honestly never thought about how it affected him, being around my mom after he knew what she'd done," she said later. "I'd been around her and what she'd done my entire life. I still loved her. I didn't think what it might have felt like for someone else to come into our home and being around her, knowing what she was really all about."

⋈

Sami had managed to broach the subject of Kathy with Shelly on a few occasions. She no longer believed the fantasy that Kathy was off with Rocky. She'd never truly believed it anyway.

One time, Shelly had been talking about Nikki, and how Nikki had been locked out of her life. Then, she added, "I wonder if Nikki told anyone, you know, what happened."

About how you killed Kathy? Sami thought. *And yes, she told Nana and the sheriff.*

Finally, she spoke. "No, Mom."

Shelly looked satisfied. Sami, however, pursued the topic, and let her mother know how she really felt.

"I'm not ever going to have a normal life, Mom. Because of what happened. I'll never be able [to] share this with my husband. It'll be a big secret forever." Sami went on. "Maybe it would be better if we told."

"What good would that do?"

"I don't think it's right that Kathy's family doesn't know what happened to her," Sami said. "Maybe we should tell the police?"

Shelly gave her middle girl the slow burn. "Are you fucking serious? Do you want to ruin your life?"

"I don't know that I can ever have a normal life, Mom," Sami said. "Not with this hanging over us."

Shelly gave her a dismissive stare. "You never cease to disappoint me, Sami."

Sami didn't back down. "Kathy's family is still looking for her," she said.

"It's better off that they don't know," Shelly shot back. "They are probably happy that she's with a man who loves her."

"She's dead, Mom."

"I know that, Sami. But talking about it now will ruin all of our lives. Do you want your friends to know?"

Sami shook her head. "No. But . . ."

"You will ruin your sister's life," she said, playing the trump card with Sami. "Tori is completely innocent in all of this. Besides, Kathy committed suicide, Sami. You know that."

Suicide, Sami thought. *Where'd Mom come up with that?*

CHAPTER
FIFTY-SEVEN

Shelly thrived on segregating people. The girls from each other. Their father from the girls. Shane, Kathy, and Nikki were isolated from everyone.

Putting a wall between people allowed her the opportunity to do whatever she wanted. People were game pieces. Toys to be abused. It didn't matter who they were.

Shelly occasionally withheld food from Tori. Not for long, usually no more than a day or two. Sometimes it was a punishment, though other times, it might have been merely because Shelly was too caught up in her TV watching to be bothered to go to the store or prepare a meal. On a few occasions, Tori found herself in the pole building digging into the depths of the old chest freezer. It had to be done very quietly. She, like her sisters, was convinced that their mother had some evil superpowers, an ability to uncover anything they tried to keep secret.

She ate frozen pancakes and carefully hid the wrappers so her mom wouldn't find out. She also made sure that she didn't eat too much of the food so that her mom wouldn't see the supply dwindling. She rearranged the contents of the freezer, shifting things around but making it appear as though it was just as Shelly had left it.

Shelly, as expected, caught on. Tori later surmised that her mother must have found the wrappers because, the next thing she knew, all of the freezer's contents were missing.

"She threw out all the food," Tori said later. "Every last bit of it. She didn't say anything about it either."

And then came more of her mother's stealth attacks.

The lights in her bedroom flooded the darkness. Suddenly the covers were yanked from the bed.

Shelly stood there with her robe half open, a breast hanging out.

"Get up. Get undressed!"

God, what now?

Tori's heart was already pounding fast, adrenaline speeding through her body, but she didn't fight her mom.

And down the stairs they went. Soon she was out in the yard, naked, doing jumping jacks or running in place in the living room while her mother sat on the sofa.

"Faster!" Shelly screamed.

Tori picked up the pace. Sometimes she cried. Mostly she just did whatever her mother said.

"You aren't even trying!"

"I am, Mom. I am. I promise I am."

"You are an ungrateful little bitch."

"I'm sorry, Mom."

"Jump higher! I want you to jump higher."

It was embarrassing. Humiliating. Any kind of refusal meant the duration of the punishment would be longer. As she did what her mother said, Tori never wondered *why* her mom was linking her punishments to nudity or pulling midnight raids on her bedroom. She only wanted it to be over.

"She was really scary," she said later. "I felt like, okay, I have no choice. It made me feel like a little person. Embarrassed. I didn't talk back because I knew it would be worse if I did."

She was *powerless.*

And yet, when it was over, the same thing always happened: "Two hours later you love her again because she'd be holding you and saying, *I'm sorry, I love you.*"

Unlike her older sisters or Shane, Tori didn't endure many repeat punishments. In fact, Shelly rarely gave her youngest the same punishment twice.

One time Shelly got the big idea that they needed to clean out one of the sheds in the back of the property.

"Right now!" she told Tori out of the blue.

As always, Tori jumped.

She followed her mom across the yard to the shed, and Shelly told her to start picking up newspapers and other garbage.

"I want you to put it in your boots!"

It didn't make any sense. It never made any sense. Yet Tori did as she was told.

"Stuff it in your underwear, you little shit!"

Tori gave her mom a quick look, but she didn't telegraph what she was thinking. She was only ten or eleven at the time, yet she knew this was bizarre.

"The weirdest part," Tori said later, "was that she'd just sit there and watch me do it. Just watching and enjoying it, I guess. I remember that was one of the first times as a kid where I was just like, *this is really weird,* like *this is really odd,* like, *there's something wrong with this.*"

Tori didn't tell anyone what was going on at home because she didn't want to get into trouble—and because she didn't think that anyone would believe her. Whenever Sami asked her how things were, Tori always told her sister everything was fine. She wondered if she was a bad girl for always getting into such trouble. She vowed she'd try to do better.

Try to get her mom to love her.

Tori was twelve when she started a journal for school. She was struggling not to be the girl in class whose father lived on an island somewhere, and whose older sisters were long gone. And whose mother abused her and the man who lived with them.

In one entry, she wrote how her favorite movie wasn't a real movie at all.

"It is a home video. I really like it a lot. It's when it was my third birthday and Mom got a kiddy pool. I seemed to really like it a lot. When no one was looking I took my birthday cake and dropped it into the pool. My mom thought it was really funny, but my sister didn't because she had it specially made for me. I just like to watch home movies."

Later, she wrote about the upcoming Thanksgiving holiday.

"I'm thankful for having all my family together at once. You see, my sister lives in Tacoma so I don't see her very much. And my dad works far, far away when he builds underground foundation and wiring for houses all over the place. My mom, I see all the time."

By then, like the others in the family, Tori didn't mention Nikki anymore. Even though photos of Nikki—and Shane—were still up all over the house, it was like her mother had erased her eldest daughter from memory.

No one saw Nikki.

No one except Sami.

That remained a big secret.

Secrets, all three Knotek sisters knew, ran in the family.

CHAPTER FIFTY-EIGHT

Shelly pushed more buttons with Ron's family behind his back. She phoned his family after taking his mother, Catherine, to a doctor's appointment late in the fall of 2001. Shelly said that she'd had to remove three fleas from Catherine's face while the two of them sat in the car. What's more, she said that she'd witnessed on several occasions Ron bossing his mother around.

Shelly also bemoaned the condition of Catherine's house and how it seemed that Ron had done nothing for his mother in quite some time. *The poor woman didn't even have a working TV!* Shelly took care of that and bought Catherine a twenty-seven-inch Daewoo. She also set up a $150 credit line with an appliance store.

When it came time to clean the house, Shelly arranged to have Catherine stay over while her house was being flea bombed. She was doing everything she could for the dear woman she considered a second mother.

And at the same time, Shelly was busy trashing her best friend. She told the family that Ron had enough money to pay the rent at his trailer court but had chosen not to do so.

"At the time they shut him out of [the rental] he had $600 and went to a lawyer instead who told him everything was legal," Ron's brother, Jeff, later said. "He had to go to court on that and the court even postponed it once so through his own negligence he lost out. He also had several chances to appear in court on the rental problem, but when he didn't show, it was decided in favor of the landlord."

On November 4, 2001, Catherine phoned her younger son, Jeff, and stated a desire to move to Michigan to be closer to him and to where her husband was buried. She said Ron was headed for court for bad checks and that there was "a federal warrant" out for his arrest. Later, she waffled on the idea to return to Michigan. She cited the cold climate there, as well as not wanting to be a burden.

Shelly inserted herself deeper into the Woodworths' family matters. She sent a short note on November 29, 2001.

"Your mom's doing well. I'm taking her picture this week for you all— and she's having her hair fixed this week for the Christmas season. I wish I could do something to help you all. God bless you and yours."

On December 2, 2001, Catherine phoned Jeff in Michigan and said Shelly had hand-delivered a letter from Ron in response to her giving away his clothes. Shelly had held the letter for some time and told Ron's brother that she'd pleaded with Ron not to send it. But he was adamant; she had no choice. When Shelly finally did give Catherine the letter, she said she did so when they were together in the car, giving her time to absorb it all as they drove around. The message was included in a Christmas card with a note: *"Give this to Mom as I don't want her to know my PO box."*

"You are one fucking stupid bitch," it began. *"I really cannot believe that you could be so fucking incredibly stupid as to think that you had the fucking right to steal my few possessions from me."*

Shelly mailed the letter a few days later to Ron's brother with her own addendum: *"Enclosed you'll find the letter that Ron had sent your mother. I feel so bad about all of this."*

Ron's sister-in-law responded with her own assessment: *"This letter was even more abusive than the last, using the F-word 22 times by Michelle's count."*

And a plan to stem Ron's abuse of his mother: *"I gave Michelle permission over the phone to screen all mail to Mom from Ron and to contact adult protective services on 12-3-01."*

✕

Jeff Woodworth continued to get calls from Shelly Knotek. As far as Ron's family was concerned, Shelly was kind, smart, and conscientious. They were far away in Michigan, and Shelly was a lifeline at a very difficult time.

Ron sat there like a stone as his family left a voice message on the Knoteks' answering machine. When Shelly came home, she played the message, then asked Ron if he'd heard it.

She later wrote Ron's family what happened next.

"Ron acted indifferent . . . but then got defensive saying, 'I don't take orders from anyone' and started a tantrum."

Ron's brother later indicated he thought Shelly was at her wit's end too. He made a note of it:

"Michelle has talked to Ron repeatedly about 'letting go' and getting on with his life but he wouldn't do it. Michelle said she was acting like his mother and not a friend and Dave said enough."

✕

It was winter break and Sami was home from Evergreen. Tori was off with friends somewhere, and Ron was working out in the pole building when a Pacific County sheriff's cruiser pulled up. A deputy got out and knocked on the front door. Shelly answered right away. Sami couldn't hear what was being said, but she was sure it was about Kathy. It had been months since Nikki had first gone to the police.

They know! she thought. *It's all happening.*

Her mom shut the door.

"Why are they here?" Sami asked, suddenly panicked. "It's about Kathy, isn't it? They know about Kathy, Mom!"

Shelly's eyes got really wide and she ran to hold her daughter.

"Oh, no," she said. "It's papers for Ron. It's nothing, I tell you. Not about Kathy."

Sami started to cry and went into her mother's bedroom. A second later, Shelly came in and held her, telling her that she was sorry for everything. She said that Kathy's death had taken a terrible toll on her too. She said she could barely live with herself because she'd let things get out of control. Shelly admitted she'd made mistakes in judgment; however, she blamed Nikki and Shane for most of it.

"They abused her so much," she said.

Sami couldn't think of a single time Nikki had ever abused Kathy. Shane might have done some, but only with their mother standing next to him telling him what to do.

"Kick her in the head, Shane!"

"I feel horrible for what this has done to you," Shelly said, crying too. "I'm so, so sorry. It won't ever happen again. I promise. If anyone ever found out, your dad and I will kill ourselves so you don't have to live with it any longer."

✕

Even though Ron was busting his butt working like a slave in the yard, Shelly kept telling Sami that she wanted him to leave, but he refused. She had only intended to help him out through a difficult time in his life, not have him live there forever.

"He needs to go," Shelly told her.

"Go where?" Sami asked.

"Just go. Get a job. Move out."

"Why doesn't he?"

"He's too attached to us. He thinks we need him."

"He's a hard worker."

"Not really," her mother said. "He is always guilting me. Telling me that he wants to stay."

CHAPTER FIFTY-NINE

Tori was twelve years old now, and she took in everything. Every. Single. Thing.

Ron had a pair of short-shorts that he wore at the beginning of his stay with the Knoteks, and a couple of tank tops too. After a while, however, Shelly took away his clothes and, as was her MO, made him work outside only in his underwear.

Tori also heard everything.

"You don't deserve clothes," her mother told Ron. "You are worthless. So don't ask me about it again. Don't even think about it. Now get your fat ass out the door and do your chores."

From 7:30 in the morning to nearly 8:00 at night, Ron would be outside in his underwear feeding the animals, weeding the garden, cutting down brush, burning trash. Whatever was on Shelly's long list of things that needed to be done.

At night, Ron would eat his dinner upstairs, alone. On most nights, Shelly would give him a couple of sleeping pills. Despite an empty bed and bedroom in the house, he slept on the floor.

If he made any noise at night, Shelly screamed at him to come downstairs, so she could punish him. Tori stayed as quiet as she could, refusing to move a muscle. She lay there, considering telling her dad what was going on, but she knew where his loyalty stood.

Telling on Shelly would only make things worse for Ron.

Tori hated what her mom was doing to him.

One time, she even tried confronting her about it. "Do you have to be so hard on him, Mom?"

"What are you talking about?"

"Ron's nice. He's a good guy."

Shelly made a disgusted face.

"If you like him so much, Tori," she said sourly, "then why don't you marry him?"

Not long after that encounter, Shelly called Tori into the living room. Ron stood still for the longest time before he spoke.

"He has something to say to you," she prodded.

"I don't love you anymore, Tori," he finally said.

Tears filled Tori's eyes. "I don't believe you."

Ron struggled to keep on message. His eyes were wet and he could barely look at the girl.

"It's true," he said, pulling himself together. "I don't."

"I knew it wasn't true," Tori said later. "She was making him say it just to hurt both of us."

Ron, in typical Shelly style, was instructed to never speak to Tori after that. There was no reason for the edict except that Shelly resented the two of them having any kind of relationship. She could see that Ron had grown fond of her youngest, and that Tori, in turn, had taken to calling him Uncle Ron. That Tori cared for Ron and worried about him must have been obvious to her mother.

As with Sami and Nikki, Shelly made it abundantly clear she didn't want Tori and Ron talking when she wasn't around to supervise the conversation. Tori didn't want her uncle Ron to get in trouble. He was smart and had a dry sense of humor. He had a kind of alternative personal style with his ponytail and his cool Egyptian jewelry that the girl admired.

They barely spoke, even though he slept most nights on the floor outside her bedroom door.

"It was best to keep quiet," Tori said years later, "because we didn't want anything to happen. The less you did that might bother her, the better."

When Tori was sure her mother was asleep and couldn't hear, however, she would tiptoe from her bedroom to where Ron slept. In the middle of the night, she'd stoop down and give him a quick, quiet hug. He'd smile and give her a little nod. Neither said anything.

Ron and Tori shared a fear of what might happen if they were caught talking.

Uncle Ron would be made to pay, and Tori never wanted to be the cause of that.

※

As had been the case for as long as she could remember, Sami was in the middle. She was the golden child. She could see her mother for what she was, yet she was seldom the target of the vilest punishments. Her relationship with her mom was as normal as it could be, all things considered. Shelly would come to Evergreen with groceries, they'd talk on the phone, or they'd go together to Target by the Capital Mall and shop.

Most of Shelly's visits were unannounced. Many had Ron along for the ride. He'd wait in the car the entire time. Sometimes for hours.

Sami and her boyfriend, Kaley, both noticed a rapid decline in Ron's appearance.

"He looks worse than last time," they said to one another. "Yeah, he's down another notch."

It was true. Ron was quickly becoming a shell of a man. He wore a woman's oversized sweatshirt. He was disheveled. The bling of his jewelry, the style that told the people of Raymond that Ron Woodworth wasn't from around there, was soon gone.

Sami recognized something was going on. But could her mom really be doing to Ron what she had done to Kathy? Later, Sami would beat herself up for not taking a stand.

Could she have helped?

※

Nikki, for her part, wasn't done trying to make things right. She didn't know what the sheriff was doing with the information she'd provided, though it didn't seem like much. She called her mother when she learned from Sami that Ron was living there.

The machine picked up and Nikki left a message.

"I know there is a man living there and you need to get him out of the house before history repeats itself."

Shelly called Nikki back right away.

"He's a family friend," she said. "He's really good with Tori. Nothing's going on."

Sami seemed to back up her mother. She'd been there almost every weekend. She was worried, but she was keeping an eye out.

"Everything is fine," Sami told Nikki. "I keep asking Tori. She's fine. She's so much mouthier than we were. She'd tell us."

"Are you sure?" Nikki asked.

Sami was positive. "She gets away with so much. She's fine."

Sami was saying what she wanted to be true. Nikki was hearing what she wanted to be true.

Everything's fine. Ron's fine. Tori's fine.

One time Sami mentioned Ron wasn't wearing shoes, which she thought was a little strange.

"But that's all," Sami said.

Oh crap, Nikki thought before trying to put it out of her mind. *Something is happening.*

)(

Dave Knotek knew it too.

He was still up in Oak Harbor on Whidbey Island, sending his paycheck home. When Shelly first told him that her good friend Ron Woodworth had moved in and was helping around the house, he had a sick feeling in his stomach. It was like a hard punch to an already queasy stomach.

Seeing it up close only confirmed what he knew.

"I'd come home on the weekends and this guy's condition was just deteriorating. She had him down in the swamp with a weed eater, barefoot and in his shorts. Cut to shit. And I'd seen her make him slap himself over and over. And she'd hide his shoes."

When Dave confronted her about Ron's lack of footwear, suggesting that they buy him a pair of shoes, Shelly just shook her head. "He keeps losing them," she claimed.

)(

On one of the occasions Ron made a run for it, Shelly told Tori to get in the car so they could search for him.

"Why are we looking for him?" Tori asked. "You don't even like having him here, Mom."

Shelly gave her daughter a quick, cold glance. "He's got all those marks on him," she said. "He'll lie and say that I did that to him. We'll all get in trouble."

"I was in awe that she said that," Tori reflected. "And even to this day . . . I think that's really crazy she was so honest about that but it's true. That's why she didn't want anyone to find Ron because he would have said all that."

When they found Ron, he got into the car. He said he was sorry and promised never to do it again.

Whenever Ron ran away—which became less frequent as the months and years went by—he didn't get very far. Like Kathy, like Shane, Ron didn't have anywhere to go. Shelly would find him, usually behind a tree or in some brush in the woods hiding or trying to make himself as tiny and inconspicuous as possible in one of the Knoteks' outbuildings.

CHAPTER SIXTY

"Tori! Get your ass out here!"

Shelly stood in the yard holding an axe.

She was Lizzie Borden to the nth degree.

"Get over here!" she yelled.

Tori went to her mother right away. There was no room for even a second of delay when her mom had that scary *Fear Factor* tone permeating every syllable coming out of her mouth.

"What?"

"Don't 'what' me. Come here."

The axe was completely scary. God knew what her mom was going to do to her, or make her do to someone else. Tori had no inkling of what she'd done to make her mother so angry, but she told her she was sorry anyway.

Shelly thrust the axe at her.

"You left this out overnight. How many times do I have to tell you to put things away?"

"Sorry, Mom."

Shelly made an irritated face. "Put this down your pants."

To anyone else, that command would be so nonsensical that the recipient wouldn't understand what she had meant. Tori knew right away. She ran the axe handle down her pant leg and into her boot. The blade rested on her side.

Satisfied, Shelly gave her a quick nod. "Now do your chores," she said. "I don't want to see that axe out of your pants until everything is done. Do you understand?"

Of course she did. Her mom was crazy. Tori limped around the yard for the next couple of hours doing what she'd been instructed to do.

It didn't stop there. With her mother, things never did.

Another time, her bed seemed lumpy and Tori pulled back the covers, exposing the family's kitchen and bathroom trash. She knew her mother had put it there, and she knew why.

"I had forgotten to take out the garbage. It was Mom's way of reminding me never to let it happen again."

She picked everything up, took it outside, then went back up and changed the sheets.

In the bathroom, Tori shook her panties and white dust fell to the floor. It was the Gold Bond that her mother routinely sprinkled inside. Sometimes when Tori was around ten, her mom would appear in the bathroom with the container of the antibacterial powder and instruct her to spread her legs and put it on her labia. The powder burned and Tori would cry out that she didn't want it.

"It's medicine," Shelly said. "You need it. All girls do."

"It really hurts, Mom," Tori said, blinking back the tears.

"Oh good God. Just buck up, Tori."

On a couple of occasions, Shelly decided Tori needed a shower.

"You're filthy," she said. "Let's go outside."

Tori followed her mother to the hose.

"Get undressed," she said.

It was cold outside, but Tori didn't say anything back to her mom. Being "mouthy," as her mom called it, was never a good idea. She took off her clothes and her mother sprayed her with the water. One time

Shelly used the pressure washer on her youngest. At least Tori was never made to wallow, unlike her siblings.

She'd seen Ron wet and cold from time to time and assumed that he'd been given the same kind of outdoor shower. They never talked about it. They weren't allowed to talk about anything.

And so it went. However, Tori experienced less abuse once Ron came on the scene. Less of the worst was better than more.

CHAPTER
SIXTY-ONE

No matter where Ron was working on the Knotek property, it was important to always be on high alert. Whenever Shelly called out, he was supposed to drop everything and get to her as fast as he could.

If he didn't answer back, for any reason, Shelly would become enraged. She'd stand there fuming and balling up her fists. Her neck muscles would tighten; her eyes would narrow.

"You fucking better acknowledge me when I call you!"

Ron started for her in a panic.

"I'm coming, Shelly Dear!" The sound of Ron's scared and anxious voice gave Tori chills.

"It was one of the scariest sounds I've ever heard still." Tori shuddered, thinking about it years later. "He sounded like he was dying every single time he said it. It was like ['Shelly Dear'] was the last thing he would ever say in his life, with such urgency and such fear."

Keeping him on his toes and frightened was only one tactic Shelly employed to "help Ron get better." A major dose of humiliation seemed also to be part of her twisted regimen.

Shelly pulled Tori aside one time while Ron sat with them in the living room.

"Did you know Ron had a baby?"

Tori looked over at Ron. He looked away.

"In Vietnam," Shelly carried on. "He got a girl pregnant and had a baby. Yes, a beautiful baby. But Ron, the piece of shit he is, didn't do anything to help the baby and it died. Probably the best thing for the baby, I think. Who'd want Ron as a dad anyway?"

Tori looked over at Ron, who was now curled in a ball.

"Ron's a good guy, Mom."

Shelly's face went red. Her features stretched tight.

"You don't know everything about him, Tori," she chided. "He's the worst of the worst and there's no two ways about it."

Ron cowered while Shelly dropped bomb after bomb. She berated him for being fat, for being gay, for losing his trailer. Whatever she could think of in her free-association style of abuse. A favorite attack was questioning his devotion to her or his love for Tori.

"You don't fucking care about us, Ron. You don't. I can just tell by watching the way you do things around here. You act like you're doing us a favor. Big guy. You are the lowest of the low. You don't care about me. Just using me. That's what you are, a big fucking user."

Sometimes she would take his interest in Egyptology and twist it.

"Oh, Ron, the gods are disgusted by you. They are. You're going to hell, you fucking, little prick."

"If you looked at him, it was like all the life was sucked out of his eyes," Tori said years later. She'd been too young at the time to recognize the parallels to what had also happened with Kathy, but she could easily see that, at some point after Ron had moved in, he'd become lost. "He didn't laugh. He didn't cry. He just sat there."

PART SIX

Opportunity

Mac

CHAPTER
SIXTY-TWO

Shelly still had a use for Ron, however, and it was an important one. Shelly enlisted him to help care for a Pearl Harbor survivor named James "Mac" McLintock, a family friend of Kathy Loreno's mother, Kaye Thomas (and coincidentally, the reason Kaye had moved her family up to South Bend in the first place). He was a big man who favored second-shelf whiskey and woodworking. He loved his black lab, Sissy, and was grateful for the mobility of the scooter he relied on to get him around his house that overlooked the Willapa River.

Shelly talked up Mac as the father she never had. She put lotion on his dry hands and made sure that he had everything he needed. She bragged to others about how much Mac loved her. She called several times a day to make sure he was doing okay. It wasn't unusual for Shelly to show up at his place once or twice daily. Tori had grown fond of Mac too. He was a grandfatherly figure, and Tori enjoyed going over to his house while her mom went about her business as his caregiver. She'd listen to his stories, and in a few instances, they raced scooters down the street.

She always let him win.

On more than one occasion, Mac told Shelly that he wanted her to live with him.

Instead, however, she moved Ron into Mac's house.

Tori knew that her mother had told Mac that Ron was gay. Mac balked at having Ron as his helper. Shelly persisted. She couldn't be there all the time, but Ron could. At first, Mac didn't like the idea of Ron bathing him and taking care of his personal needs; however, in time, the two of them worked things out. Ron was over there nearly every day and, sometimes, he slept over.

While there were other bedrooms in Mac's house, Tori noticed that Ron wasn't occupying any of them. She ventured into the basement and opened a tiny, windowless storage area. Inside, she found some of Ron's things, including some blankets. The space was small, almost like a tiny jail cell.

Mom's making him sleep in there, she thought.

Another time, she found some bedding in a firewood storage area under the entryway to the house. Unlike the basement cell, this space was open to the air. The dirt floor was damp.

Even in Mac's house, away from Shelly, it was clear she still controlled Ron.

He's sleeping wherever she tells him to, Tori thought.

☓

Lara Watson hit the roof when she heard through Sami that Shelly was caring for an elderly man named Mac. She hadn't been happy about Ron hanging around the Knotek place either. Something was going on. She was sure of it. She immediately phoned Deputy Bergstrom at the Pacific County Sheriff's Office. She asked about the Kathy Loreno case, and Bergstrom told her that the case had gone cold.

He was in the midst of a big trial and would get back to it as soon as he could, he told her.

"I keep working it when I have time," he'd said.

That didn't sit well with Shelly's stepmother at all. She phoned her local chief of police, Dale Schobert, who urged her to give the Pacific County authorities a chance to build the case.

"They are probably working it behind the scenes," he told her.

That scarcely satisfied Lara. All she could think about was how Shelly had done the unthinkable, and she worried about what she might do next.

She also checked in with Shane's maternal grandparents, who she knew had been worried about Shane, and they said the same thing. They hadn't heard from anyone either. Sami also said she'd never been directly contacted, which wasn't strictly true—she'd just never called the sheriff back. And Nikki was never contacted after she reached out the second time, following her statement about Kathy.

Not a single word.

CHAPTER
SIXTY-THREE

Shelly was floating on air when she told Tori the news. James McLintock was going to leave his estate to his old black lab, Sissy—but "after Sissy dies," she went on, "Mac's house and everything goes to me."

Tori thought the news couldn't be better. After her mom's termination from her job as a senior citizen caseworker, she'd seemed a little lost. And decidedly more abusive. The idea that she was heir to Mac's estate flipped the switch a little. It filled her mom with plans.

Any plans that distracted Shelly from how to make someone beg for mercy were very welcome around Monohon Landing.

Mac assigned Shelly power of attorney on September 7, 2001. It came at a very good time for the Knoteks, whose financial circumstances were beyond dire. Shelly had juggled and cooked the books to such an extent she could barely manage her own lies. Dave didn't know how bad things were financially until his wife called him and said he needed to ask for an advance on his wages. He balked, so Shelly took matters into her own hands. She applied for a payday loan in Aberdeen on September 25, 2001. She listed the family's monthly income at $3,500.

Dave started coming home on weekends more often, and the yelling increased. Tori would make loud noises in her bedroom in hopes that the commotion would jolt her parents into toning it down, but that never really worked. While she loved her dad more than anything, she began to resent him for coming home. It seemed that her mother bottled up a lot of her anger at Ron until her father arrived to carry out whatever punishment he'd been instructed to do.

The yelling was always about two things—money and their houseguest, Ron.

"You need to do something about Ron," Shelly told Dave.

For his part, Dave didn't have to ask any follow-up questions. Shelly steamrolled him with a litany of infractions Ron had supposedly committed.

"He took a crap in the yard," she said one time. "I *saw* him. Coming around a corner and there he was. We can't have that."

With his wife looking on, Dave tore after Ron and grabbed him by the shirt, pulling Ron so hard he lost his balance.

"Don't ever do that goddamn kind of thing around here."

Ron was stunned, but he had a way of deflecting with sarcasm or a look of annoyance.

Was that a smirk?

Whatever it was made Dave even more angry.

"Are you listening to me?" he asked, pulling Ron closer.

Ron didn't answer, and Dave slapped him on the side of the head. Ron looked even more shocked.

"I won't," he finally said. "I won't do it anymore."

X

In time, Shelly had found—maybe even *created*—a compliant victim in Ron Woodworth. He almost never rebuked her ridiculous, incessant, and cruel demands. He barely blinked no matter what she did to him.

Or had him do to himself.

Shelly's scream was like a shot in the dark.

"You fucking prick! Do it!"

Tori, suddenly awake, crawled out of bed to investigate the startling noise. It was the only time she saw this particular punishment in action. Later she'd recall hearing it occur multiple times.

Ron stood in his underwear on the porch. His body was stiff, his eyes glazed over. *From fear? Drugs?* Shelly stood facing him as she bullied him into hitting his face with both hands with as much force as he could.

"Harder!" she yelled at him. "You have to learn, Ron!"

Tori couldn't understand how anyone could do that to themselves. He was striking his face repeatedly so hard that his head jerked back with each self-inflicted blow.

Shelly kept up with her ugly party mix of epithets and commands.

"Faggot! Lazy fag! Don't make me hit you myself! Tell me you're sorry!"

Ron wasn't crying, but this time he seemed scared.

"I'm sorry, Shelly Dear," he said.

"After all I've done for you, you pay me back with nothing but excuses. You make me sick, Ron. You really do. You make everyone sick. Your own mother was right when she told you to get lost. I was an idiot to take you in. You goddamn ungrateful fag!"

Tori heard her mother continue to shout obscenities, but all Ron said was, "I'm sorry, Shelly Dear."

His face went red and he was crying. For some reason, he kept doing as she commanded. It was like he was hypnotized. It went on for at least a full five minutes. It might have been longer. Tori, like her sisters before her, found that time stood still when their mother tortured her victims.

Tori retreated back to bed, cinched up her blankets, and put the pillow over her head. As she'd done hundreds of times before, she tried to block out everything. What her mother was doing was so wrong. So harsh.

When she heard the slapping and yelling again, Tori summoned the courage to confront her mother.

"Why are you making Ron do that, Mom?"

Shelly seemed exasperated and let out a breath. It was as if her daughter's question, not her own behavior, was beyond bizarre.

"Can you see he's been bad?" she asked. "He deserves it."

Tori was unconvinced. Even if Ron had been bad, he hadn't been *that* bad. And Shelly's demands were impossible to meet.

I want this garden weed free by the morning!

I don't want you to use the bathroom in the house!

Why are you shitting outside?

Tori tried another approach. The obvious one, the one that she hoped would appeal to her mother's sense of humanity.

"But it's hurting him," she said.

Shelly gave her a hard look. "Go upstairs and stay there. This has nothing to do with you."

Tori went up to her room. While she recognized that someone had to speak for Ron, she figured that pushing her mother further would only make things worse for him. Her mom had no sense of humanity. Trying that approach had been a dumb idea. *What was she thinking anyway?*

Ron continued to make mistakes, continued to be "bad." At least Shelly thought so. He was in a glue trap, and there was likely no way he couldn't avoid her wrath. Tori witnessed another confrontation over bodily fluids.

"What's this, Ron?" Shelly asked him another time. She held up a cup of urine.

Ron looked at the cup, and then cast his eyes downward. "I had to go to the bathroom and I didn't want to wake you."

Her rule! That's what she wanted!

"You are disgusting me, Ron," she said. "I can't have this kind of thing going on in my house. This is my house, Ron! Your nasty habits make me sick."

"I'm sorry, Shelly Dear."

She handed him the cup.

"Drink it!"

Ron didn't hesitate. He put the cup to his lips and drank every drop.

A couple of weeks later, Tori saw Ron dump a cup of urine out the window. His eyes caught hers.

"Don't worry," she said. "I won't tell Mom."

And she didn't.

No one wanted to make Shelly angry.

Tori didn't say a word to Ron because she loved him. She didn't want him to suffer because of her.

One time Ron was out weed whacking, and her mother was in a foul mood over the slow speed at which he was working. It wasn't his fault. The machine was acting up. The sound of the engine stopping and starting was making Shelly madder and madder. Tori could feel the energy and it was scary. She went out to the yard to show Ron how to keep the gas-powered garden tool running.

To stop her mother from doing whatever it was that she would do.

Tori nearly gasped when she reached him. Ron was hunched over the weed whacker, struggling mightily to make it run. He was nearly naked, his bald head and back badly sunburned. But that wasn't the worst of it. His feet were bloody and the skin of his hands was shredded.

"Uncle Ron," Tori said in a voice so low her mother couldn't hear. "I'm so sorry."

She wished he'd bolt. Never come back. Get as far away as he could. Far, far from her mother. It didn't matter to Tori anymore that her mom's abuse of her had softened in direct relationship with the escalating attacks on Ron. She was stronger. She'd be able to survive it.

When her mom decided Ron needed to move into Mac's house for much-needed around-the-clock care, Tori felt a surge of relief.

He'll be safer there, she thought. *Things will get normal again. Whatever that is.*

CHAPTER
SIXTY-FOUR

Normal is relative, and normal didn't have much staying power at Monohon Landing Road.

On February 9, 2002, Tori was getting ready to go to a football game at Willapa Valley High when her mother got ahold of her to tell her she was at the hospital.

"Mac fell," Shelly said, her voice a little shaky. "He's hurt bad. I'm coming to get you right now."

Tori loved Mac. Just like she loved Ron. She was a girl who wanted more than anything to have a caring family around her. Her sisters were grown and her father was largely absent. Surrogate family members like Mac and Ron meant everything to her.

Or at least as much as her mom would let them mean.

When her mom picked her up, she seemed anxious, though not hysterical. She muttered something about an accident and that she didn't think Mac was going to live.

"It's bad," she repeated. "Ron was there when it happened."

Tori felt sorry for Ron. He was a gentle soul and he must be overcome with worry. By the time they arrived back at the hospital, nurses informed them that Mac had indeed died. Tori burst into tears and melted into her mother's arms.

Shelly didn't seem broken up at all.

Indeed, she was nearly giddy. She'd been left $5,000. There was the matter of his dog, Sissy, of course. But Sissy was old. She couldn't live much longer, and then Shelly would inherit Mac's house, worth more than $140,000.

How Mac died was a bit of a mystery. At first, Shelly was vague about it. Ron had made the call to 911, saying Mac had fallen and hit his head. The authorities didn't seem too concerned either. Tori later gathered that the examining doctor referred the case for further investigation by the coroner and the prosecuting attorney's office when he confirmed Mac died as a result of acute subdural hematoma caused by a blunt impact to the head. It was *possible* that the impact had been caused by a fall. Ultimately nothing further was investigated.

And then it was done. Mac was gone. Just like that, Shelly was flush with cash. Things were definitely looking up.

Indeed, a few days after Mac died, on Valentine's Day, Tori padded downstairs to find her mother wrapping up the greatest box of chocolates she'd ever seen.

She wrote in her school journal a day later:

"I was sure they were for me. I tiptoed upstairs like I never saw a thing and then about ten minutes later I came downstairs and sure enough they were for me!"

Despite the inheritance—the money; the house in South Bend; the dog, Sissy, now chained up outside—before the last chocolate was devoured from the big box, Shelly had resumed her old ways. It was like she just took in her good fortune like a big gulp of air. Money, something she'd chased her entire life, was all right, of course.

But her old games?

Much, much more satisfying.

CHAPTER
SIXTY-FIVE

What happened at Mac's house in South Bend quickly morphed from a shared tragedy to a personal opportunity. Shelly used the episode as the catalyst for a new attack against Ron. It was cruel beyond measure and it came up all the time. Once, when Ron was back working in the yard at Monohon Landing, Tori overheard her mother screaming at him about it.

"You killed Mac! You're a murderer!"

When Ron tried to defend himself, she pushed him into the dirt and then came back inside the house.

"He murdered Mac," she told Tori as she stomped around. "I can't live with a murderer!" Tori didn't know what to think. She'd thought Mac's death was an accident of some kind. Besides, she couldn't see Ron hurting anyone. Not ever.

Another time, the three of them were seated in the kitchen. Tori was minding her own business, and Ron and her mother were in the middle of one of their disagreements.

"How would you feel if a murderer was living in your house?" she asked him.

Ron didn't answer. He just kept his eyes turned downward.

"It doesn't feel good," Shelly went on. "Not at all. You killed Mac, Ron. You are a goddamn murderer."

Again, no response.

Tori never believed a word of it. Shelly might have sensed her reluctance to agree that Ron was a killer, so she kept employing new ways to bring up the subject.

In time, however, the strangest thing happened. Ron started to agree with Shelly.

"You're right," he said. "I killed him. Please don't tell."

Shelly twisted the knife.

"Don't disappoint me, Ron. Don't you ever. I don't want to tell, but you need to know you disgust me. You're a murderer."

Another time, her mom took a break from the TV to tell Tori her latest version of what had happened at Mac's house the day he died.

"He fell out of his wheelchair and bonked his head real hard. Ron just stood there and let it happen. Waited too long to call for help in time to save him. Ron's a useless prick, Tori. I know you see some good things about him but think about it. He's a murderer! He killed our Mac! Mac's like your grandpa!"

In yet another version of Mac's demise, Shelly said the elderly war veteran had fallen into a coma and Ron left him to die.

"He didn't even call me until it was too late," she said. "I call that murder, Tori. I really do. The sight of that fag makes me sick."

Don't call Ron that, Tori thought, but all she said was, "I didn't know about that, Mom."

While Shelly professed contempt for Ron and what she said he'd done to Mac, she also spewed vitriol over Mac's will.

"Lawyers really botched it up," she explained to Tori. "I'm going to tell them that Sissy got hit by a car and died. You need to back me up. It's no big deal, but I need you to understand that story is very important to our family."

"Okay, Mom," Tori said. She thought it was a little strange but not so terrible. After all, her mom was going to get the house anyway. Her mom had done unthinkable things to her and Ron, but she wouldn't really hurt the dog.

"Once we fix up the house and sell it," Shelly said, "we'll have the money to move up to Oak Harbor and live as a family again."

For most kids, that might be a dream come true. All Tori could think about was how badly her parents fought when they were together.

Living under the same roof every day would be a nightmare.

The absolute worst.

⋊⋉

On March 19, 2002, a little over a month after Mac's death and nine months after Lara and Nikki had first sounded the alarm about what had happened to Kathy Loreno, Lara Watson received a message to call Deputy Jim Bergstrom.

Finally, she thought.

Lara had already heard that the old man Shelly was caring for had died.

"She killed him," she told the deputy.

"You don't know that," he replied.

"She poisoned him, I bet."

"He was old. Sick for a long time."

"Who is taking care of the dog?" she asked.

"Shelly is," he said.

"He left her the house," she said.

"Right. And she's caring for his dog."

Lara pushed it. "The dog is probably being poisoned too."

"The dog is fine," he said. "Patrol saw the dog."

Lara moved on. She figured Shelly had probably killed Mac. She was absolutely sure that Kathy had been murdered. Nikki was not a liar. Not by any measure.

"I don't know how you run things in Pacific County," Lara finally said, "but this is not right at all. You need to do something. You need to find out what happened to Kathy Loreno. Have you talked to Sami?"

He said he still hadn't been able to reach her.

Lara wasn't buying any of that.

"She's in Raymond every weekend, deputy. She's worried about her little sister. She goes there to make sure that Tori's okay. Not being hurt. Does this compute at all?"

Deputy Bergstrom insisted he understood, but what more could he do? Sami had refused to call him back.

Lara hung up. She didn't believe he'd tried at all.

※

Sami continued her clandestine relationship with her older sister. She defended Nikki to Tori when Tori would parrot how disrespectful and rotten Nikki was, but only to a point. She didn't want to call attention to the fact that they had remained close. Tori might tell. Like Sami herself had regrettably told on Nikki and Shane when they were growing up. Their mother had a way of weaseling out details and then blaming the messenger.

In May 2002, a few weeks after Lara's call to Deputy Bergstrom, Sami snuck down to Sandy, Oregon, and attended Nikki's wedding at Lara's wedding venue. Sami was happy for her sister. Actually, thrilled. Nikki had found a great man and was living a life that had been impossible to imagine when they were growing up.

When she was forced to wallow.

When she was told she'd never be anything.

That no one would ever love her.

Sami, who still wanted to love their mother more than anything, hated the fact that Shelly was excluded from the wedding. She understood the reasons behind it, of course. *Why would Nikki's tormenter be invited?*

Even so, Sami said later, "I felt bad that they were estranged."

Without telling anyone, she wore a special ring on her finger. It was a "mother's ring" with Nikki's, Tori's, and her birthstones set in a gold band, a gift Sami planned to give Shelly the next day, Mother's Day. The ring was another small secret in a family that had kept and buried countless secrets.

By wearing the ring, Sami felt, "it was kind of like my mom was there at the wedding."

$\rtimes$

After Mac died, Dave Knotek wore out the rubber on his truck tires with more trips home. Their marriage had been in trouble in the past, but they were working together to try to find firmer footing. Dave couldn't function without Shelly. Not really. Although he knew their relationship had been toxic, he couldn't stop loving her.

For her part, Shelly was telling him that she needed him too. That now, more than ever, was the best time to start over. Moving out of Pacific County for good and never looking back was the only way they'd be able to survive. She was under stress over the estate and Ron was giving her all kinds of trouble.

After one of their weekend reunions in June 2002, Dave left Shelly a florid love letter. As he often did, he called her by her pet name, Bunny.

"I hate leaving you here. It breaks my heart so very much. I want to be close to you all the time in my life."

He said he would check on rentals or a lease option up in Oak Harbor. They needed to get out of Raymond and make a fresh start.

"Wherever I am I can always feel your touch and that goes right to my heart. I feel your love for me even though I don't deserve it. I love you ever so much forever and ever."

He wouldn't say it out loud, and never to his wife, but Dave knew deep down that their marriage couldn't survive much longer, not without a big change.

𝕏

While her husband was firmly on her side, other forces were at work to make matters far more difficult than Shelly thought she deserved. In fact, she was baffled by how badly she and her husband were being treated after assuming possession of Mac's house. Neighbors—led by a retired Pacific County sheriff—questioned whether the Knoteks even had a right to the deceased's estate. The sheriff was suspicious about what had gone on there.

Shelly had no idea why she was being treated so harshly. All she ever did was be kind to Mac and treat him like he was her father. She'd brought him soup. Enlisted Ron in caring for him. She'd even had Ron do Mac's yard work. If there had been a kinder person than she, she couldn't think of one.

Shelly called her lawyer again on September 4, 2002. The lawyer made note of the call and notified another of Shelly's lawyers that something needed to be done about the harassment.

"The police in South Bend stopped by a number of times to check their identification and generally make life miserable for Michelle and her husband. One police officer even indicated to Dave that he should be careful tonight when he was driving."

Every bit of scrutiny seemed to fuel Shelly's anger at everyone and everything, especially at Ron. Months after Mac died, she continued to hurl her accusations at Ron.

"You killed Mac, Ron. You fucking killed him!"

"I didn't, Shelly. He fell. He fell out of his chair."

"Liar! I know what you did, and the police are going to come and get you. They will. I swear it!"

The ongoing threat that he'd be arrested and sent to prison for Mac's murder hung over Ron. He would slump down in the car if they drove past a police cruiser. Whenever there was a knock on the door, Shelly would insist that he hide.

"Don't make a sound! They'll take you and put you away for good!"

Tori knew what her mother was up to. Shelly had Ron live in fear because she was actually worried that, if the police picked him up, he might tell them all the things she'd done to him.

CHAPTER
SIXTY-SIX

The last time Sandra Broderick saw her old friend Ron Woodworth was over a meal at Slater's Diner in Raymond in the summer of 2002. Ron looked weak and unwell. She was shocked by his transformation, both mentally and physically. Ron had been witty and sharp. He had a warm kind of personality that brought people in close. This Ron was far from that. He told her that he'd been given a trio of medications by Shelly for depression. Sandra watched warily as he took the medication with his food.

"The pills are helping, but I still have headaches." He took a green pill, then a brown pill, then a white capsule while they sat in a booth at the diner. "Seeing a doctor and a psychiatrist from the state too."

"He was dirty and unkempt," Sandra remembered. "He used to care about his appearance. He was spaced out, irrational, and incoherent."

The more he talked, the more Ron's old friend from the military felt her concern grow. She could plainly see that Ron was in serious trouble. And she told him so.

Ron just looked at her blankly. Nothing she was saying seemed to be tracking. He was in a fog, completely clueless as to how thin and weak he'd become.

"He wasn't the Ron I'd known for twenty years."

Not long after the meal at Slater's, Sandra received an unexpected and very welcome call from Ron. He indicated, for the first and only time, that there were some things going on with Shelly that were bothering him.

"She has my cars and won't give them back to me," he said.

Sandra was incredulous. "Won't give them back?"

"No," he said. "I keep asking."

The disclosure troubled Sandra enough to drive down from her place in Iron Springs for surveillance of the house on Monohon Landing. She drove by slowly and noted that Ron's tan and blue cars were parked out front.

Sandra didn't stop to inquire.

"I didn't want a confrontation with [Shelly]," she admitted.

If she had stopped, she might have seen what Shelly was able to hide.

Sami was also alarmed by the changes she saw in Ron. She asked her mother about his significant weight loss.

"Is Ron okay?"

Shelly went into full-on defensive mode. "What do you mean by that?"

"He's not sick or anything?"

"No."

"He's lost a lot of weight, Mom. That's all."

"He needed to lose weight, Sami. He was fat. He's eating healthy. No more junk food. He's in the best shape he's ever been. He has muscles where he never knew he had them before."

Her mother crowed about how much the work around the house had been helping Ron get in shape.

"He loves being outside and doing chores," she said.

Then Shelly cut off all of Ron's hair, including his beloved ponytail. Sami cornered Ron in the yard and asked about it when she was sure her mother wouldn't be able to overhear.

"I like it this way," he said. "I like it all gone."

She also inquired about his dental problems. He appeared to be down to a single remaining tooth in front.

"Oh, those other teeth were fake anyway," he dismissed. "I'm waiting to get dentures, Sami."

Of course, this wasn't going to happen. When Ron's teeth had started falling out, Tori had asked Shelly why they didn't take him to a dentist.

"He needs dentures, Mom," she said.

Shelly dismissed the suggestion out of hand.

"He can't get to a dentist because he has too many warrants out for his arrest. They couldn't treat him. Besides," she added, "dentures are too expensive."

CHAPTER
SIXTY-SEVEN

The last time Nikki saw her mother was at the Olive Garden in Olympia in 2002, the year Mac died. Nikki was hesitant about the get-together, but she figured she had nothing to lose. *Maybe things would be better?* Sami had continued to report to her sister that Tori was doing fine.

"She says Mom is weird, but she's treated fine. Not like us."

Shelly had dressed up for the occasion and looked good. It was apparent almost at once that her nice appearance was merely camouflage.

She was the same woman she'd always been.

"She was so rude to the waitress," Nikki reported. "Belittling her, sending things back. I kept thinking, you know, *I don't need this. I don't need to be part of this.* It was mean, ugly. Seeing her was a terrible mistake."

Nikki didn't tell her anything about her life. She'd shut that down before dessert.

"I never saw her again after that."

※

Tori Knotek kept a brave face. She never said a word to her sisters or anyone about what was going on at home. Not because she didn't want her mother to be held accountable for what she was doing, but because she feared the dire consequences of poking a bear.

With all that she'd seen, Tori was terrified of what her mother might do to her. And she worried that it was all her fault somehow.

She wrote to her mom in her journal:

"I know that sometimes it might seem like I don't understand you or I just don't want to, but that's wrong. Very wrong. I always can understand you and I will always want to understand you. I am just sick of me disappointing you and Dad so much. I know it's my fault."

Though she couldn't quite put it into words, on some level Tori knew her mother was only happy when someone else was suffering. There had to be a word for a person who found joy in another's pain. Whatever it was eluded her. To smile when someone screamed? To revel in the agony of a cut, a burn?

Why was her mom wired that way?

On a couple of occasions, Tori heard her mother tell Ron to get under the big desk in the living room, which was adjacent to her bedroom. The sound of furniture moving brought her to see what was happening.

This time.

"You are going to stay there," Shelly said, "until I hear your cry."

Ron had stuffed himself under the desk. "I'm sorry, Shell Dear," he said.

"You're not sorry enough, you good-for-nothing faggot!"

Ron started to make crying noises.

That made Shelly even angrier.

"You goddamn faker!" she railed. "I know you are faking!"

Tori asked her mom if she could let Ron out.

"No," Shelly said flatly. "He's being punished. Leave him alone. He's been very bad. I don't want to go into the details. Just leave him."

A little while later, Tori noticed that Ron had been liberated. It wasn't for long, though. Soon, he was back under the desk, crying.

She was pretty sure by then the tears were real.

CHAPTER
SIXTY-EIGHT

When Pacific County sheriff's deputy Jim Bergstrom attempted to serve a restraining order against Ron, brought forth by his mother, the deputy caught a glimpse of Ron on the porch as he pulled into the Knotek place. It was in the spring of 2003. Ron, a thin, spiderly figure, shot the deputy a startled look and then fled into the field through a narrow opening in the fence.

"Hey, Ron!" Bergstrom called out. "I'm only here to serve papers on you."

After Ron vanished into the woods behind the house, the deputy gave up and knocked on the door. He waited. And waited. He finally left when no one answered, even though he was pretty sure someone was home.

Someone had been.

Fifteen minutes later, dispatch took a call from Shelly Knotek. She was irritated. Agitated. Concerned. She wanted to meet the deputy in front of the Raymond post office to find out what was going on. There, Bergstrom told her about the restraining order and his need to serve Ron.

"He's not living with us now," Shelly said, looking Bergstrom right in the eye. "He's living up in Tacoma."

"I don't appreciate being lied to," Bergstrom shot back. "I saw him at your place. He ran away. I know he was there."

Shelly, as always, had a quick comeback. She was always skilled with the redo.

"He probably ran away because there are warrants out for him. He's sick. I've been taking care of him. He has a heart condition."

She went on to promise that she'd have him call.

Before leaving, Bergstrom asked about Kathy Loreno. He told her Kathy's family was still worried that she'd just disappeared with that trucker boyfriend. He told Shelly that one of Kathy's brothers had tried to find his sister with a private investigator and her mom had run a missing person ad in the paper.

"I haven't heard a word from her in a long time," Shelly said.

No one had.

The encounter with the deputy seemed to rattle Shelly—and it had nothing to do with Ron. It was the idea that there were still questions about Kathy's whereabouts percolating among her family—and law enforcement.

A little while later, Shelly told Sami that she'd run into Kathy's mother, Kaye, at a grocery store.

"She was as sweet as ever," she reported to her middle daughter. "Loved catching up with her."

Sami highly doubted that the encounter had ever occurred. At first, she wrote it off as her mom's obsessive need to lie. Lying was like taking a breath to Shelly. Sami could never grasp why her mother felt compelled to lie when saying nothing at all would be a smarter course.

Then it dawned on her. Her mom's motive about her so-called encounter with Kathy's mom was merely a way to test the waters, an excuse to revisit the Kathy story.

"Do you remember the name of her boyfriend?" she asked.

Sami was tentative. "Rocky?"

It was a pop quiz. A game show. It was a cattle prod to a fake truth.

Shelly snapped at Sami. "Think! Do you remember what kind of job he had?"

Sami stepped up her game.

"Trucker!"

And so it continued. Shelly drilled Sami repeatedly about what Rocky looked like. How in love Kathy had been. How she'd gone off to live a life that she'd always dreamed about.

"If the police come, do you know what to say?"

"Yes, Mom," she said. "I do."

On and on it went—in person and over the phone. Shelly would fire questions and scenarios over at her daughter. Sometimes Dave would get the same treatment. In all cases, it was about making sure that everyone understood the stakes involved.

"Our family will be ruined. Think of Tori! She'll be in foster care!"

Yet all the preparation in the world wouldn't—*couldn't*—have prepared Shelly for what happened next as the heat on the burner went from medium to high.

X

Tori and her mom sat in the car while Shelly sifted through the mail. Bills were almost always ignored as she looked for things that mattered to her—a check from her husband, an offer from some cheesy catalog company for something she didn't really need.

And most certainly couldn't afford.

Shelly opened a letter, and instantly the mood in the car changed. Her face went white and her hands began to shake. Her eyes stayed fixed on a letter. It was addressed by typewriter solely to her, postmarked in Olympia on April 18, 2003.

"The gunshots you heard last night were from Kathy. Like the Lord Jesus Christ, SHE also arose from the dead and is back to revenge you. Ashes to ashes . . ."

Shelly freaked out. They'd all heard a gunshot the previous night when someone shot out a neighbor's security light.

For the next several days, Shelly repeatedly asked Tori if anyone had been coming around asking about Kathy.

"This is important, Tori. Has anyone?"

"No, Mom," she said. "I promise."

"Think!"

"No. No one."

Tori didn't understand her mom's over-the-top concern. Kathy, whom Tori could barely remember, wasn't dead. She had run off with her boyfriend. She was living a happy life. Why would Kathy want to take revenge on her mom for anything? Kathy was her mom's best friend.

Shelly reported the letter to Dave, who had no clue where it would have come from. Neither thought that Nikki would betray the family. Maybe someone from Kathy's family had heard something and wanted to avenge Kathy's death? But if that had been the case, Dave and Shelly agreed that they'd have gone to the police.

As far as they knew, that hadn't happened at all.

Shelly, in full-on frantic mode, called Sami at her teaching job in Seattle, a couple of hours away.

Sami's supervisor pulled her aside.

"Your mom's on the phone."

"I'm in the middle of class."

"Seems important."

Sami had talked about her mother with every manager or supervisor she had. Knowing how her mom could be, she considered it a pre-emptive strike. She knew that, whatever it was, her mom would keep calling until she got her on the phone.

Sami got on the phone.

"Kathy!" Shelly barked. "Has anyone been asking you about Kathy?"

The Pacific County sheriff had tried, but Sami had dodged the authorities.

"No, Mom," she said.

Shelly persisted. "No one?"

"No, Mom. No one. What's happening?"

Shelly told her about the letter.

The letter scared Sami. It meant that someone outside of the Knotek family was onto what her mother and father had done. Someone out there was digging into what had happened and using the threat of an anonymous letter to shake things loose.

"That doesn't make sense," she said, though, deep down, she knew it did. If she'd lost someone and thought that another party knew, she'd find a way to get some justice.

Kathy deserved justice.

She thought of the necklace Kathy had given her on her birthday. She thought of how Kathy always had time for the girls, doing their hair, making them laugh with a story. She could think of a million good things about Kathy.

"I know," her mother said. "I don't know what's going on. Do you? Sami?"

"No. I promise. I have no idea."

Sami hung up. She almost hoped Kathy's family *had* put the letter in the mailbox. Kathy's family, she thought, needed to know what had really happened.

CHAPTER
SIXTY-NINE

Shelly studied the Kathy letter like a forensic examiner. She held it to the light. She rotated it in every direction. She scrutinized the postmark. After all of that, she couldn't come up with a decent guess as to who might have sent it.

Anyone could have. Even Shelly knew she wasn't in line to win any popularity contests in Raymond.

The threat in the anonymous missive didn't make Shelly retreat or try to tone down what she was doing to Ron. Instead, she wandered around the house in her half-open bathrobe carpet-bombing Ron with epithets. No matter how hard Ron tried, he couldn't do anything right.

His failures at pleasing Shelly were legion.

Tori spied on her mother and father in the yard one weekend when her dad came home. Ron had fallen off the roof, where he'd been cleaning shingles, and was lying on the ground, crumpled and battered. Instead of rendering aid, Dave ordered Ron to get up and do it again.

Without a word of protest, Ron gathered himself, climbed back onto the deck banister, and jumped off again. Tori was sure he'd broken a leg.

"I remember going back upstairs and he fell again and then I heard my dad smack him down. It sounded really hard. I heard Ron yell. I'm assuming it was on his face, but I don't know. And why? I don't know why."

Maybe he was moving too slow or was too clumsy, she thought.

It happened once more.

And again.

On a separate occasion, Tori heard her mother telling Ron to be a man and jump. She went to look and could see Ron, wearing only underwear, climb to the rail and hold himself up with the support post. His feet were bloody and he was crying.

This time, Ron, in his quiet, unforceful way, resisted some.

"I don't want to, Shelly Dear," he pleaded.

"Just get it over with," Shelly said. "I don't have all night."

And off he'd go, landing with a thud in the gravel with his bare feet.

"Get up! Do it again! You are a piece of shit and you need to be punished."

Ron somehow managed to get back up to the rail and do it all over again.

How Ron could even walk at all mystified Tori. Every step was a struggle. It wasn't only that his feet had been cut on broken glass buried in a hole in the garden, or that he'd been forced to jump from the roof or porch rail. It was also how her mother attended to his wounds.

Tori watched her mother and sometimes her father in the way another driver slows and rubbernecks at a car crash. She didn't necessarily want to see, yet she couldn't really turn away.

Shelly took a pan of hot water off of the stove, steam rising as she carried it out to the pole building. Tori heard Ron yelp as Shelly and Dave made him plunge his bruised and bloodied feet into a combination of hot water and bleach.

"I remember the smell of it was like the worst smell ever of my life," Tori recalled years later. "It was like the smell of bleach and decomposing flesh, like it was burning his skin off. And it just was terrible. He smelled like he was rotting, literally the smell of dying flesh. He smelled like that for a month. Up until the very end."

Even as he declined, Shelly continued her practice of never letting Ron wear shoes while doing yard work or calisthenics outside. His feet hit the gravel so hard from the new jumping punishment that his soles split open and oozed blood and pus.

She'd get out her bleach bottle and pour the caustic liquid over them and tell him to shut up and stop crying.

"Yes, Shell Dear," he'd say.

Other times she'd boil water on the stove, fill a tub with it, and make him soak.

"One night she made the water too hot, I think," Tori recalled. "And he ended up burning his feet to the point where skin started falling off. That's when my mom started to wrap his feet up with stuff."

The night his skin peeled off was the last time Ron slept in the computer room outside Tori's bedroom on the second floor. The girl, then fourteen, thought it was because he could barely walk up the staircase. After that, he slept mostly in the laundry room, the pole building, or outside on the porch. His feet were bundled and bandaged, and he barely spoke. He certainly never complained.

Years later, when Dave Knotek was told that bleach actually damages human skin, he seemed genuinely surprised. Shelly had used bleach by the gallon on Kathy, Ron, and even the girls. In fact, they never made a trip to the grocery store without replenishing the household's bleach supply. Despite everything he'd witnessed, however, Dave still couldn't comprehend that his wife would do anything that would hurt anyone on purpose.

Shelly probably didn't know that bleach was bad either, he said.

CHAPTER SEVENTY

Like Kathy a decade prior, Ron was not getting any better. He was on the very edge of a black hole with Shelly's foot placed firmly on his back. She acted concerned. She no longer berated him for killing her surrogate father, Mac. She even toned down the name-calling.

Shelly called Dave at his job in the summer of 2003 to say she was worried. She might have been a little panicked too. She tried to make arrangements to drop Ron off at a homeless shelter in Aberdeen. Ron wouldn't hear of it. He flatly refused.

It was like she was stuck with him. She wanted him gone. He'd become more than she could handle.

During the call, Shelly said Ron had attempted suicide by jumping from the limb of one of the alder trees.

"What happened?" Dave asked.

"He said he was trying to kill himself."

"Really?"

"Yeah," she said. "He knows how serious we are about taking him to the shelter."

Dave didn't have much feeling for Ron either way. He was mostly concerned about having him around Tori in his underpants all the time, or how Ron's presence weighed on Shelly.

Shelly laid more groundwork.

"He said he couldn't cope with leaving and wanted to do everyone a favor and end it all," she went on. "Said he was sorry. 'I'm such a burden and my life is such a failure. I'm starting to burden you, Dave, and Tori. I don't know what else to do.'"

Ron had been lying on a bench on the back porch for a couple of days. Shelly had been feeding him whiskey while telling Tori that he was sick, yet making promises that he was going to get better. Tori wanted to believe her mother. *But those feet.* They were so swollen he could barely move them.

"I'm taking him to Mac's tomorrow where he can rest a little," Shelly told her.

"All by himself?"

"He'll be fine. Won't you, Ron?"

Ron was weak and drunk. He managed a slight nod.

"Are you sure, Mom?"

"I'm going to check on him every day. Don't worry."

The next morning, when Tori woke up, she noticed Ron was nowhere to be found.

"Where is he?" she asked her mom.

Shelly looked right at her. "I took him to Mac's this morning."

Tori's window was over the driveway—a gravel driveway that didn't allow for anyone to sneak in or out without making a distinctive and loud crunching noise.

"Oh," Tori said, knowing a lie when she heard one. "I didn't hear you leave."

✗

Ron had been gone for a few days, and Tori and her mother were sitting on the sofa in front of the TV.

"You can't tell anyone about Ron," Shelly said.

Seriously, Mom?

Tori didn't have a clue what part she couldn't tell. The list had to be a hundred pages long.

"What?"

Shelly gave Tori a stern, almost threatening look.

"If you tell anyone, especially Sami, I'll disown you. I swear I will. I'll shun you for the rest of your life."

That was a threat.

The room became very quiet.

"I wouldn't say anything," Tori said. She didn't ask her mother why she had singled out Sami. Sami never spoke ill of their mother at all. At least not to Tori. Sure, she said that their mom was weird, but whose mom wasn't a little weird to a teenager?

"Tori," Shelly said, "if the cops come around, I need you to tell them that Ron left and is living in Tacoma."

Tori swallowed hard. It was a lie. A big one.

"Okay, Mom," she said. "That's what I'll say."

Once that was settled—as big a fib as it clearly was—Tori noticed a change in her mother's personality. Shelly became kinder toward her. She was back to being her mother's Turtle Dovey. She made nice meals for the next few days. She didn't force Tori to strip and reveal how her body was changing.

Yet whenever Tori asked about Ron, she'd be dismissed.

"He's fine," Shelly would say.

Tori pushed a little. "I want to see him."

"He's resting. He needs rest, Tori."

"Okay, but I miss him."

"He's fine," Shelly insisted. "I see him every day. Sometimes twice a day. I've been going over there every morning at seven to take him food and check on him."

Tori could have started her own list of her mother's lies right then. Ron wasn't going anywhere. He was stuck at Mac's. As for her mother taking care of him? That was another lie.

"I never once heard her start the car and leave in the morning," Tori later said. "I would have heard her. Besides that, she'd never get up that early for anything or anyone. My mom slept in because she'd been up all night."

Tori asked about Ron every day.

"Why do you keep asking about Ron?" her mother asked.

"I like Uncle Ron."

"Well, he's fine and you need to stop asking all the time."

Tori persisted.

"I want to see Uncle Ron."

"Okay," Shelly finally said. "Fine. But I'm too busy. He's too busy. Maybe in a day or two."

And then the good times, the meals, the I-love-yous ended.

Shelly enlisted Tori in doing the chores while Ron was gone. Weeding, feeding the animals, organizing the kitchen—whatever he had done, Tori was told to take care of it. *All of it.* All to her mother's peculiar satisfaction too.

"I wish Ron was here," Shelly told Tori. "He's so much better at doing the chores than you are."

When Tori didn't clean the dog kennel to her mother's satisfaction, Shelly told her to crawl inside, then she locked the door.

"That'll teach you! How does it feel to be treated like your precious puppy? You stupid asshole! You think a dog likes lying in his shit? How do you like it? Shit! Shit! You are so fucking lazy, Tori!"

Tori stared at her mom through the wire bars of the kennel. It crept into her thoughts that maybe she deserved this. Maybe she hadn't done a good enough job? Her mom was always so sure.

"I'm sorry, Mom!"

Shelly turned on the hose and sprayed her until Tori was soaked to the skin in cold water mixed with dog feces.

"So fucking useless!"

CHAPTER
SEVENTY-ONE

It was about time. Sami had been surprised and pleased when Shelly had called out of the blue to say she'd finally decided to allow her little sister, Tori, to come up to Seattle and spend a few days with her. It was the first time ever.

The three met for dinner at the Olive Garden in Olympia, a good halfway meet-up spot. Right away, Sami noticed something was terribly wrong with her mother's right hand. It was badly swollen. Her thumb was more than twice its normal size and looked as if it might even be out of joint.

"You need to go to the hospital," Sami said.

Shelly appeared to shrug it off. "Seriously, Sami. I'm fine."

She wasn't. Throughout the meal, Shelly was short with the staff. She was on edge. She didn't look well either. Shelly had always prided herself on her looks, but she'd gained weight and her hair was a mess. It seemed she'd lost some teeth too.

"She looked crazy," Sami recalled. "She was agitated, all over the place. Something was going on."

On the drive back to Seattle, Sami had two surprises for her little sister.

"Tonight, you're going to try sushi for the first time. I'm taking you to Bento's in Greenwood."

Tori made a face. "I'm not sure about that," she said.

Sami gave her a smile. "You'll love it."

"What's the other surprise?"

"We're going to see Nikki tomorrow."

All of a sudden, Tori was panic-stricken. She was not only terrified of seeing her sister for the first time in seven years, but she didn't want to carry the burden of defying their mother. Her mother had spent years telling her what an evil person Nikki was, how she was selfish and cared about no one. That she was the worst sister ever.

"No. I don't want to see her."

"She loves you," Sami said. "You know that, right?"

Tori really didn't. "I guess," she said. "But I don't want to tell Mom."

Sami gave her a reassuring smile. "You're going to see her no matter what you say."

The sushi was a middling success. Tori managed a California roll just fine, but nothing else. Inside, she was in turmoil. She could barely sleep that night, she was so nervous about seeing Nikki again. *What if Nikki didn't like her?* Nikki had been such a huge influence in Tori's life—taking care of her, playing with her. And then poof! She was suddenly gone, and made out to be a terrible person by their mother. Tori had had no idea that Sami and Nikki had stayed in contact over the years.

But the prospect of seeing Nikki was only part of what kept Tori up that night. She also worried about what was happening with Ron back home. She'd pondered that throughout the meal at the Olive Garden, listening to their mother lie to Sami about him moving to Winlock or Winthrop or Tacoma. She knew that he was too weak to go anywhere. He probably needed to be in a hospital.

Maybe, she hoped, her mom would take him to one.

⋊⋉

When the three Knotek sisters gathered at Duke's Seafood & Chowder House on Seattle's Lake Union the next day, it was, for Tori, like encountering the most amazing woman she'd ever seen. Her sister Nikki was twenty-eight, all grown up. So beautiful. Poised. She even smelled wonderful.

Seeing her big sister for the first time in years, Tori would later say, was the biggest deal of her life. Even after she'd been bombarded by the lies that her mother flung to keep the estrangement intact, Tori knew right in that instant that she had missed Nikki with all her heart.

"You are so beautiful," Tori told her.

"So are you."

Sami pulled the sisters together. She was the middle girl, the one who had lived on both sides of the divide.

No one talked about how terrible their mother was during the meal. Or how misguided their father had been. They all just reveled in this moment of reconnection and reunion.

"Remember, Tori," Sami said. "We don't have to tell Mom. This lunch with Nikki can be just between us. Understand?"

Tori agreed, though she knew that was easier said than done. Their mother had a knack for digging into all corners of their lives to find things they'd prefer to keep private. With Shelly Knotek, there were no secrets.

Except her own.

CHAPTER
SEVENTY-TWO

It was after two in the morning on July 22, 2003, when Dave's phone rang and woke him up at the jobsite on Whidbey Island. He'd been sound asleep, and it was hard to make sense of the call. It was Shelly, of course. Not normal Shelly. Not demanding Shelly. This Shelly spoke in a halting, weary voice.

"You need to come home," she said, her voice rising a little. She was speaking quietly.

"What's going on?" Dave asked, suddenly very much awake.

His wife danced around the subject.

"It's not good," she said. "We got something going on here. It's about Ron."

Dave didn't ask his wife of fifteen years for any specifics just then. They'd been together long enough for him to know that no one asked Shelly for more than she was willing to reveal. She told him that Tori was going to spend time with Sami in Seattle, and that she needed Dave in Raymond as soon as he could get there.

Dave had been home the previous Sunday, and he'd seen Ron recovering from what he and Shelly had insisted had been a fall from a tree. His finger might have been broken in the fall, as well. Dave also recalled that Ron's feet were bandaged, and there were burns on his head and chest from an accident Shelly said he'd had when burning brush in the yard. There were bruises too. Lots of them. Again, all purportedly from some accident.

At Shelly's urging, Dave had again told Ron that he needed to move out, but the man had refused to vacate Monohon Landing. One time Dave offered him cash, $270, to leave town, but Ron was steadfast in his refusal. He didn't want to leave Shelly.

"You need to get the hell out of here, Ron," Dave said, raising his voice to make a point.

Ron had refused to go. His only comeback was that he'd hurt or kill himself if he had to leave.

Dave was in hot water with his boss for one thing or another and didn't dare ask to leave the job to get back down to Raymond.

"I can't make it home until Friday," he told Shelly. Friday was a long way away.

Despite Shelly seeming nervous and upset, she didn't balk at the delay.

"She never told me he was dead," Dave said later of his wife's early-morning call. She didn't have to. "I knew it. I knew why too."

His gut reaction was correct.

Ron was indeed dead.

Shelly claimed to have found him dead on the back porch. She noted that there had been a heat wave and he'd taken to sitting out there to let the fresh air circulate over his wounds. She told her husband that she worried someone might blame her for all those wounds—all the burn marks, cuts, and bruises across Ron's body.

Shelly insisted she'd tried to revive Ron before realizing he was gone. Once she accepted that he was dead, however, Shelly had dragged Ron's corpse to the pole building and shut the door. There, she dressed him in clean sweatpants—clothing that she'd refused to let him wear when he was alive—and put the body into a couple of sleeping bags.

Next, she removed all the camping gear from the top of the freezer, opened the lid, and put the body inside. She returned the camping gear to the top of the freezer, arranging it so that no one—especially Tori—would know that any of the gear had been moved. Shelly considered every detail.

After all of that was done, she made the call to Dave.

CHAPTER
SEVENTY-THREE

When Dave came home at the end of the workweek, Shelly told him that Ron's body was wrapped in sleeping bags hidden inside the freezer in the pole building. Dave felt like a zombie. The idea that this was happening again was more than he could bear. He'd seen it all coming. He knew that there could be no good end for Ron as long as he stayed around Monohon Landing. He was a troublemaker, just like Shelly had said. Troublemakers, well, make trouble.

Goddamn it, Ron!

How could you do this to Shelly?

Dave struggled as he pulled Ron's body from the freezer.

How could Shell have managed to put him in there?

She's superhuman!

Dave never looked at the remains. He didn't want to. Instead, he silently went about the business of doing what he'd done before. His wife's bewildering physical strength again came to Dave's mind when he tussled with Ron's body and tried to slide it into a couple of black plastic contractor bags he'd taken from the jobsite on Whidbey Island. Dave shook while the bags kept slipping as he tried to get them around Ron.

Getting rid of a body did not get easier as he got more practiced at it.

He stood there in the pole building among the bric-a-brac of his life with Shelly and the girls—the old clothes, the toys they'd outgrown, the camping gear from the times when they'd done things as a family. Next to the freezer, Shelly had stacked Ron's belongings, a tableau of his life and interests: His books on Egyptology. His glasses. The jewelry he'd proudly showed off in the days before he'd been stripped of who he was. The clothes he'd ceased to wear, because Shelly had dictated how he dressed. All piled up and ready for a quick removal.

"I tried to save him," Shelly insisted as she lurked nearby, wringing her hands. "I did CPR, but it didn't work. He was too weak. Oh God! I tried so hard. I'm so scared, Dave."

He was too.

"They're going to think we did some kind of abuse on Ron," she said. "The police will point fingers at us."

Dave knew she was right. *And why wouldn't they? How had they let this happen in the first place?*

He told Shelly he could handle it on his own and she should go inside and get herself together. He carried Ron's body through the back gate, fighting every step of the way to hang on to the slippery bags.

There was a single hitch, and it was a big one. Pacific County was in the midst of a burn ban due to hot, dry summer weather. Dave couldn't cremate Ron, as he'd done with Kathy. He couldn't dispose of the ashes at Washaway Beach. On the other hand, a cremation wouldn't have been practical, burn ban or not. The barn that had once blocked the view of the yard was gone, and a streetlamp had been put nearby, casting light over the scene. Someone could see a fire and report it to the authorities.

Dave retrieved a number-two shovel with a spade edge and a blue plastic tarp from the pole building, and like the construction worker he was, he planned out a burial pit. It would need to be three or four feet deep, with enough space to lay the body flat. He wanted to go deeper, but the earth wasn't forgiving. It was near hardpan. The dirt went onto the tarp so that the grave wouldn't be detected. Dave had a plan to make it look like it had always been there.

Dave placed Ron's body on his side and shoveled the dirt over the body. When he was satisfied, he put ash from the firepit over the fresh soil. Next, he put a layer of fir branches on top.

Shelly stayed away while her husband went about the task at hand. She never wanted to be part of the dirty work.

He stood back in the dark, removed his work gloves, and studied what he'd done. It looked good, but it was only temporary. He'd need a more permanent solution. That would have to wait until the burn ban was lifted. He took the tarp to Mac's house in South Bend and stashed it there.

As usual, even after everything unraveled, Dave defended Shelly and put no blame on her.

"I love her dearly," he said. "There's no way she caused any abuse on Ron or Kathy. She just didn't call when Ron passed on. It was just out of fear of what happened in the past. And like I say, my wife worries about everything and she was just looking after her family again. She's just being the protector that she always is. I don't see where she had done anything wrong at all."

CHAPTER
SEVENTY-FOUR

Back in Seattle, Sami and Tori were coming down off the high of their reunion with Nikki. It had been the best day ever. Tori had alternately missed and feared Nikki over the years, but at that moment, she could see her mother's manipulations for what they were. It shouldn't have surprised her, but it did.

Shelly wanted to control people. She loathed any scenario in which she wasn't the center square. It was like their family was a cult of some kind: Nikki had escaped first, then Sami. The world outside of Raymond was a more beautiful—and happy—place than Tori had ever thought possible. She was Dorothy from Kansas, transported to the colorful world over the rainbow. It was obvious who their mom had been in that scenario.

Her mom. The thought of Shelly snapped Tori back to her biggest fear. She obsessed that she wouldn't be able to keep the reunion a secret.

"Yes, you can," Sami insisted. "I have. You can."

"I don't know," Tori said.

Sami remained upbeat, encouraging. "I do. Because I know you."

Sami retrieved some laundry from the dryer, and the two of them sat down and started folding.

"Funny story," Sami went on. "I remember when Mom used to wake me up in the middle of the night and dump out all my drawers, I mean everything, out on to the floor. She wanted me to make sure everything was matched and if I had a sock that wasn't, look out. I had to look for it all night. Like until three in the morning."

Tori sat there quiet for a minute.

"Mom does that to me," she finally said, looking up and meeting her sister's gaze.

Sami felt her heart race. *No,* she thought. *Fuck. No. No. This can't be. Not Tori.*

"I had asked her every time I saw her if she was okay," Sami said later. "It was my job to protect that girl. But I failed. I did. I didn't ask the right questions. I didn't tell her what I knew. I just asked if she was okay. If Mom was okay."

"What else does Mom do to you, Tori?"

Tori looked at Sami, who was crumbling in front of her eyes, and gave her a truncated list of the things their mother had done to her. It was a kind of bingo of Shelly's standard punishments—the same things she'd done to all of them—to Shane, Kathy, Nikki, and herself.

"Does she let you go to sleep?" Sami asked.

"No."

"Does she make you do things naked?"

"Yeah."

"Lock you out all night?"

"Yeah."

"On the front porch?"

"Right."

Sami was crying by then. She put her arms around her sister.

"Why didn't you tell me, Tori?"

"I don't know. I thought it was just me, I guess. I didn't know Mom did any of that before. I thought you and Nikki had a happy childhood."

Sami knew where she had to go next. This was her chance, an opening to ask for a dose of reality from her little sister. "Did she do anything to Ron?" she asked.

Tori started to cry. She could see that her sister's question wasn't really a question at all. It was a statement.

A truth.

Tori gulped some air. "Yes," she said. "All of it. And other stuff too." She took in her sister's reaction. She wasn't shocked. She took it like it was meant to be, a confirmation of what she likely already knew.

"How did you know about this?" Tori asked.

Sami swallowed hard. "She did it before. She did it to all of us. She did it to Kathy."

Kathy had never left Sami's mind. She could play back every image she'd ever collected in her brain growing up at the Louderback House or the farmhouse at Monohon Landing—the good and the ugly. Lately things had become clearer. It might have been the letter sent by whomever it was. It might have been the guilt she felt for not backing up her older sister when Nikki went to the police. Though she would have, Sami told herself, if the sheriff had tried harder. She would have braced for her world to come crashing down if she'd thought for one second that Tori was being abused.

Tori had seemed okay. And the police hadn't followed through.

So she didn't tell.

Sami delved deeper. "Did Ron ever try to run away?"

Tori nodded. "Yeah, lots of times. But Mom and me always found him and brought him back."

"Kathy did too," Sami said.

"Did Mom make Kathy do weird stuff? Chores?" Tori asked.

"Yeah," Sami said. "She had to do the dishes naked."

Tori retrieved an early memory of Kathy from the house in Old Willapa. Tori had been around two years old. Kathy was in the bathroom on the main floor. She wore a thin lime-green nightgown. Her hair was falling out and she moved very slowly.

"What's wrong?" Tori had asked Kathy, but before she could answer, her mother hooked an arm around her daughter and yanked her away. Shelly didn't say anything, but after that, Tori knew that she wasn't supposed to ask those kinds of questions. It wasn't her place to talk to Kathy. Not like that.

Now Sami and Tori held each other and cried. They held nothing back.

Except maybe one thing.

Sami could barely speak. Inside, she knew she had to say the words to her little sister.

"Mom killed Kathy," Sami choked out. "They burned her in the yard."

CHAPTER
SEVENTY-FIVE

Shelly stood in front of the kitchen sink, falling apart. She'd never looked worse. She'd gained more than twenty pounds over the past year. Her red hair needed a Clairol refresh. That was on the surface, of course. Inside, the combination of the anonymous letter and Ron's demise had crushed her bravado, the self-assuredness that typically gave her the confidence to do the unthinkable without batting an eye.

Dave was the first to broach the need to come up with something to explain Ron's sudden departure from Monohon Landing. Coming up with cover stories was well-trod territory for the Knoteks. Kathy was off with Boyfriend Rocky touring the country. Shane was in Alaska, fishing off Kodiak Island. Nikki had left Raymond to pursue a new life in Seattle. They hadn't merely vanished; they'd gone somewhere they'd always wanted to go.

No one seemed all that interested in Ron, though. That was good. It would work in the Knoteks' favor.

Dave, who had always been passive in their marriage, could see that Shelly was flailing. He came up with the initial plan. Inside, he was a wreck too, but they both couldn't be undone by emotions. One of them had to pull it together.

"He was staying at Mac's for the last couple of weeks," he suggested. "He was looking for a job."

"Right," Shelly, said, almost by rote. "We gave him some money for bus fare."

Dave took a breath. He was not a master of fiction, even though living with Shelly meant learning to lie.

"I gave him a ride to Olympia to catch the bus," he went on. "He decided to go to San Diego."

Shelly brightened a little. "Right. He was talking about that." The idea seemed plausible enough to calm her a little. She worried about what Tori would think, but convinced herself that her daughter believed everything she said.

"I'll tell her when she gets home from Sami's," Shelly said.

Dave thought that was best.

That night they practiced the story over and over, backward, forward, adjusting a little when tiny cracks in logic worked their way into the conversation. Ron needed money. He needed some food. New clothes. Everything that had eluded him at Monohon Landing was woven into the story line.

And yet there was room for doubt. The slightest error, the tiniest blip in the story, could be their undoing.

As a backup scenario, Shelly played out the concept that Ron had been suicidal over Gary again. She told Dave that when she was bandaging his feet in the bathroom shortly before he died, Ron had a full view of the open medicine cabinet.

She'd also made a discovery in one of the outbuildings, she said.

"I found these in the chicken house." She held out a pair of amber-colored pill bottles. "Ron must have taken these."

Dave didn't look closely at the bottles. He didn't need to. What Shelly was saying made sense. Ron had been distraught. He had, in fact, threatened suicide several times. Dave thought back to the time Ron received the restraining order from his mother and how that had crushed him. He'd threatened suicide over that too. There was another time when he told Dave that he'd wished he'd just die so that everyone could be better off.

"That's how I feel," Ron had said.

CHAPTER
SEVENTY-SIX

This isn't happening. Not again. The realization that Shelly was doing to Tori what she'd done to the older Knotek sisters was devastating to Sami. She and Tori talked into the early-morning hours. It was a horrific matching game—what had happened before, and what was going on now. Tears and rage fueled the conversation. Regret too.

And fear. Lots of fear.

There was the question that Sami dreaded above all others. She'd been thinking about Ron and how he was supposedly off getting a new job somewhere, even though the last time she'd seen him he didn't look like he could do any work of any kind.

"How's Ron?" she asked.

Tori didn't need to answer with words. The look on her face told Sami what she needed to know.

"I think he's dead," she said. "I think Mom did something to him too."

That brought more tears and a wave of emotion fell over Sami too. She thought back to her mother's recent calls. She'd been in touch more frequently the past couple of weeks. Shelly had told her during one conversation that Ron was looking for work out of the area.

"Up in Winlock," Shelly said. "At a trailer park. We really need him to get this job. I need you to pray for it. Pray that he gets it."

Something about her mother's story hadn't seemed right. Whenever Sami talked with her little sister, Tori said Shelly told her that Ron was staying over at Mac's place, helping to get it ready for sale.

"It's time for him to get out on his own," Shelly said.

"I guess so," Sami had agreed, not knowing what else to say. The last time she saw him, Ron had been a mess. There was no way he could go out on his own anywhere and survive.

She kicked herself for not doing more. She'd seen the problems with Ron. She knew the warning signs. Yet in order to survive, she'd swum in a sea of denial. No life preserver. Just Sami bobbing along until a wave would suck her downward.

And drown her.

Sami pulled herself together. It was after two in the morning.

"We need to tell Nikki," she said.

Ж

No one expects good news from a call at that hour. A car accident. A heart attack. Some kind of tragedy that can't wait until morning.

Nikki took the call.

It was worse than anything she could have imagined.

Sami told her about the abuse that had been going on. All that she'd missed. How Tori was locked in a dog kennel and sprayed with a hose. The nudity. The withholding of food. And Ron Woodworth.

"She did the same thing to Kathy, Nikki."

"I don't know what we should do," Nikki said. She was in a completely different world than she'd been when she went to Raymond and made the first complaint about their mother, almost exactly two years earlier in July 2001. She was happy. She had a man in her life that she loved. She didn't want to rock the boat by revisiting what her mother had done.

"We have to get Tori out of there," Sami said.

Nikki knew Sami was right, though getting the police involved hadn't made a difference before. And Nikki wouldn't put anything past her mother or father when it came to what they might do in revenge. Her mom had tortured a woman to death and lied about it. She'd made Nikki complicit in her scheme to fool Kathy's family into thinking she was off touring the country with Rocky. She'd forced her to wallow in the mud nude. Dave Knotek wasn't any better. He'd tossed a brick through a window to get her fired from a job. He'd tailed her up in Bellingham. Dave was Himmler to her mother's Hitler, blindly doing whatever evil bidding she'd demanded.

"It didn't work last time," Nikki said.

Sami knew that was true. She also knew that there would be hell to pay for turning in their parents. They'd all go down in flames one way or another. People might wonder why they hadn't gone to the police sooner. They'd wonder how they could have looked the other way.

Sami took a breath. "Maybe Tori can manage to get through this, you know, like we did."

Nikki wasn't sure, though given all likely outcomes, she let herself believe that was the best course. The sisters worked to convince themselves that it would be okay.

"She's fourteen," Sami went on. "She only has a few more years."

"I know. She can do this."

"She can."

"But if she can't, Nikki . . . If she can't do this, we need to get her out of there," Sami said.

Nikki agreed, and eventually brought up the subject of Shane.

Sami had accepted the story that Shane had run away, though they'd barely looked for him.

"Mom did something to Shane, Sami," Nikki insisted.

When it came to Shane's absence, the two oldest Knotek girls had only ever talked about it in whispers. They kept going back to the birdhouse their mother insisted he left for her along with a sweet little note.

Nikki had always been the most skeptical. "Shane would never have left her that note with the birdhouse," Nikki said. "He hated her guts."

"Okay, Nikki," Sami reasoned, "but Mom wouldn't really hurt us. Shane was our brother."

)(

When Sami hung up her phone, she went back to Tori.

"We need to figure out what's best," she said. "Do you think you can give us some time, maybe wait this out? You'll be eighteen in four years."

Tori said she wanted to do what was best for everyone, but she was filled with righteous anger. More than anything, she wanted her mom to pay for what she'd done to all of them.

"She needs to be stopped," she said. "You know that, Sami. She's evil. She's probably the worst person in the world. Look at what she's done. Look at the things she did to Kathy and to Ron and to you and Nikki."

As her sister talked, Sami replayed her mother's greatest hits over and over in her mind. She could see everything that had happened with perfect clarity. There was no arguing that their mom probably was the worst person in the world.

But she's our mom. The only mom we'll ever have.

Sami went silent, and Tori filled the quiet of the space between them.

"I can't do this anymore, Sami."

Sami held her sister. She was desperate. She knew that everyone's life would go up in flames if the truth came out. Even so, she'd found a way to navigate her mother's treachery.

She hoped Tori could too.

⋈

There were more tears on the drive down to Olympia to meet up with Shelly in the Olive Garden parking lot. The visit that was supposed to be the highlight of the summer had turned into a nightmare with the realization that what had been done to Kathy Loreno had also been done to Ron.

Before they parked next to their mother's waiting car, Sami told her sister one last thing.

"If she says Ron is gone, then that means he's probably dead."

Sami had been crying. Her eyes were red, and it was obvious that their mother noticed it.

"Everything okay?" Shelly asked.

Always quick with a joke or a way to deflect, Sami answered right away. "Yeah," she said. "Just so hard to say goodbye to my little sister."

The sisters hugged and cried together while Shelly watched from the driver's side of her car. It was a long, painful goodbye. Finally, they detached, and Tori got into the car.

Shelly started the car. "What was that all about, Tori?" she asked as she put it in gear for the drive back to Raymond.

"Just a great weekend. Going to miss her."

Shelly probed a little and Tori told her she didn't feel well.

"I have a bad headache, Mom." She leaned her head against the glass of the passenger window and closed her eyes, pretending to fall asleep.

I don't want to talk to you, she thought.

When they pulled up into the driveway at Monohon Landing, it felt like a foreign land. Tori had only been gone a few days, yet in her mind, this already wasn't her home anymore. It wasn't a place she even understood. Everything looked and felt weird.

"Ron got a job," her mom said.

Tori knew it was a lie.

Ron's dead.

While her mother had been mostly quiet on the drive, she let a harshness creep into her voice when she told Tori to feed the dogs. Her tone was the opposite of her sisters'.

It was cold.

Mean.

Cross.

Tori went and did what she'd been told to do. Inside, she felt sick and scared. Her world was turned upside down. But she wasn't alone. She had her two sisters. They loved her, and they knew what kind of a monster their mother truly was. That, more than anything, emboldened her. It made her want to go to the authorities and tell them everything.

Yet Sami had urged her to wait. Tori understood where Sami was coming from. She also knew that if there was a price to pay, *she* would be the one stuck with the bill. It wasn't the punishments that frightened her. She'd survived just fine up to that point. What worried her was the idea that the reunion with her big sister would be only a one-time thing.

"I knew that if I didn't say anything," she said later, "I might not get to see Nikki anymore."

That wasn't acceptable to Tori. Not at all. She wasn't going to lose her big sister a second time.

Going to the police wasn't only about making her mother pay. It wasn't even vengeance. It was her way of stopping all the madness so she could be with her sisters again.

Shelly studied her daughter, her eyes scanning Tori from top to bottom. It wasn't a gaze of interest or the look of love for a daughter who had been missed around the house for a few days. Shelly had the eyes of an apex predator. She had a way of sizing people up.

"Is everything all right?" she asked.

"Everything's fine, Mom."

"You're lying."

"No. I'm not."

"Come here, I want to hug you."

"I don't feel good," Tori said. "I feel kind of sick. I'm getting a runny nose."

Shelly gave her a cool look. "Oh? I can help. I have something for that."

She disappeared and returned with a couple of tablets.

"Take these."

⋈

Sami became frantic when Tori called her later that night and told her their mother had tried to give her a couple of pills, but Tori had only taken one.

"What? What did she offer you?"

"Some pills."

"What kind of pills?"

"Yellow ones. For my nose."

Sami grew desperate, remembering the time her mother had given her some pills and she couldn't even walk. Or all the times she'd fed pills to Kathy, leaving her in a stupor for hours. Her mom was always passing out medication and telling the recipients it would make them feel better when it only served to make them compliant. Or get them out of the way so she could watch TV or sit around unencumbered by having to address the needs of anyone else in the house.

"You need to throw it up, Tori. Right now."

Tori balked a little. "Mom wouldn't hurt me," she said.

Sami drew a breath. After all they'd talked about, after every detail Sami knew to be true, she probably had the better grasp of what Shelly could, would, and had done. Nikki had confided in Sami that she thought at one time her parents had plotted to kill her, that she thought they were going to make her disappear after Shane vanished, because they didn't trust that she'd stay silent forever.

No one could.

"You don't know her, Tori. You need to get that out of you right now!"

Her sister's urgency was a jolt.

"Okay," Tori said. "How?"

"Try to make yourself throw it up!"

Tori said she would, although deep down she knew she couldn't. She was afraid that if she threw up, her mom would find out and be angry with her. Maybe hurt her. She sat there in her room for a minute. She felt groggy. Whatever her mom had given her made her feel strange. She went out in the yard and poked around, all while thinking her mother was onto her.

She called her sister a second time that night.

"Get me out of here," she said. "I can't find Ron. He's dead, Sami. I know it."

"Are you sure?"

"Yes. Please."

Sami pushed Tori to try a little harder. She didn't want to go to the police. She'd seen how it went down when Nikki told them about Kathy. It was a losing proposition.

"Are you positive you can't just do this for a couple more years?"

The request was ludicrous, and they both knew it.

"No, I fucking can't, Sami. Mom's a killer. She'll know. She'll probably kill me too. You know what she's capable of, Sami."

"Okay," Sami said. "We'll get you out."

"I need out now," Tori said. "This has to stop."

CHAPTER
SEVENTY-SEVEN

The next morning, while her mom tucked herself in front of the TV, Tori went into the pole building, continuing her quest to find any sign of Ron. It didn't take long. A heap of his personal effects, including his underwear, sat on top of the freezer, as did some bloody bandages that had been wrapped around Ron's feet after soaking the feet in boiling bleach water. The bloodstains were old, brownish, but Tori knew that's what they were.

Holy shit, she thought. *Why is all this here?*

She stood still a minute, trying to sear what she was seeing into her brain. She wanted to catalog every single item in case her mom came to get rid of it all. Without knowing her own plans, Tori took some of the bloody items and hid them in the chicken coop.

Next, she searched the house for anything else that had belonged to Ron. He didn't have much by then—a few books and less than a drawer of clothes—but everything was gone. She looked for a pair of jeans that had become too loose and were stashed away in one of her older sister's dresser drawers. That, too, was gone.

She made her way to the firepit. Her parents had been acting strangely, and her mother's admonishments to stay away from there were more than a warning. Even having heard the story from Sami, it was hard to even think about what had happened to Kathy when Tori was a little girl.

Tori needed more evidence. Something the police might be able to use to determine that Ron had been killed and disposed of somehow.

Maybe in the same way her sisters said Kathy had been.

Quickly and quietly, she leaned over and picked at the branches she'd suspected her father had placed over the burn pile. The earth had been smoothed over.

They've already cleaned everything, she thought. *They know that someone will come.*

Finally, her heart pounding harder than it ever had, Tori scooped up some dirt with ash and hurried back to the chicken house. She assumed that Ron had been disposed of in the same way her sisters said Kathy had. Her hands were shaking but she wasn't crying. Tori knew that what she was doing had to be done.

Her mom had to be stopped.

When she went back inside, it was as if nothing had happened. Her mom was sitting there. Doing her thing, which amounted to very little at all. Tori went upstairs.

Shelly went about her business. She wrote out a change of address card for Ron's Lowe's credit card account, putting Monohon Landing as his old address. She didn't have a new street address for him; however, she'd apparently settled on a city for Ron. Not Winlock, Winthrop, or any other place that far away.

She put down Tacoma.

CHAPTER
SEVENTY-EIGHT

Raymond was a million miles away. At least it sometimes felt that way. Nikki didn't like looking back. She was married. She was going to build a family despite what her mother and father had done to her. How do you explain wallowing in the mud to anyone? Or the cruelty that her mother had inflicted upon Kathy?

Or Shane.

What about him?

On August 6, 2003, Nikki and Sami drove down to Pacific County to tell the sheriff what they knew to be true. They were as scared and nervous as they'd ever been in their lives. The drive was punctuated by what-ifs and then long stretches of anguished silence. Tears too. What was happening was big. Bigger than them. Big because it was overdue and, the sisters knew, likely too late to save Ron. It was Nikki's second time sitting down with Deputy Jim Bergstrom. The first time had been an epic failure. Nothing had come of it at all. *Why hadn't anyone helped?* It couldn't be laid solely at the feet of Sami for not talking to the sheriff. In fact, Bergstrom and another deputy had been at Monohon Landing to inquire about Ron. They knew he was holed up there and that Shelly Knotek's history was less than stellar.

Around town, people called her Psycho Shelly.

They also knew Kathy Loreno had last been seen alive in Shelly's company. And that Ron had been the one to call 911 when Mac had supposedly fallen from his wheelchair, leaving Shelly the ultimate recipient of the World War II vet's estate.

With tears and long pauses to work up the courage for what they needed to say, the Knotek sisters gave their story—the same one Nikki had told before. This time was different. This time, they were believed. Others from the prosecutor's office and law enforcement came in and out of the interview room at the Pacific County Sheriff's Office. Deputy Bergstrom and members of the prosecutor's staff recorded everything they said. It was at once shocking and painful. Nikki and Sami saw the outcome as twofold: a rescue operation for their little sister, and accountability for their parents for everything they'd done.

"If Ron's dead," Nikki told the deputy, her voice breaking as she looked him squarely in the eye, "you could have stopped it."

Bergstrom didn't reply, which was fine by Nikki; there probably wasn't anything he could have said that would have made any difference anyway.

After disclosing nearly every appalling detail, they got back in Nikki's car for the drive home to the Seattle area. It was pitch dark and the moon hung high in the sky. They were emotionally beaten. Sad and angry at the same time. And scared. But mostly they thought about their little sister and how her world was going to be rocked when Child Protective Services arrived the next morning to get her.

"She's going to be okay," Nikki said.

Sami agreed. "She's stronger than we were."

Nikki tossed and turned all night, unable to shake any of it from her mind. When she crawled out of bed, she called the one ally that she'd always had growing up, her grandmother, Lara. When she couldn't get her on the phone, she e-mailed her.

"You need to call me. I was in Raymond until 1 a.m. last night. CPS is taking Tori out of the house this a.m. at 8:00. Mother and Dave did something very bad AGAIN! I was with Pacific County prosecutor and Sami came with me too."

※

Tori phoned Nikki a couple of times wondering what was happening with the police.

"What am I supposed to do?"

"Just hang on, Tori."

"How long? I can't stay here."

"We're getting you out. I promise."

Later that same day, Shelly called to discuss Sami's upcoming birthday plans.

"Dad's taking you surfing!" she said.

"I'm so excited," Sami said, straining to keep her voice from betraying what she'd done. Despite everything, it was hard for Sami not to warn her mother. *"Pack your shit and run. You need to get out of there, Mom! They are coming to get you!"*

She didn't, of course. She'd never been more frightened in her life. There was no stopping what was about to happen now.

※

Tori was only fourteen, but she was strong. While she waited all night and the next day for her parents to get arrested, she called Sami again and again.

"They haven't done anything," she said of the sheriff. "Mom's still home. I'm still here. What's taking so long?"

Sami wasn't sure. She thought once they'd come forward, things would move quickly. They all thought that. She was worried too.

"I know they are working the case," she told Tori.

"You keep saying that," Tori said, "but I don't know."

Sami did her best to calm her little sister. She could see that, while Tori's edges were fraying, she remained clear and with a sense of purpose.

"I hid Ron's clothes in the chicken coop," Tori told her.

"Good. That's good."

Tori also prepared for the authorities to comb through the house for evidence. She wrote a note on white-and-pink-lined paper with a cheerful bumblebee flying across the top.

> *Dear FBI, police, etc.*
> *Please don't ruin all of my things when you're investigating. Nothing of interest is here anyways. Please leave all of my personal belongings alone. Please find the animals good homes.*

CHAPTER
SEVENTY-NINE

When the knock came the next morning, Tori stood by the front door. She didn't open it right away. She didn't want her mother to know how glad she was that the sheriff had finally arrived. As she watched him approach, the fourteen-year-old recognized Deputy Jim Bergstrom as the man who'd come by the house on an earlier occasion asking about Ron.

When Shelly joined her, she leaned into her daughter and whispered, "What did you do? Did you say anything?"

Tori looked right at her mother. She didn't flinch. She didn't bat an eye.

"No, Mom. No."

The deputy told Shelly that he—and caseworkers for CPS—were there for Tori. They were taking her in on suspected child abuse. Shelly immediately went into outraged overdrive. Tori could tell that her mom was scared too. She didn't say much, just repeated that she didn't understand what was going on.

Bergstrom followed Tori upstairs where she collected a change of clothes and some personal items. Her face was white, and a slight pinkish rash appeared by her ear and down her neck. It was a familiar marker. Even when she couldn't say how scared or worried she was, her body showed how she felt.

Tori whispered in the deputy's ear.

"You need to get a search warrant and come back," she said. "In the pole building there's a bunch of Ron's stuff. I'm pretty sure my parents are going to burn all of it. I put some stuff in the chicken coop. To hide it."

Just outside the door, she told another officer that her mother had given her two small yellow pills a couple of weeks ago. Tori had only taken one of the pills, which had made Shelly angry.

"Well, then," she'd said, "you don't trust me."

When Tori told her story to Pacific County investigators that afternoon, she minimized most of what had happened to her. She said what she knew about Ron and how she thought he was dead. She didn't know anything about Kathy because she had been too young at the time. She was careful in what she said because, in her mind, there was always the chance that they'd release her back to her mom.

If they send me back home, what will my mom do to me? she thought.

She later said that she had only told the police "like ten percent of the bad stuff."

Investigators, however, understood that 10 percent of a nightmare is still a nightmare.

𝕏

Sami looked at her phone and tried to steady herself. It was the call she'd been dreading. She considered letting it go to voice mail and maybe even pretending she'd never gotten the call.

It was her mom's number.

Shit had hit the fan, and it was about to splatter all over Pacific County.

"Mom?"

There was no "Hi, honey" or anything like that. Just a rapid-fire launch into what had happened.

What Sami and her sister had made happen.

"They took Tori away just now, Sami! The police!" Shelly exclaimed. "They came and got her for child abuse. I don't know what's going on? Do you?"

Sami took a breath and played dumb.

"What's going on, Mom?"

Shelly was fuming, sputtering. Her sentences ran on. "I've never even laid a hand on her. I don't think I've ever even grounded the girl! And every time I did, I took it back."

Her mother's lies always seemed so convincing.

"Oh Mom," Sami said. "I'm so sorry."

In many ways, that wasn't a lie. Sami was sorry for so many things. Sorry that she hadn't seen the warning signs that her sister was being abused. Sorry she hadn't been more skeptical with Ron when he told her he was okay. Sorry that she hadn't backed up her sister when Nikki and her grandmother told the authorities about Kathy.

Sami also felt sorry for her mother. Shelly sounded desperate. She was trapped and clawing through the phone to get out of her situation, a situation of her own doing. She thought that it was all about Tori. *Oh boy.* She had no idea that Tori being taken from Monohon Landing was only the tip of the spear.

Shelly was reeling by then. "Did she say anything when she stayed with you?" she asked. "That she and I didn't get along?"

Again, Sami, the peacemaker, the middle kid, the one who had almost been her mom's favorite, lied.

"No, Mom," she said. "Nothing."

"Do you think Nikki would have called the cops or said something about Kathy? And that's why they took Tori?"

"No, Mom," Sami said. "No, she wouldn't do that."

Sami made a quick call to Nikki.

"Mom's freaking out."

"Good," Nikki said. "She should be."

Nikki made the mistake of picking up the phone to hear her mother's tirade that someone had complained about how she'd been mistreating Tori and how she'd been taken away by Child Protective Services.

"Ripped from my arms for no reason!" Shelly screamed.

Nikki didn't know what to say. She didn't want to tell her mom that she and Sami had been the complainants or that Tori herself had played a part in her own emancipation from Monohon Landing.

"I'm sorry, Mom," she said.

Of course, she wasn't. In fact, after all Shelly had done to her, Kathy, Shane, Tori, Sami, and Ron, how could anyone sympathize with a predicament that was her own doing?

"I'm going to get to the bottom of this right away!" Shelly swore.

She said that the cops were out to get her. *Tori was not an abused child. She was the opposite. She'd been spoiled. Given every advantage.* Shelly could see no reason why anyone would want to harm Tori in the ugly way the authorities had suggested.

Shelly spat out more anger, excuses, and denial, and the call mercifully ended.

Nikki began to feel a little uncertain about what she'd done, the storm she and her sisters had created by telling the truth. She e-mailed her grandmother that she was falling apart and was thinking that her mother might be innocent of any wrongdoing.

Lara fired back a response. She'd talked with the police and county prosecutors for more than two hours and was beginning to feel the constant drip of the investigation and its stop/start impact on everyone.

"I told them about Shelly calling you last night and they said . . . You are NOT to answer the phone from her. DO NOT . . . It is imperative!!!!! Shelly is running around screaming at everyone blaming them . . . She is like a cornered RAT . . . Get that restraining order and block the phone . . ."

Lara knew Shelly better than anyone. She'd watched her stepdaughter operate and work things in a way that were at utter odds with the truth. If the sky was blue, Shelly had a way of insisting it was green. She was a master manipulator. This time she wasn't going to get away with what she'd done.

"Your mom is now putting stuff into your mind and accusing everyone else for talking about her. The authorities said DO NOT FALL for it."

The police weren't talking either. There was no way to find out what was going on except by calling home. Sami and Nikki needed an update.

At the end of the day, Sami sucked up the courage and called her mother to see what was happening in Raymond.

As expected, their mother was frazzled.

"They won't let us talk to Tori," Shelly said. "We still don't know what's happening or why."

Sami had never heard her mother spinning around like that, both enraged and confused. Dave, who'd come home from Whidbey Island, got on the phone and asked Sami if she knew anything.

"No," she said. "I don't."

He, too, was out of sorts, anxious and confused. It was as if Dave Knotek hadn't a clue that anything out of the ordinary had ever taken place. Sami loved her dad. She knew that he had to know, because he was there! She was sure that whatever bullshit her mom had made him do was not his fault. At least not completely. She saw him as a victim and an accomplice at the same time.

"Well then," he said, "I'm going down to the county to find out what I can."

That night, the blue glow of the TV flooded the yard as Pacific County cruisers snaked past the Knotek property. Shelly watched a marathon of crime shows and flipped through the phone book in search of a good lawyer. Dave drank, popped antacids, slept out in his truck. Or tried to sleep. Shelly might have been oblivious as to what the real end game was, but he knew. It wasn't all about Tori. And he knew that all of his wife's bravado about how careful and smart they'd been to cover their tracks with Kathy didn't apply to Ron Woodworth. He'd been moved from the freezer and buried in a big hole in the backyard. He wasn't really gone at all. Dave was pretty sure that Ron's body would be found.

And when it was, everything would be all over.

The next day, Dave left Shelly at Mac's house to go find out what was happening with Tori. Between watching TV and hunting for a lawyer, Shelly had inserted a pair of messages written on Bratz-branded Post-it Notes into the blue-flowered bag that Dave carried with him to Child Protective Services for Tori.

The first: *"What is going on?"*

And the second: *"Did you say anything?"*

X

Tori had indeed said something. So had Nikki. Sami too. Lara had also weighed in. They found out others had too. Kaye Thomas had even run an ad in the *Willapa Harbor Herald* with her daughter's photograph and the headline "Missing Person."

And yet none of what any of them had to say would lead to an arrest.

Dave Knotek took care of that all by himself.

Unable to locate Tori, he went to the offices of the Pacific County sheriff. He was tired. Beaten down. He was exceedingly nervous too. When the investigators asked if he'd consent to an interview, Dave couldn't think of any reason not to. He didn't need a lawyer. He'd never abused his little girl and neither had his wife.

As it turned out, that wasn't what they asked about. They focused on Ron and Kathy. Dave stayed firm that he and Shelly had done nothing wrong, though little chips soon began to fall from his story and he started to cry. At one point, he said he needed to use the bathroom; the interrogators agreed, and one followed him down the hall.

Just outside the bathroom, Dave broke down and told the officer where Ron had been buried and where Kathy's remains had been scattered after her body had been burned in the firepit.

Deputies picked up Shelly at Mac's house. She was confused. Indignant. She clearly couldn't understand why anyone would ever think she'd done anything wrong.

She was all about helping people, after all.

Nikki cried when she got the news her parents had been arrested. Her dad had admitted to disposing of Kathy's and Ron's bodies, but nothing else. He hadn't pointed the finger at Shelly, and for her part, she'd kept her mouth clamped shut.

There was a tragic irony to the date. It was Kathy Loreno's birthday. Missing for a decade, the woman who'd told the Knotek girls not to help her, out of fear that something would happen to them, would have turned forty-five that day.

Nikki sent an e-mail to her grandmother.

"The police are going to search the house and the property today. Cross your fingers they find stuff. But I think the confession from Dave on disposing of the bodies might be enough along with our statements. We all have to remember that mother is pretty smart, and she manages to weasel her way out of A LOT of things. I hope this won't be one of them."

As the whirlpool of truth began to pull Shelly and Dave downward, there was the matter of the other person who had vanished in the night.

Shane.

PART SEVEN

Truth

Shane

CHAPTER EIGHTY

The day after her parents' arrest, Sami and her boyfriend, Kaley, went out for a steak dinner at the Metropolitan Grill in Seattle to celebrate her twenty-fifth birthday. Despite everything that was happening, Sami told herself that having a birthday celebration would be a small life raft in a raging sea. To many, such a response would have seemed strange, but Sami was a girl who'd spent her entire life trying to chart a course that at least made her life appear normal. No matter what. She'd played high school sports wearing leggings to hide the evidence after a beating. She'd made excuses when her mom didn't come to pick her up, as though a walk home was what she needed.

With each bite, she swallowed a little more of what was going on in her mind. She tried to make a joke of some of it, but it wasn't funny. It was hard to even think. Newspapers and TV had been flush with stories about her parents. Pictures of Kathy supplied by her family were on TV, as was Ron's driver's license photograph.

"Tale of abuse, deaths unfolding in rural Raymond."

"Raymond couple befriended 3 strangers who then disappeared."

"PROSECUTORS IN RAYMOND PURSUE POISONING ANGLE."

The reality of what was happening back in Raymond took the oxygen out of the birthday celebration, and the couple left the restaurant.

As they drove through Tacoma, Sami's cell rang.

It was her grandmother.

The call started with a short pause as Lara tried to frame the words in a way that didn't hurt. There was really no way to do that.

"Shane's dead," Lara said in a shattered voice. "Dave confessed to killing him."

Sami dropped the phone and started screaming. "He's really dead! He's dead! Shane!"

Kaley tried to comfort her, but there was nothing he could do but drive. Sami screamed until her throat hurt.

She'd consoled herself through the years with the thought that Shane was off somewhere, happy. Maybe having kids. Living and working and being a grown-up version of the kid he'd been at Monohon Landing and before. Now the fantasy went up in smoke. *Gone.*

It had been a game she played with herself. It was also a hope that in the end was a lie.

"I looked for him over the years," she said later. "In a crowd on the street. I knew that something was wrong and that he wouldn't just disappear, but I wanted to believe that he was out there being happy."

)(

Dave Knotek would admit to a lot of things that he'd done. The murder of Shane Watson, however, was one subject that never really made its way to a full, recorded confession. He and the sheriff's investigators were out at the property when he finally conceded that his nephew was gone.

"Shane's in the ocean," Dave said, standing on the edge of the field as criminalists and dogs scoured the property.

Later, he told investigators that he'd come into the pole building and found Shane playing with the rifle—something that he had explicitly told him never to do.

"Shane, give me the gun!" he claimed he'd demanded.

The teenager refused.

"Give it to me," Dave repeated.

When Shane continued to balk, he said he'd tried to wrestle the gun away, when all of sudden, it fired. After he saw what he'd done, he went back inside the house in a panic.

The three girls were upstairs. He was sure no one had heard the shot. He immediately told Shelly what had happened, and she started crying. The two of them went outside.

"I want to see him," Shelly said.

Dave held her back, refusing to let her see Shane's body. He started to cry too, and Shelly had clutched him like a baby.

"What are we going to do?" she asked.

At that moment, he didn't know. He was petrified. Too scared, he'd later insist, to report the accident in the pole building.

If that's indeed what it was.

※

Nothing could be worse. Nikki wrote an e-mail to her grandmother after learning Shane had been murdered too.

"I seriously don't think I can handle much more of this. I wish I could have a quiet life. I never do terrible things and I stay out of trouble. I can't turn on the television without seeing my mom."

She'd always known there was a significant possibility that Shane had been killed, but she'd wanted more than anything to believe he was okay. She was horrified to have to truly confront the idea that something she'd told Shelly might've led to what happened to Shane.

CHAPTER
EIGHTY-ONE

The day after Kathy Loreno died in the summer of 1994, Shelly had been a caged animal, pacing the floor of the Monohon Landing house as though there were no way out of the trap that she'd created for herself and family. She cried. She scolded. Mostly, she seemed determined. She even made a vow.

"I'm not going to let anyone take this family down," she said.

Dave, who'd done his wife's gruesome dirty work, told her everything would be all right. "No one will. I promise."

Shelly wasn't convinced, and she immediately focused on the two oldest. Shane and Nikki were close. They were out working in the yard together, talking. Shelly told her husband she knew what they were talking about and she didn't like it one bit.

"They are going to tell," she said.

Dave disagreed. "No, they won't. Nikki is blood. So is Shane."

"Shane's *not* our blood," she said. "He's going to tell. He's going to ruin the family."

"He won't," he said. Though, of anyone in the household, it was obvious to Dave that Shane was indeed the weakest link.

Shelly kept at her husband. She was the record album that skipped a track. She called him at work. She reminded him the minute he got home. A storm was coming and the boy in the house was the cause of it. He'd be their complete ruin.

"We need to get rid of him," she said.

Dave didn't have to scratch his head or ask for any more information. He knew exactly what Shelly meant. The only solution to ensure that the rest of the family would survive was eliminating Shane from the picture, but Dave didn't like that idea at all. Shane was like a son to him.

"I don't know," he told her.

Shelly loathed weakness and ambivalence. "You do. You'll figure it out. It has to be done."

Shane, it turned out, *was* ready to do something about what was going on in the Knotek family. He told his confidant, Nikki, that he had something he needed her to see.

"But you need to keep it a secret." He was dead serious and spoke in his quietest voice. He told Nikki to meet him in the pole building. While Nikki looked on, the cousin she considered more of a brother pulled three photographs from a hole he'd cut in a small, plush teddy bear.

They were Polaroid images of Kathy, naked, black and blue, crawling on the floor.

"They murdered Kathy," he said, setting down the photos. "You know it. I know it. We need to tell the police. Your mom is psycho and your dad is seriously fucked up too."

"Where did you get those?" she asked.

"Swiped them from your mom."

Nikki kept her eyes on the photos. She didn't know what to say.

"I'm going to take them to the police," Shane went on. "You want in?"

Nikki, as scared as she'd ever been, finally answered.

"Okay," she said. "Let's do it."

They talked about finding the right time and making sure that they had a game plan for when the police came and arrested Shelly and Dave. Nikki told Shane that she was all in. She wanted her mother in jail. She wanted her to pay for what she'd done to all of them, especially Kathy.

The bloody snow. The kicks to her head. The shower that ran red with her blood. The rancid smells of those smoothies her mother made for Kathy.

"I hate Mom," she said to Shane.

"I do too," he said.

Good. They were on the same page.

Shane had always been her ally. She agreed with everything he was saying, but inside she was worried. "What if they don't believe us?"

Shane slid the photographs back into the fluffy filling of the stuffed animal.

"The photos are proof," he said.

Nikki continued processing the plan and the consequences. She wanted to go to college and create a life far away from Raymond. Although her mother picked away at her self-esteem, there was still part of Nikki that knew she was strong enough to make it. The truth would feel good, and it would right a very big wrong. All of that was incontrovertible. She thought about her siblings and how they'd be parceled off to foster care. What would happen to them? Would they end up with relatives? Or strangers? Would they be worse off than they were now? Tori was adored and happy. Sami seemed to navigate Shelly's abuse more effectively than Nikki did. She didn't rock the boat. Things were bad for her and for Shane, although they weren't terrible at the moment.

Nikki could barely sleep that night as she wrestled with Shane's plan. She didn't want him to tell. She didn't want the family torn apart.

The next morning, she saw her mother. Her stomach was in knots. "Shane has pictures, Mom."

Shelly stopped what she was doing and studied Nikki. "Pictures of what?"

"Kathy."

Shelly flew into a rage. "Where?" She went over to Nikki and grabbed her by the shoulders.

"In his room," Nikki said, stepping back a little. "In his teddy bear."

Nikki knew it right then. She had lit a fuse. In that very second, she wished she could take it back. She saw the shark look in her mother's eyes. It was the same look that the dogs had when Shelly tied them to the apple trees and told the kids that the animals were fine. How, they, too, could skip a meal or two.

Ravenous. Determined. Just one bite.

Nikki would spend more than twenty years trying to understand what led her to tell on Shane that day. She loved him. She thought of him as a brother. They were united in their hate for Shelly and Dave. They wanted both of their parents in jail. If anyone deserved to go to jail, it was them. Not for what they'd done to her either. It was for Kathy.

She asked herself over and over why it was that she'd betrayed Shane.

"I didn't want to get him in trouble," she said. "I just was so scared that if he told, everyone would know about what had happened. I didn't say that he was going to show the pictures to the police. I only said that he had them."

Shelly sounded the alarm and called Dave the second Nikki told her about Shane's photos. Dave didn't understand what she was talking about at first.

That irritated her even more.

"I'm telling you he has a photo of Kathy," she said. "A photo of her that he is going to take to the police. We need to find the photo!"

"What is the photo of?" Dave asked.

"I think it was taken after she died. A Polaroid. It's going to make us look bad. We didn't do anything wrong, but a photo like that . . . it will ruin us. You fucking have to find it."

Dave was exhausted from the drive from Whidbey. The idea that there was photographic proof of what had happened to Kathy jolted him into alertness. Dave started looking the minute he got home, but the teddy bear was nowhere to be found. He went through the out-buildings and even dug in some places in the yard where Shane might have hidden a photo. At the same time, Shelly had torn up the house.

Neither found the photos.

Next, Dave confronted Shane.

CHAPTER
EIGHTY-TWO

Nikki heard yelling coming from the woodshed. It was her mother's voice. Her father's too. The voices were loud and violent and completely terrifying. Every now and then, between the breaks in the adults screaming, Nikki could make out a yelp coming from Shane.

It was like the sound of an animal getting hit. With an electric cord. With the handle of a shovel. With a fist.

"What were you going to do, Shane?" Shelly was screaming. "You ungrateful fucking piece of garbage! You won't ruin our family. You won't be the cause of sending your sisters off to some shithole state institution!"

"No," Shane said.

"You were going to tell!" Dave yelled. "You were going to ruin our family! You piece of shit! Why in the fuck would you ever want to do that?"

It went on and on. And then silence.

The next time Nikki saw Shane, he was black and blue.

"They beat the fuck out of me," he said. "About the pictures of Kathy."

"That's what she does, Shane," Nikki said. "I'm sorry. I'm really sorry."

Nikki felt terribly guilty for what had happened, although as far as she knew, Shane wasn't aware that she'd been the one to tip off her parents.

"It was my fault," she said later, blaming herself for what happened.

)(

Shelly wouldn't let up.

"What are we going to do with Shane?" she repeatedly asked Dave.

He knew she meant what was *Dave* going to do. That she meant killing a teenager who was like a son to him.

Every time Dave came home, Shelly pressed him on a plan to commit murder. And when he just sat there, in a near stupor because he didn't know what to say or how to placate her, Shelly would make her own suggestions on how it could be accomplished.

"I need it to look like an accident," she instructed him.

"Right." Dave wished the conversation was about any other subject. "An accident? I don't know, Shell. I don't know if I can."

She suggested taking Shane up into the woods to cut wood and have a tree fall on him.

"An accident like that," she said.

Again, Dave was unsure. "It would be pretty hard to do that."

Wrong response.

Shelly flew into a rage.

"You need to fucking man up. Grow a pair. Jesus! What kind of a man are you? Do you realize what's at stake here? Our girls! Do you want him to tell and then ruin our lives for what he did to Kathy?"

Shelly was never part of any blame. She'd tell everyone that Shane had been Kathy's abuser. That her husband had. That she had no idea what was going on when she wasn't there to take care of Kathy.

"You know that Shane killed our Kathy! We both know it. He deserves to die for what he did. Dave, be a man!"

Dave promised that he'd get it done. He told Shelly he was taking his time and thinking it through, considering the best plan, but inside hoping she'd forget about it.

She didn't.

※

For the longest time, nothing happened. At Shelly's instruction, Shane and Nikki hid under the neighbor's house listening for any clue that they might have heard or seen something about Kathy. *The screaming out in the yard during the waterboarding? Maybe the acrid smell of the fire?*

Nothing.

The summer flew past, and the kids returned to school. Christmas came and Shelly made a big deal out of it as she always did, piling up the gifts and then taking them away. Shelly didn't drink, so New Year's Eve was a quiet one at home.

Everything was relatively calm until February, six months after Kathy died.

Nikki woke up in the middle of the night. A noise had interrupted her sleep. *Something happened.* She looked around her room and listened carefully. The house was silent. She went back to sleep, wondering if the noise had been part of a dream.

Not hardly.

CHAPTER
EIGHTY-THREE

It was February 1995. Late. Quiet. Pitch black outside. Dave retrieved his .22 from the cab of Old Blue, and went into the pole building to find Shane. He felt like an automaton: one foot in front of the other. The door was shut. He twisted the knob and went inside. The light went on. He didn't say a word.

Dave fired the rifle into the back of his nephew's head.

Blood oozed over the cement floor.

Shane was gone.

Dave was numb as he bent down. He hadn't wanted to kill the boy. He hadn't thought he *could* ever kill him. But it was as if he'd been programmed, harangued into it by the pretty redhead he'd married.

The woman he loved despite everything.

The woman that could look at him when their bank account had been overdrafted to kingdom come and say it was the bank's fault. "They keep screwing up our account! I'm going to complain tomorrow!"

The woman his dad had spotted as a fraud and troublemaker from the minute he'd met her. "Sawdust for brains if you stay with her."

He went back inside to tell Shelly what he'd done.

"I killed Shane."

Shelly's mouth dropped open like a safe hurled from a ten-story building. She appeared to be in complete shock. It was as if her husband's actions had come out of the blue.

"You did what?" she asked, her eyes growing very wide. "You killed our nephew? Why?"

Seriously, Shelly?

Dave didn't know what to make of her just then. It was what she'd begged him, harassed him, cajoled him into doing nearly since the day Kathy died.

"What are we going to do now?" she asked.

"What we did with Kathy," he said.

Shelly liked the idea.

It had worked before.

After composing himself, Dave returned to the pole building and put Shane's body into a sleeping bag and carried it to a space near the workbench. He poured some bleach into a Home Depot bucket of water and did his best to clean up the bloody mess. He had promised his wife there would be no trace. No DNA. Nothing would be left behind to indicate what might have happened.

And then he waited for a chance—when the girls would be away from home—to burn the body.

The next morning, the girls woke to the birdhouse and the tale that Shane had run away to Alaska to fish. A day or so later, Shelly offered the girls the chance to stay overnight with friends—a rare occurrence that each jumped at.

This time, when Dave burned the body, he did so without the aid of the accelerants or the metal sheeting he'd used with Kathy. No tires. No diesel either. He only used wood and kept putting more on top of his nephew's body until it vanished into ash and bone. It took all night and a portion of the next morning—longer than Kathy's cremation had.

The metal sheeting he'd used on her had, he reflected, been very effective.

When the ashes were cool enough, Dave shoveled them into bags for the familiar drive out to Washaway Beach. He parked his truck, looked around to make sure no one was watching, then dumped the ashes into the white-foamed surf of the Pacific.

When Nikki, Sami, and Tori returned home a day later, the burn pile was out.

A short time later, Dave brought in an excavator and pushed the dirt down the hill to a tangle of blackberry bushes.

Shelly insisted they report to the Pacific County sheriff that Shane had run away. Dave made the call, telling the deputy that his nephew often disappeared for days at a time.

"Came from a screwed-up family," he said, adding that he and his wife had looked everywhere.

The deputy thanked him for the report, and Dave told Shelly that they were instructed to "just let it go."

Shane was gone. The body was gone. Next on Dave's and Shelly's minds was the weapon used to kill the boy.

$$\lambda$$

The short carbine .22 rifle used to shoot Shane was indeed a problem. Dave didn't want it around the house. He was sure that someone would find it and somehow discover the truth about what had happened to Shane. He was a nervous wreck when he came up with a half-baked plan that Shelly approved. He drove north out of Raymond to a remote logging road, and when he was sure no one was looking, he got out and buried the weapon in the dirt. The gun that killed Shane was like Edgar Allan Poe's tell-tale heart, always mocking Dave, reminding him of what he'd done to his nephew. Shelly, too, was absolutely certain that, despite how isolated the location was, and how careful her husband had been, someone would surely stumble across the gun and figure out what had happened.

"You need to go get it," she'd said.

So that was what he did. Two weeks later, Dave went back into the woods to retrieve the gun and bring it back to the house. He put it in the firepit and burned it.

"I was hoping the stock would melt or something," he said later. "But it didn't."

Dave handed what remained of the murder weapon to Shelly, who stored it in the back of a cupboard. He never saw it again.

CHAPTER EIGHTY-FOUR

Even after Shane's murder, Shelly stayed on the hunt for the Kathy photos. The photos that Shane had were proof of something that couldn't be explained away. Not easily anyway. She tore through the house when the girls were away at school. She looked through the outbuildings, poking under boards and pulling away clutter in the pole building.

They had to be around there somewhere.

Shelly didn't know it at the time, but at least one other image of Kathy also existed, on a roll of undeveloped film stashed in a drawer in the living room. Shane had taken the photo of Kathy, naked, crawling on the living room floor. It was horrific and sickening. Kathy was clearly struggling. She must have been cold. She was trying to move from one room to the next, and it appeared that she was too weak and too abused to stand.

Kathy had been reduced from a person to an animal.

"We have to find the pictures," Shelly reminded Dave as she rifled through the kids' rooms and the kitchen junk drawer. She couldn't let go of the endless quest to get the photos and destroy them.

"If someone gets his or her hands on it," she said, "we'll be in hot water."

Hot water? That was an understatement typical of his wife. Dave, however, was aware that life as they knew it would be over. He was in this mess with Shelly up to his neck. He'd help search and then she'd start over a few weeks later, tearing up the place again looking, berating Shane for his double cross.

"He would have betrayed us," she said.

Around that time, she started to embellish the story of Shane running away by telling the girls that he had just called.

"He said he'll call back," she said.

Another time before leaving the house, she told the girls, "If Shane calls while I'm gone, be sure to find out where he is."

Dave pulled his wife aside.

"You need to keep the story simple," he said. "Don't keep adding to it. He ran away. He's gone."

Shelly couldn't help herself, though. Thinking ahead, she made a notation on a calendar about when the boy had run away. She added other notes as time went on, recording the few times she and the girls piled into the car and made trips around Pacific County looking for her nephew.

She'd been great at searching for him in the past. This time, however, nothing.

Dave even missed work a few times on fruitless searches for Shane. The girls believed that their father was doing the best he could to find their cousin.

Years later, he claimed that he thought about Shane every day. Every night too.

"Killing someone is something you never get over," he said. "Not even for a second. It's always there."

CHAPTER EIGHTY-FIVE

Nikki and Sami stayed in constant contact after their parents' arrests, avoiding TV when they could, though that was nearly impossible. The Raymond Torture Killings, as their mother's and father's crimes were summarily dubbed, invaded all the space around them. TV accounts played up the angle of a house of horrors in the middle of a bucolic oceanfront community. It was *Arsenic and Old Lace*. It was *Mommie Dearest*. It was *Psycho*. Everyone was talking about the Knoteks.

Except the Knotek girls. Nikki, Sami, and Tori never said a word to the media. It was a promise they'd made to each other.

Shelly and Dave were held on multimillion-dollar bonds and faced all kinds of charges, from murder to concealing a death.

While the Knotek sisters had all wanted justice for Kathy, Shane, and Ron, it still didn't feel great to see one's life through the lens of the media—a reflection of something at once foreign and familiar.

Their parents had killed multiple people.

They'd done the most cruel and vile things anyone could do to another person.

And so much of it had happened right before their eyes.

It took only two weeks for Sami, then twenty-five, to get guardianship of Tori. Sami, who was then living alone in a one-bedroom apartment off Greenwood Avenue in Seattle, made arrangements to get a two-bedroom apartment. She felt good about the opportunity to give her sister a fresh start, away from their parents.

X

Shelly knew that Sami was her best target—Dave was also in jail, Tori was a minor, and after everything she'd done to her, Nikki was a lost cause. Shelly had to have realized there was no way back into her oldest daughter's life. She barely even tried.

But Sami, a classic middle-kid peacemaker, was a pleaser.

Nearly from her first day in jail, still pending trial, Shelly sent Sami letters from prison with lists of items she needed. She wanted everything and anything that her daughter would provide her, and she was very specific. A certain bra. A special robe. A particular tube of lotion. Her tone was demanding, and demeaning. Even from jail, Shelly acted certain that whatever she desired was owed to her.

Sami dutifully packaged up what she was told to send. Even though she knew Shelly belonged right where she was, picturing her there all alone made Sami sad, as did the idea that everyone else in there had comfy underwear and nice bathrobes, while her mother was just getting what the state gave her.

She didn't tell either of her sisters that she was helping their mother, though Nikki picked up on it one time when Sami let slip that their mother was struggling behind bars.

"Are you sending stuff to Mom?" Nikki asked.

Sami deflected the question at first, then conceded that, yes, she had been.

"A couple times," she said. "It wasn't a big deal."

Nikki couldn't believe her ears. "Are you serious? After all she did to us? You're *helping her*?"

In a way, Sami still felt she didn't really have a choice.

"She's controlling you," Nikki said. "Don't you get that? She's doing what she always did."

ⵝ

In February 2004, six months after his arrest, Dave Knotek pleaded down his first-degree murder charge for killing Shane Watson to second-degree murder, and pleaded guilty to unlawful disposal of human remains and rendering criminal assistance. While the Knotek girls made it clear that helping their mother would mean the end of any relationship he might ever have with them, Dave insisted that he wouldn't assist in Shelly's prosecution. For her part, Shelly was desperate to make sure Dave kept his mouth shut—even though Washington's marital privilege laws could keep him off the stand. It wasn't what he'd say on the stand, anyway, that her daughters knew would concern her. All he had to do was back up what they had seen and said.

Which he did.

He was sentenced to a little under fifteen years in prison.

And then it was Shelly's turn.

Pacific County prosecutors told the victims' families they couldn't make the first-degree murder charges stick against Shelly. No body for Kathy. No bones and ash under the bed. An autopsy on Ron that couldn't prove how exactly he'd been injured—or by whom. Given the condition of his remains, it would be hard to say what had actually killed him. Kathy's and Ron's supporters figured the case was too big, too involved, for the county to do what really needed to be done.

Nikki, Sami, and Tori knew that their mother was smart, devious, and the kind of person who would never accept blame for anything she'd done.

The boiling water.
The bleach.
The weeks in the pump house.
No food.
No clothes.
Everything was a lie, or facts were misconstrued.

Ten months after her arrest, Shelly entered a so-called Alford plea of guilty to the charges. An Alford plea can be rather perplexing; it's a plea that allows the defendant to plead guilty yet assert innocence at the same time. It's also a plea that allows the defense and the prosecution to save face—and money—by avoiding going to a trial that would almost surely result in a conviction. The plea probably saved Pacific County a measure of embarrassment too. The media wouldn't rehash the missed warning signs by the police that Shelly and Dave were involved in nefarious deeds. No one could deny that Ron would likely have still been alive had Nikki's story of Kathy's murder been more aggressively pursued by the sheriff's office. Maybe Mac would have lived longer too.

Ultimately, both sides worked out a tentative sentencing agreement for seventeen years.

At sentencing two months later, Shelly looked beat down. Her hair was scraggly, and her Clairol red had long since faded to a mix of gray and reddish blonde. Her jail-issue orange jumpsuit loosely hung on her frame.

No one from her family was there to support her.

She spoke to the court before the judge pronounced her sentence. Her words sputtered through some tears.

"In this jail and in this courtroom and in this community," she told the court, "and everywhere else I'm known as some kind of horrible monster. I'm not. I've made such horrible mistakes though. Kathy was my friend, she had value and she had purpose. She would have been there for me. I wasn't there for her a lot. I was not there when Kathy died. Not there for her."

Shelly pointed the finger at Shane and Nikki, claiming the teenagers had been Kathy's abusers.

None of it was her fault. Not Kathy. Not Ron.

"I believe I am not guilty of murder, of deliberately causing her death. But a mother is the most responsible for her home environment. She was mistreated in my home and now she's gone. I'll never get over it and I don't deserve to."

The sentencing judge took it all in while both sides said their piece. The prosecutor noted how convoluted the case had been and how it was possible the truth of what happened might never be known.

The Alford plea, unlike many plea bargains, didn't require her to tell the court what she'd done.

Shelly seemed surprised, however, that her words did not have the desired effect on the sentencing judge. Instead of sympathizing with her, he added more years to the tally. While Shelly's mouth hung open, the judge sentenced her to more than twenty-two years—five more than the seventeen she'd agreed to—for the second-degree murder of Kathy and for the manslaughter charge relating to Ron's death.

Nobody was happy. Everyone was satisfied.

For a woman who lived to control others, who reveled in telling people what to do and how to do it, it was fitting justice.

Shelly Knotek wouldn't be in charge of anyone or anything for more than two decades.

EPILOGUE

Dave Knotek was released from prison in 2016. He lives on the Washington Coast and, despite health challenges, works long hours at a seafood processing plant. He's thin and struggles being on his feet all day. The only thing that keeps him going is his relationship with his daughters Tori and Sami. Nikki refuses to see him, which he understands. He says that the remorse he feels for his role in what happened at the Louderback and Monohon Landing houses hasn't left him. He knows it never will.

Nikki can neither forgive nor forget. She can only move on, raising her children in a way that her mother could never understand. With love. Respect. She knows that what happened to her has altered her life in ways that are invisible, but though she chooses to think the best of people, she can't do that when it comes to her parents. Nikki tries not to think about her mother. While she's told her oldest children that their maternal grandmother is in prison for doing something very bad, she's refrained from sharing any of the details. Her heart remains heavy and full of regret for her part in what happened to Shane and Kathy. Being a victim herself has never been an excuse for Nikki.

Shelly Knotek will be released from prison in 2022, at which time she'll be sixty-eight. She continues to maintain that her conviction was a mistake, claiming that she misunderstood the Alford plea. None of her daughters have seen her since she left Pacific County, though a visitor to the women's prison in Gig Harbor, Washington, says Shelly's hair is white now and that she's fighting cancer.

At least that's what she says.

From her big house in Raymond, Sami thinks her mother was a bad seed, someone whose evil nature was unfortunately given the opportunity to flourish. "I'm not sure she would have killed anyone if she had been born into a different family, a different town, married a stronger man," she theorizes. "Mom liked to torture people. It just went too far, and she found she had a taste for it. I don't know."

As for her father? She loves him, but she wrestles with what happened even today.

"I don't care what my mother did or how powerful she was," Sami said. "If my mom put a gun to my head and said you need to shoot your brother, there's no way I would have. Nikki too. No way. But our dad did."

Tori, now at a new job, has a few moments of nostalgia for the mother she had once loved. She doesn't miss Shelly at all, though she does miss having a mom. Luckily, her sisters were able to fill that role. While she's managed to forge a close relationship with her dad and recently spent Christmas with him, Tori wants nothing to do with Shelly.

Shelly tried, of course.

She wrote to Tori in care of Sami after she was sent to prison about how she was overjoyed that her youngest daughter had so many people in her life to love and care for her.

"I've chosen so badly in life. I've made so many mistakes and wrong choices. Ones I regret so much. But you are not like me. Please never believe what you've heard. There is more to it all."

Sami never delivered that letter.

"My little sister didn't need to see it," Sami said. "She's smart and happy and Mom has no place in her life."

The Knotek sisters gather together several times a year, mostly at Nikki's place near Seattle. Nikki returned to Raymond in 2018, for the first time since the case broke. It was hard, but Sami was there as Nikki revisited memories of their mother. She remembered a few times when her mom was kind—attentive, even. Those good memories brought tears. Sami also returned to the Louderback and Monohon Landing houses for the first time that fall. She had a visceral reaction to the bathroom at Louderback and the place where Nikki had been made to wallow. Tears came. Smiles too. She pointed out a fish pond that Kaley had made and the spot where he'd park his car to drop her off, honk, and flash his lights until Shelly gave up and let her inside.

The sisters text and talk all the time. They see the insanity of the things their parents did, the horror of what happened while they were growing up. While Shelly may have sought to keep them apart, to control them forever, she underestimated the strength of their bond.

Sisters forever. Victims no more.

AFTERWORD

By Katherine Ramsland, PhD

From the inside, a violent home looks starkly different than it does to outsiders. Children who grow up with cold, narcissistic, or sadistic parents don't know that a caretaker with the potential for extreme cruelty is not the norm. Even when they see a contrast in the families of friends, they've already been robbed of the ability to challenge parental authority. Instead of seeking help, they hunker down and adapt.

Increasingly more offspring of serial killers—mostly daughters—are speaking out about being related to the most monstrous of all offenders. They're victims too, they say, and they are. You can find them on talk shows, on podcasts, and inside the pages of their own memoirs. Melissa Moore, the daughter of "Happy Face Killer" Keith Jesperson, even developed a TV series in which she introduced relatives of serial killers to members of families whose loved ones were victims, hoping for healing for all.

Some offspring are blindsided, like Kerri Rawson, the daughter of Dennis Rader, Wichita's "BTK" serial killer. A decade after his arrest in 2005, she described to a reporter her anguish and humiliation upon learning that the doting father she'd loved all her life had murdered ten people—including children—in her hometown. In *A Serial Killer's*

Daughter, she describes the difficult process of trying to understand why he did it and how to get on with her life.

Yet others are not surprised at their criminal parent's double life, because they'd witnessed open displays of abuse and rage. Some even led police back to their home. Terrified and shamed by feelings of betrayal, they nevertheless hoped to right wrongs and stop monsters.

Such is the story of the daughters of the abusive killer, Michelle "Shelly" Knotek. A woman whose beauty and sex deflected suspicion, she ruled her home and subjected her children and her tenants to horrifying torment. Using cover stories and a caretaker's persona to hide her sadistic cruelty, she got away with her violent behavior for years. She manipulated her third husband into helping to cover up her crimes, even to kill for her.

It seems impossible that anyone could command such extreme compliance, but successful predators use a variety of tools to ensure success. They're patient and observant, and they plan and prepare. First, they look for compliant people with few resources: their own children or elderly parents, friends in need, homeless people, the mentally ill, or those without family ties. Then they pursue a program of steady erosion of their victims' ability to resist. Even in the face of outrageous behavior, such people will be too frightened, docile, confused, or incapacitated to retaliate or seek help.

Having only superficial emotional attachments to truth and moral behavior, predators train themselves to imitate trustworthy behaviors like honesty and compassion so they can exploit what people expect. If confronted, they can pivot in a split second and slip their cover story into place with ease. They know what they want and what it will take to get or achieve it. Knotek used a contrived persona of charm and success to falsely engender trust in potential new victims. Once she drew these flies into her web, she brought out the stinger.

Some predators are sadists, described as the great white sharks of deviant crime. Their capacity for criminal cunning is unequaled, as is their capacity for harming others. They're happy only when they have crushed the lives around them, usually with mental and physical abuse. They enjoy whipping, binding, burning, hanging, electrocuting, stomping, piercing, or choking victims into unconsciousness and then reviving them. Controlling others with pain empowers them.

A bent toward sadism forms during certain associations in early adolescence, coupled with a callous temperament that needs control and lacks remorse. Even so, more than one-third of sadists report discovering their perverted propensities well into adulthood; they enjoy the sense of authority that arises from having their way with a vulnerable and submissive human being, and their fantasies grow increasingly more sophisticated and perverse. Because they seek stimulation, they become quite inventive in the types of cruelties they inflict on others. The usual nurturing that accompanies parenthood means nothing to them.

Dr. Michael Stone, a forensic psychiatrist and the inventor of the 22-point scale of evil, includes cases of "parents from hell" when he describes what goes wrong in an institution we regard as the ultimate arena of safety and protection. He labels as evil those parents who present a normal social persona to shield the harm they do in private. They serve their own needs and desires at the expense of their relatives, especially their children. The more pleasure they derive from acts of torment, the more they indulge. Indeed, Stone reserves the "most evil" category—level 22—for psychopathic torture-murderers, with torture as their primary motivator. They thrive on inflicting pain. Whenever they tire of one torture implement, they find or create another. They prefer to keep their victims alive as long as possible, acting out their most damaging fantasies, but know that ultimately, these people must die.

Victims who want to get help recognize how difficult it would be to convince authorities of the sadist's behavior. They know that if they try but fail, the punishment will be severe. So, they often decide to just wait it out and hope they can eventually flee. Even the sadist's accomplices, once caught, might wonder how they crossed a line they'd never believed they'd cross. Once they looked the other way during torture or committed a heinous act at the sadist's behest, they were compromised. They had little choice but to continue. Skilled predators know how to stay in control.

Even when sadistic parents are caught, convicted, and sentenced, the nightmares continue for their children. Some shun the media, change their names, get therapy, and hope to live their lives as normally as they can. Others seek out a public forum. No matter which route they take, the offender has stained their souls. They might end up with sleep or eating disorders, an inability to sustain healthy relationships, or unrelenting episodes of PTSD. Perhaps they unwittingly abuse their own children or feel an uncontrollable urge to lash out at people they love. The more they learn about the abnormality of their early lives, the more potential there is for the damage to affect significant areas of their adulthood. They might even fear that they'll pass along a genetic infection, so they watch their own kids with increased vigilance.

The sadistic predatory "caretaker" can have a devastating ripple effect on the lives of surviving victims that can take years to heal. Even when they finally understand what was done to them, they often suffer from feelings of guilt. They might even still love the parent who hurt them, not quite accepting the enormity of the abuse. They might respond when the parent still tries to control them from prison. This is difficult for outsiders to understand, but no matter what form it has taken, home is still home.

Victims of abuse can still love the monster. This ambivalent loyalty might just be the predator's ultimate form of damage.

Dr. Katherine Ramsland is a professor of forensic psychology at DeSales University in Pennsylvania. She has published more than one thousand articles and sixty-five books, including The Psychology of Death Investigations; Confession of a Serial Killer: The Untold Story of Dennis Rader, the BTK Killer; *and* The Mind of a Murderer. *She presents workshops to law enforcement, coroners, and attorneys and has consulted for several television series, including* The Alienist, CSI, *and* Bones. *She also writes a regular blog for* Psychology Today.

ACKNOWLEDGMENTS

The subject matter is dark and scary, but my overwhelming feeling while writing this book was one of hope and appreciation. That has everything to do with Nikki, Sami, and Tori. I am so grateful to the brave Knotek sisters for trusting me with their story. I grew up in a family of brothers, but if I had been so lucky as to have a sister, I would wish for any of these three. Each reminds me that as terrible a person's starting point in life might be, it's where one ends up that really matters. And each one of them is living proof that, no matter what, the love of family is the one thing we can always count on.

I'm also indebted to their father, Dave Knotek, for meeting me to talk about the very worst of his own journey through life with Shelly. I honestly didn't know what to expect, but now I see him through Sami's and Tori's eyes. I know that he will never minimize or try to shed his culpability in what happened in Raymond. He will spend the rest of his life atoning for what he did, and he only helped me write this story because his girls wanted him to.

Lara Watson is everything you'd want your grandma to be. I will never forget our interview in Portland and her consistent support for telling the story since moving to sunnier climes. I also thank her youngest daughter for the photographs that helped me put the faces to the names of family members.

Shelly continues to be the game player she always has been. We exchanged a number of letters and she agreed to meet me, but then kept putting me off, telling me she was too busy to find the time. We had a brief phone call too. For more than a year, I stayed somewhat hopeful that we'd connect for an interview. Silly me. She's like so many of her ilk, a victim of circumstances that have nothing to do with anything she's ever done.

Many thanks to Kelly Paananen for the haunting memories of her sister (and for the cookies she brought back from New York). I know her heart is still heavy from the loss of Kathy. It's a hurt that never goes away. Thanks to her brother Jeff Loreno too. I also appreciate the time and perspective Kaley Hanson and his mother, Barb, provided me on one of many visits to Raymond. And huge gratitude goes to Pacific County Senior Records clerk James Whorlton for saving the day when a file went missing.

That leaves the publishing side of this book to recognize. I'm supremely grateful to Shannon Jamieson Vazquez for the great care and insight she provided during the editing process. She challenged me to dig deep, and while, admittedly, it was painful at times, it was exactly what I needed to do. And to the team at Thomas & Mercer and Amazon Publishing . . . what can I say? Gracie Doyle and Liz Pearsons, you are awesome—and you know an important story when you see one. I am the luckiest author ever.

I haven't written a true crime book in many years, so people ask: Why this book, why now? Shelly Knotek occupies a kind of strange space in the annals of true crime. Everything she did was the action of a monster—so horrific, so cruel. And yet, so unknown. She skated under the radar with the passage of time and the Alford plea. There was no sensational trial. No real public airing of all that she'd done.

Nikki, Sami, and Tori wanted the world to know what their mother had done. It's a warning to the vulnerable that will cross her path when she's finally released. All worry that she'll do it again.

ABOUT THE AUTHOR

Photo © Claudia Olsen

#1 *New York Times* and Amazon Charts bestselling author Gregg Olsen has written more than thirty books, including *Lying Next to Me*, *The Last Thing She Ever Did*, and two novels in the Nicole Foster series, *The Sound of Rain* and *The Weight of Silence*. Known for his ability to create vivid and fascinating narratives, he's appeared on multiple television and radio shows and news networks, such as *Good Morning America*, *Dateline*, *Entertainment Tonight*, CNN, and MSNBC. In addition, Olsen has been featured in *Redbook*, *People*, and *Salon* magazine, as well as in the *Seattle Times*, *Los Angeles Times*, and *New York Post*. Both his fiction and nonfiction works have received critical acclaim and numerous awards, including prominence on the *USA Today* and *Wall Street Journal* bestseller lists. Washington State officially selected his young adult novel *Envy* for the National Book Festival, and *The Deep Dark* was named Idaho Book of the Year.

A Seattle native who lives with his wife in rural Washington State, Olsen's already at work on his next thriller. Visit him at www.greggolsen.com.